LAO-TSE

LAO-TSE

LIFE AND WORK OF THE FORERUNNER
IN CHINA

Received in the proximity of Abd-ru-shin
through the special gift of
one Called for the purpose

GRAIL·FOUNDATION·PRESS
G A M B I E R , O H I O

Lao-Tse: The Life and Work of the Forerunner in China
contains the translation according to the sense
of the original German text. In some cases
the words of the translation can
only render the original meaning approximately.
Nevertheless, the reader will come to a
good understanding if he or she absorbs inwardly
the meaning of the contents.

Original German edition:
Lao-Tse: Leben und Wirken des Wegbereiters in China

Paperback edition, Third edition, 1995.
Only authorized edition.

Library Systems and Services Cataloging-in-Publication Data

Lao-Tse, Lao-Tzu: life and work of the forerunner in China/
received in the proximity of Abd-ru-shin through
the special gift of one called for the purpose.
p. cm.

Translated from the German.
ISBN 1-57461-008-2
1. Lao-tzu 2. Taoists—China—Biography.
I. Abd-ru-shin, 1875-1941.
BL1930.L357 1995 299'.51463 B—dc20

Printed on recycled paper.

THE SEER OPENS WIDE HIS EYES AND SEES.

BEFORE HIS GAZE ARISES LIFE WHICH

HAS BEEN INDELIBLY ENGRAVED IN THE BOOK

OF THIS GREAT CREATION:

Li-Fu-Tai sat in front of his little house in contemplative repose. Over him arched a deep blue sky, but he did not look up at it. On all sides spread undulating green rice-fields, but Li-Fu-Tai heeded them not.

He had withdrawn completely into himself; his soul was greeting other souls in other realms.

A small yellow dog came prancing up, and sought to draw the man's attention to itself. But all its droll antics, its merry yapping, were in vain; the man's soul was not in his body.

With its pointed white teeth the animal took hold of Li-Fu-Tai's blue robe. But when the man did not respond to this either, the little dog scampered straight back into the house.

A woman emerged from it and approached the man. But when she perceived the absent expression of his features, she silently picked up the pails from the ground and withdrew.

Now all was quite still around the dreaming man.

From afar a white cloud, a strange shape, sailed towards him. It came nearer, ever nearer, and took the form of a huge dragon.

When it had come very close to Li-Fu-Tai, it seemed to descend. The shimmering head of the cloud-dragon emerged out of the blue sky, and a voice like the rushing of the wind, now loud, now low, was heard:

"Hear me, Li-Fu-Tai! Shang-Ti sends me to speak to you. Return from the Gardens of the Souls!"

The man's figure remained motionless, but his soul obeyed the call. And it listened to the tidings brought by the Messenger of Shang-Ti, who began afresh:

"Human soul, hear me! With faithful devotion you think of your people, pondering day and night on how you can break the sway of the demons. But your power is too weak; you know that. Nor have you been prepared to absorb thoughts of Heaven, and to pass them on to those who are in need, and implore Shang-Ti for them. But be it known to you:

9

"For a long time now a soul has been prepared in one of the Highest of the Gardens above. It has absorbed supreme wisdom, and has been given the ability to draw strength from the Light whenever it may be needed.

"This soul is destined to be a leader of your people, and Shang-Ti has chosen you to prepare the earthly home for it. That is to be your reward for your loyalty towards Shang-Ti and towards your people. Speak, Li-Fu-Tai, will you receive this soul and guard it as a gift of the gods?"

And Li-Fu-Tai's soul bowed down and pledged itself before Shang-Ti's Messenger. Then it returned to the body.

Li-Fu-Tai fell to the ground, touched Mother Earth three times with his forehead, and prayed. At that moment he knew what had taken place, and was overcome with deep reverence. The cloud, however, vanished. A clear blue sky smiled down upon the blessed human being.

His wife returned from the watering-place. He went to meet her, took the pails from her and carried them into the little house. Not for a moment did he think of sharing with her what he had just experienced. There was time enough to tell her about it when the soul that had been prepared had made its entrance.

They had lived together for five years, and the gods had not yet blessed their union. Now Li-Fu-Tai knew why this had to be so. This child was to be permitted to grow up in seclusion.

But he, Li-Fu-Tai, now had to prepare himself and reflect daily upon the sacred writings which told of the gods, and above all of Shang-Ti, the highest of all gods.

He must send out his soul ever more consciously into the Gardens of Light; he must become at home there, to be a good guide to the coming soul. And he must look after his earthly possessions better than before, so that the coming one would not suffer want.

In the following months his wife Wu-Li often marvelled at her husband's diligence. But it pleased her. She felt that she was being given a new task, and she prepared herself for it joyfully.

Anxiously she took heed of all the advice given to her by experienced women. She must not leave the house after sunset, so that demons would not be able to approach and frighten her. She must search for and always carry with her all kinds of herbs, to attract good spirits.

10

For all manner of spirits filled the air; she could not be too careful, evil be drawn to her and the little growing child. And how very necessary was to guard against being envious or spiteful, lest the coming soul be forced to enter the body of a fox, for instance. Each of the women neighbours had different advice.

Wu-Li listened to it all, until one day she found that much of it was contradictory. Whose advice was she to follow? It did not occur to her to discuss it with her husband. No doubt, like most men, he believed that women lacked sense, making it impossible to speak seriously with them. She would not even risk exposing herself to a rebuff.

One morning she went very early to the watering-place, which nestled among tall fan-palms. The emerald green moss that grew all round it made a fine cushion to rest upon.

Wu-Li was kneeling down to draw water when she perceived a lovely female figure, such as she had never before seen. Everything about her was luminous and bright, even the long hair that enveloped her like a mantle.

But how strange: to Wu-Li it seemed as if she could see the trunks of the palm-trees right through the figure. Was it a heavenly messenger? It could not be a demon. Even though Wu-Li had been told that demons sometimes assume magnificent forms, this woman spoke to Wu-Li's soul, and she calmly abandoned herself to the blissful feeling aroused in her by the manifestation.

After gazing for a long time, Wu-Li ventured to ask:

"Who are you, and whence do you come, most beautiful one?"

"I am a servant of Kwang-Non, and I come from the Gardens of the Souls. A soul is about to enter you. You are to cherish and protect it, and be ever mindful that Shang-Ti, the Sublime One, sends it to you! Prepare yourself to receive it worthily.

"This soul is to accomplish great things. But you must banish all thoughts of demons from your mind. They cannot approach you so long as your own thoughts do not attract them. Pray unceasingly to Shang-Ti, call to Kwang-Non, and blessing will be spread about you like a sacred mantle.

"Avoid associating with the neighbouring women; go into the woods and seek out the holy places. Prepare an altar in your home and make offerings of flowers."

...e bowed in prayer, letting her forehead sink on to the ... overwhelmed by the holiness of the moment. When ... and the woman looked up, she found herself alone.

...lay Wu-Li set up an altar at the best place in the ... enquiringly at her, as though awaiting an explana- ...ot ask in words, he received no reply.

...mazed, he watched as the little house-altar was set up. Wu-Li's small hands spread the finest, most richly embroidered silken cloth over the lacquered table. Then she placed a bronze incense-bowl in the centre, and two precious vases with flowers on either side of it. That was all.

Now Li-Fu-Tai had to ask, for he missed all the signs of ancestor-worship, such as amulets, statues and writings. An altar was being set up at which to worship; that much was clear. But if he, the master of the house, was to say his prayers there, he also had to find out to whom they were directed.

"Will the Blossom of my house not tell me to whom she dedicates the altar?" he asked pleasantly, although he was annoyed at having to enquire at all.

He had been about to put the question brusquely, but then he remembered that harmony was to prevail in the home which was permitted to shelter the approaching soul. Now he himself was surprised at how little effort it cost him to be pleasant. But greater still was his surprise at his wife's reply: "Altar and offering are intended for Shang-Ti."

Never yet had an altar been set up to the highest of gods in an ordinary dwelling-place! Li-Fu-Tai stared at his wife, aghast. Could the anticipation of the joy bestowed on her have confused her senses? He must try to dissuade her from this presumptuous undertaking.

He turned towards her kindly, and was about to speak, when he saw a luminous female figure standing by the altar. She raised her hands in blessing over the incense-bowl and flowers, also over Wu-Li, who had dropped to the ground in worship. So his wife too saw the Luminous One? Marvelling, the man reflected upon it, as he slowly sank to his knees beside Wu-Li.

Then the Messenger of God began to speak. In a clear, soft voice she announced that Shang-Ti had graciously accepted the altar and flower-offerings. The couple should not cease to pray. Their little house must become a temple of God, in which peace and joy should reign.

Then the gracious figure disappeared; but through their joint lofty experience husband and wife found each other, sharing what they had been permitted to see and hear. –

AGAIN SOME MONTHS had passed. Li-Fu-Tai had to leave his home for a few days, because it was the time of the great markets, where silk and rice were sold in exchange for food supplies.

For Wu-Li the time spent by herself passed quickly. She had various things to prepare for the coming soul. Moreover, in her small garden she grew the most beautiful flowers for the daily offerings on the house-altar.

These flowers, however, had long aroused the envy and curiosity of her neighbours, from whom Wu-Li had so obviously withdrawn.

So long as her husband was present they had not dared to ask; but they wanted to take advantage of the days when Wu-Li was alone with the little yellow dog, in order to get to the bottom of the secret that was obviously associated with growing the flowers. Between them they had agreed on how to persuade the woman.

Early in the morning the nearest neighbour came to ask for fire, because hers had gone out during the night. Wu-Li was startled. Where the fire goes out, all is not well with the household. In any case she would not have the woman in the house. She asked her to wait in the garden.

That was exactly what the neighbour had wanted. She went from one plant to another, closely inspecting the flowers. When Wu-Li returned with burning chips of kindling, the visitor was in no hurry to carry the fire back into her house.

"You have glorious flowers, Wu-Li," she began flatteringly. "There is probably not a woman in the whole neighbourhood who can boast of such a display. What do you do with the flowers that you cut every day?"

"I take them inside and enjoy them," came the quick reply.

"That you can also do in the garden; there is no need to cut the flowers," murmured her neighbour. "We too want to enjoy them. Will you not give me some of your flowers?"

13

Wu-Li was at a loss for a reply. Then her neighbour bent down to pluck a stem with three magnificent white bell-shaped blooms. But before she could do so the little dog, which had remained unnoticed, came bounding up. It growled fiercely at the stranger, to whom at that moment it seemed big and dangerous. With a cry, she let go of the stem and rushed off with the kindling, which by now was almost burnt up.

Wu-Li caressed the animal, and was glad to be rid of the inquisitive woman. But peace was not to be hers at present. Soon afterwards another of the neighbouring women appeared, saying that she wanted to make a pilgrimage to the temple of the goddess Kwang-Non, many miles away. She intended to make her an offering of fruits, rice and flowers; Wu-Li should give her the white bell-shaped blooms. But just these had been grown by Wu-Li for her altar.

"Shang-Ti," she implored inwardly, "Thou hast sent me word that I may call upon Thee when in need of help. Let not the flowers be taken; they are for Thee!"

Hardly was this quiet prayer completed than she perceived the Luminous Messenger, and repeated after her the words which she spoke:

"She who wishes to make an offering to the goddess must take flowers that she has grown herself. What good will it do you to offer the magnificent white blooms? The goddess would surely know that they come from Wu-Li's garden."

"You are right, I must not offer up another's flowers."

With these words the neighbour took her leave, and the Helper also vanished again.

Wu-Li plucked the much-desired white flowers, and carried them prayerfully to the house-altar. There she cast herself on the floor, and thanked Shang-Ti for his help. Then she sat down to her embroidery. She had promised Kwang-Non a cloth to cover the incense-bowl, in gratitude for the gift of the pure soul about to come to her.

Slowly and thoughtfully she selected the threads, drawing them through the fabric with care. She had received a good education until she had gone with Li-Fu-Tai as his wife. Wise, good women lived near the temples of the principal deities, and spent their lives in helping others.

As she worked, the young woman mused upon all this. She was still very small when her mother died. Her father, a high-ranking warrior, was absent most of the time. At home, however, she had only brothers, all of whom were older than the small sister, who was given little attention.

So the child was entrusted to the good women, and grew up in their care, together with a number of other little girls. They had a strict upbringing, and were allowed to learn many things. Some were trained to serve in the various temples of countless goddesses.

Wu-Li tried to recall all the names, but smiling, she had to abandon the attempt. Even in those days she had hardly known the names of the goddesses, and why they were worshipped. Was that wrong? The good women had rebuked her sharply for it, and many a tear had she shed over it. But the gods could not be angry with her on that account, else they would not now entrust this soul to her care. How she looked forward to the little child!

Quietly she began to talk with the little soul, and it seemed as if the unborn child answered.

"You must forget that I am coming to you from the Sacred Gardens, you who wish to be my mother. You must teach and guide me as though I were quite an ordinary child, otherwise I shall not be able to fulfil my task."

"What task awaits you, soul?"

"I am to fight and destroy the demons and blaze the trails for the light spirits to the souls of men."

"So you will be a warrior on earth?" asked the woman with a gentle sigh.

"I shall not fight with earthly weapons. The demons must be vanquished spiritually."

"Can I be of help to you, coming soul? Tell me, what may I do for you?"

"Establish peace and harmony all around me from my first breath on earth, remain in the Truth as you now stand in it, and you will help to prepare the soil on which I can thrive. You will help to forge the weapons which I shall need for battle."

"O soul, who sends you?"

"I am sent by One Who stands far higher above you human beings than Shang-Ti. Can you imagine that? Shang-Ti is only one of His servants. He is sublime and mighty, wise and just."

Trembling with awe, the woman heard the words. She was about to speak, but her voice failed her. Finally the question burst from her lips:

15

"What is the Name of Him of Whom you speak thus?" But she received no reply.

She sat for a long time, lost in deep thought. Then she went over to the altar; her prayer however did not seek Shang-Ti, but the Sublime One Who was above all others. And something completely new flowed through her, a feeling of happiness and new strength, such as she had never known before.

From this day on she prayed only to the Sublime One, but she could not tell Li-Fu-Tai about it. Deep awe of the holiness of what the coming soul had imparted to her sealed her lips.

The days passed in tranquil uniformity, until the hour when the old neighbour laid the new-born babe in her arms. It was a boy, of delicate frame and very light complexion. The old woman pointed this out to the priest who was to bless the boy, and he in turn questioned Li-Fu-Tai about it. The proud father, who tried hard but in vain to appear indifferent, was able to tell him a great many things.

"Look at me, worthy Father of the temples," he said. "My complexion too is lighter than that of all the neighbours. Time may have made the difference less obvious, but it is quite apparent in the days of the holy ablutions. The reason for this is that my forefathers were not born in this region, but came here to settle from over tall mountains."

"Do you know from which country they came?" the priest wanted to know.

"They called it Tarim, and tradition has it that the whole configuration of the country was totally different from this, as were the plants and animals."

"Why then did your forebears leave this special land?" the priest asked, a little mockingly.

Li-Fu-Tai had an answer to that also.

"The knowledge of what happened long ago was transmitted from father to son. The ancestor who emigrated with his sons did so at the behest of one of the gods."

The priest interrupted him:

"Which god could have directed him to do so?"

"I do not know," said Li-Fu-Tai somewhat hesitantly. "The name which came down to us bears no resemblance to any of ours, and yet my fore-fathers were pious men."

"What was this name?" the listener asked urgently.

"It sounds something like Yahwa," replied Li-Fu-Tai.

"Yahwa, Yahwa?" mused the priest. "You are right; we know of no god by that name. The actual name must have been distorted through transmission. Indeed, that is very likely. Continue your story!"

"The command received by my ancestor, Li-Pe-Yang, was roughly as follows: Go south across the high mountains. Shun no danger. You will be safe from wild beasts and impassable ravines, for you are protected.

"When you have crossed the mountains, continue your journey south, but at the same time turn a little towards the rising sun. You will come to a fertile land where the men wear red buttons on their black caps. Look around there. A plague has left land and dwelling-places without owners. If you find a piece of land that you like, go to the priest and ask him for it. Tell him that I sent you, and he will grant your request."

"A strange tradition," said the priest, amazed. "Do you also know why your ancestor had to come to this particular place?"

"We were told that too," affirmed Li-Fu-Tai. "The voice is said to have told him that from this part of the Middle Kingdom a Light before whose radiance the demons would flee should one day shine over the whole realm."

"And so that his descendants might partake of this Light, your ancestor undertook the arduous journey?" the priest reflected. "Truly, such selflessness deserves especial honour from you. I see you have set up a beautiful altar there. Make regular offerings; it will bring the child the blessing of your ancestors."

The priest left the little house with dignity. But something new had dawned on the soul of Li-Fu-Tai. What if this child were destined to bring the Light? Surely it must be so!

Perhaps this new-born babe was the ancestor come back again! In that case the little child should have been named Pe-Yang! Why had he not thought of it? Now the priest had blessed the babe as Li-Erl; the name had seemed beautiful and appropriate to him and his wife. Now the child must bear it until one day his deeds should justify a change of name.

Quietly Li-Fu-Tai went to the bedside of his wife, who was gazing blissfully at the little Li-Erl. He was truly a lovely little boy. Wu-Li had gently pushed aside all the amulets and herbs with which the neighbours had covered the new-born in order to protect him from demons and magic.

"You are protected, my little warrior of the Supreme One," her lips whispered, and it seemed to her that the child was smiling.

THE NEXT FEW YEARS passed without any special events. The truly pious disposition of the mother knew how to maintain peace and harmony, and thus also joy and happiness in the home, although at times it was not easy.

Li-Fu-Tai lived in the constant expectation of discovering his ancestor in his son. At the very least this boy was bound to be completely different from all other sons of men. He watched the child constantly, but at the same time he suffered many a disappointment. Li-Erl developed exactly like other healthy children. In time he learned to walk and talk, he fell into the water and reached into the fire. When he got into some childish mischief, the father was annoyed by his son's naughtiness. But his mother tempered the punishments and softened the rebukes without much ado. To her all the child's actions that annoyed the father seemed to spring from the same source: an immense thirst for knowledge. That was what the mother perceived in every one of her child's deeds. He asked few questions, preferring to find his answers through experiencing.

But despite these occasional vexations, it seemed as though the house was a playground for all good spirits, as though an air of heavenly peace wafted through it.

That was apparent to the few visitors who called from time to time, either to trade with the father or to set the deft hands of the mother to work. Sometimes they even asked about the gentle atmosphere that filled the little house. It was attributed by some to the special altar in Li-Fu-Tai's home.

In the morning and evening Wu-Li took her little son to the altar, and accustomed him to saying his childlike prayers there. She tried to tell him of the Sublime One. The priest had taught her special prayers for her son to say. She said them with him, but always added petitions and thanks from her own heart as well.

Li-Erl soon did likewise. To him it seemed natural to express all his wishes at the altar, but also to take his every joy there.

One day – he must have been about three years old – his mother found him touching the ground before the altar with his forehead, and imploring:

"Sublime One, I am hungry!"

Smiling, Wu-Li picked up the child and asked:

"Why do you not ask me?"

The child gazed with large eyes into hers and replied:

"Everything comes from the Sublime One; if Li-Erl asks Him, He will certainly tell you."

Not very long after that Wu-Li found the child in the twilight, engaged in animated, subdued conversation with someone whom she could not see. The little one stood before a mat and said, just as his mother approached:

"I understand you very well, Tsin-Hi. I will ask my father, but you must help me, so that he will not say I am too young."

Then the boy bowed with all propriety, as if to take leave of a very distinguished guest. Who had taught him that? Where had he seen such things?

For a moment Wu-Li wanted to ask her child with whom he had been speaking, but at the same time she knew that Li-Erl would never say, moreover indeed, would never be allowed to say. After all, she too had spoken to no one of the vision which she had before the birth of her child.

Any foolish question of hers would make the child shy, and disturb the harmony. For his part Li-Erl told her nothing about the meetings with Tsin-Hi (Son of Heaven), to which he was apparently quite accustomed. Keen observation revealed that after them the child's eyes were more radiant than usual, and that he was happier and more light-hearted.

When his father returned home the next day after a brief absence, and greeted his little son, he asked as usual:

"Is there anything my little light-seer wants?"

Light-seer was the pet name which his father had given him, thinking of the ancestral tradition. The mother found the name very fitting, because the child appeared really to see and to love only that which was luminous, avoiding darkness in any form.

Usually the boy answered his father's unfailing question with a smile, but today he said: "I was already waiting for my father to ask. I have a very great wish." With these words he slipped from his father's side and cast himself down before the altar.

19

"Sublime One, help me! I would like to learn to read and write."

Had the picture not been so touching, the father would have had to laugh at the earnestness with which the boy, who was still so little, aspired to adult knowledge.

"Come to me, Li-Erl," he said kindly. "Why will my son not wait until the time for learning has come?"

"Because there is no time to lose."

"And what will you do with the acquired knowledge?"

"I need it for my life."

The answers came quite calmly and naturally.

But the father wanted to find out whether his son was really in earnest. He explained to him that the Chinese language was very comprehensive. Ordinary scholars could learn only about a third of it. That of course was enough for trade and commerce.

Those who devoted themselves to learning, who wanted to read books and perhaps even write their own, had to learn about twice as much. While he, Li-Fu-Tai, had some knowledge of this second stage of the language, it had taken him some twenty years to acquire it.

"Then teach me that, my father," begged the boy. "Afterwards we must find other teachers."

"I believe that what I can show you will satisfy you," said his father, half amused. But the child shook his head earnestly, and begged:

"Let us begin at once, I have no time to lose."

Every day now the three-year old practised the intricately formed words of his language with brush and drawing-ink. His father soon realised that he was a very inept teacher. His command of what he was to teach was inadequate, despite many years of earnest study. The child, however, grasped everything with the greatest clarity, and retained what he had once been told.

Contrary to expectation, a teacher was soon found.

The priests who lived and taught near the temple refused to admit so young a child among their pupils, and rebuked Li-Fu-Tai for aiming too high with the boy. Somewhat dejected, the father set out on his homeward journey. Li-Erl was anxiously awaiting the news his father would bring. What was he to tell him?

Lost in thought, he was oblivious to the road, and collided with a man whose outward appearance attracted his attention.

He was an elderly, poorly-dressed man, whose garb differed markedly from that worn in the neighbourhood. His bronze-coloured face was very wrinkled; bushy, almost white brows shielded the deep blue, shining eyes. These eyes gazed enquiringly at Li-Fu-Tai, causing him to apologise almost against his will, and to stammer something about "deep thoughts".

"What was the subject of these thoughts?" asked the stranger kindly. His voice was pleasant and his speech articulate.

"I am looking for a teacher for my son," answered Li-Fu-Tai almost hastily.

But then he was annoyed with himself, for of what concern to the stranger were his affairs?

The latter, however, seemed not at all surprised; he simply said:

"Then we had to meet. You seek a teacher, and I a pupil. Yet I know not whether I may find what I seek this very day."

"So you are a wise man?" said Li-Fu-Tai, amazed. "Perhaps you can help me then. My son would like to learn to read and write our language. The pious fathers refused to admit him. I do not ask your services for nothing; I can pay for them," he added with a certain pride.

The elderly man regarded him keenly.

"How old is your son?"

That was the very question the father was afraid to answer. He evaded it, and told how eager a pupil little Li-Erl was. For a short while the learned man listened to him, then he said emphatically:

"You must answer my question; everything depends on it."

"His circle of years has not yet closed four times," said the father hesitantly.

At that the figure of the old man straightened.

"Let us go to your house," he said almost joyfully. "I must see the boy."

After that they did not speak another word until Li-Fu-Tai's little house came into view. At the doorway stood Li-Erl, looking out. But when he saw that his father was not alone, he abandoned his intention of running to meet him. Instead he hid behind all kinds of household effects that lay outside the house, and had first to be called.

21

Now the old man and the child stood face to face, looking intently at each other. It was as though their gaze became merged. Then the aged man placed his bronzed, wrinkled, but finely-formed hand on the boy's head, murmuring soft words.

"I will be a teacher to your son for as long as he can still learn from me," he said, turning to the father. "Solely for this purpose have I come here from distant lands."

Li-Fu-Tai stared incredulously at the speaker. Could it be that again someone had travelled here from far away for the sake of his child?

"Are you permitted to tell me who sent you and whence you come?" he asked diffidently.

"Later," said the old man. "We must now decide on how to arrange things. Is there room for me in your house?"

Li-Fu-Tai said that there was not, but offered to build a separate dwelling for the learned man next to his own.

"What shall I call you?" he wanted to know, and learned that the teacher wished to be called Lie-Tse. Whether that was his real name remained unsaid.

Now Wu-Li, who had been working with the silkworms, joined them. Without restraint, she approached the stranger and greeted him like a welcome guest. Amazed, Li-Fu-Tai gazed at his wife, who was usually so shy.

"Do you know who this is?" he asked her. Without hesitation she replied:

"He is the kind wise man who will teach Erl. He will live with us and be a father to us. I am grateful to him and to Shang-Ti for it."

"How do you know that?" her husband pressed her further.

"I have seen him three times at night in a dream, and spoken with him. We know each other quite well."

Wu-Li said it cheerfully, unaware that she was uttering something special.

But all the time Li-Erl stood there blissfully happy. He could wait until the wise man had time for him, because later he would surely always be there for him.

The very next day the building of the house began. Bamboo-poles were fitted together. Wu-Li brought mats and silken covers, small bronze vases, and vessels – pure white and painted ones – made of choice white clay. Such bowls had not long been available, and only rich people could afford them. Even before everything was completed, the instruction of the child began. It was obvious that the little one knew far more than his teacher had expected, more even than his father had realised. The instruction filled virtually the whole day, for Lie-Tse did not allow the child to leave his side; he made use of every conversation to instruct him.

Some time had passed; the wise man was living as a revered and intimate member of Li-Fu-Tai's household, when the latter resumed his former enquiry into the whence and wherefore of Lie-Tse's coming.

The boy had already gone to rest, and now Lie-Tse recounted:

"Far, far from here is my homeland; we call our country Tibet, and rarely does one of our people leave his native soil. But even in my youth I had received a message from the gods that I should prepare myself to be one day a teacher and helper to a Truth-bringer. Thus I have spent the greater part of my life in waiting and learning; I almost feared that I had missed the time, and been found unworthy.

"Then finally, three nights in succession, tidings came to me of the boy to whom the Highest of all gods wished to send me. I made ready, not knowing what land I was to look for.

"But having passed beyond the borders of my homeland I came upon a group of travellers who called to me that for some days now they had been waiting for me; they were to guide me safely to my pupil. They had brought a small, nimble horse for me, also provisions enough for a journey of several weeks.

"When at last this village lay before us, they declared that our destination had been reached. They took their leave, and at once set out on their homeward journey. I could not even show them my gratitude in anything but words."

"He who sent them will reward them," said Wu-Li pensively.

Again Li-Fu-Tai had to marvel at his wife. Whence did such knowledge, and the confidence towards the learned man, come to her?

But the latter nodded kindly to her:

"You are right, Wu-Li," he said, "I had the same thought, and was not concerned."

"Did you not ask the people who had sent them?" asked Li-Fu-Tai almost vehemently. "They might well have been impostors?"

"Do I look as though impostors could find anything of value on me?" smiled Lie-Tse. "Besides, they spoke of my pupil, of whom no human being knew. So it was clear to me that in some way or other God had sent them to be of help to me."

"You say God," Li-Fu-Tai thoughtfully picked up the words of the old man. "Do you not believe in the gods? Which god do you mean?"

"Him, the Only One, the Sublime One, Whom we call by the unutterable Name. Him Whom your wife worships at your altar and Whom your son too has already learned to revere."

"And the gods whom I worship?"

"They are His servants," replied Lie-Tse calmly.

Perhaps he had expected Li-Fu-Tai to enquire further. But the father of the family withdrew pensively into his inner being. He knew very well that he had taken a special soul into his care; he realised that because of this his way of living and thinking would change, indeed would have to change; but he wanted to proceed with care. He was averse to undue haste. For the time being he regarded it as quite sufficient to allow the presence of this learned man for the sake of his son.

The neighbours took hardly any notice of the old man, whom they probably regarded as a kind of servant. He entered into no conversations, but if addressed he answered pleasantly.

When the boy was about six years old, Wu-Li and Lie-Tse deemed it time for him to be taken into the temple. His father, who had also been consulted, left the decision to the learned man.

So the day came when Li-Erl was to see the inside of the temple for the first time. It was only a small, unpretentious pagoda, barely rising above the buildings that surrounded it. But Wu-Li had always marvelled at the woodcarvings inside and out, at the lacquered works and the bronze vessels, as being the most beautiful to be seen. She was convinced that the little one, whose heart was so receptive to beauty, would come home overwhelmed. Instead a very weary child stepped over the threshold, responding to his mother's eager questions only with a smile.

"Can you explain what has had such an effect on Li-Erl?" his mother asked their companion. He too looked as if he would have preferred not to speak, but then he said:

"The boy cannot reconcile that which is alive in his soul with what he saw in the temple. Much time will yet have to pass before he is able to comprehend that human beings drag the Divine down to their level in order to be able to worship It."

"I do not understand you, Lie-Tse," said the mother, quite confused.

"Then you will be all the better able to understand what is happening in the soul of your child."

How often Wu-Li had experienced things like that: the old man seemed to speak in such simple words, yet the sense behind them remained obscure to her. For some days the boy continued pensive; then on a walk he spoke to his teacher about his thoughts.

"What do they do in the temple, Lie-Tse?" he began rather plaintively. "All the pictures which they revere as gods are demons! Just look at them, surely you must notice it too."

"Well, you see, Li-Erl, the people wanted to have pictures of the gods. But they had nothing to go by. They did not want to make them look like human beings; that did not seem exalted enough. But the unearthly things they saw were only demons. So they formed the gods in the image of demons, merely adding the qualities which they revered in them."

"What do the gods say to that?" the child wanted to know. "Surely it cannot please them."

"No, it does not; that is why they chose a soul above, who is to come and show men what is right."

"Will that be soon?" Li-Erl asked eagerly.

"The soul is already on earth. As soon as the time has come, its task may begin. But tell me, child, what can you learn from this experience in the temple?"

The boy hesitated for a moment before replying, but then he cried:

"That men should not make images of the gods; for they cannot do it, and spoil everything."

"Do you now realise why your mother has placed no statue on the house-altar? She cannot put it into words, but her soul knows and intuitively perceives all that. You have a very good mother."

As he finished speaking, Wu-Li approached the two, who were just returning from their walk. The boy smiled at her, and once again she felt the connection with him and with the Gardens of Light.

Li-Erl now visited the temple regularly, for it was part of the plan prescribed to Lie-Tse from above that the future Forerunner should be acquainted with everything. It was not to be made easy for him to find the Truth.

Lie-Tse told him very little, usually letting him find even the answers to his own questions for himself.

WITH ALL THIS, years went by. The boy had become a youth, who had mastered even the third stage of the language, had read widely, and at his teacher's wish associated with the priests.

As he did so, it was obvious that Li-Erl was not by nature a fighter. When his views and those of the priests differed – as often happened – he was silent and sought a bridge, or at least an understanding. That won him friends among the men, who otherwise would undoubtedly have rejected his thoughts as unacceptable.

But his teacher considered that the time had come for him to see a more important temple, and to make the acquaintance of more learned men. That had long since been the wish of his father, who was very proud of his intelligent son. But he stipulated that Lie-Tse should go with the young man. Moreover, they were accompanied by two servants, who were to look after them.

The parting from his mother was hard for Li-Erl; nevertheless he looked forward to all the new things he was to see. He also shared his teacher's view that the journey should be made on foot if they were really to enjoy it. He wished to see everything that could be seen on the way, to get to know everything that he did not yet know.

There was plenty of it. First they journeyed towards the sunset. After a few days the landscape changed, and the hilly plains of his homeland disappeared. The rocks rose ever higher, forming mountains and whole mountain-ranges. Also different trees grew there: conifers instead of the wide-spreading palms.

Li-Erl looked about him with open eyes, and had a thousand and one questions for his teacher. Then suddenly he became quiet. Lie-Tse, who was afraid that the strain of walking might after all be too great for the lad, looked at his pupil anxiously. However the anxiety left him at once: this was not the look of an overtired person! His eyes sparkled, there was a smile on his lips, but Li-Erl was evidently preoccupied with something of which his teacher had no knowledge at present, nor did he enquire.

In the evening, as they were resting under the starry sky, the youth began:

"Do you see them too, my father – the good spirits that inhabit the mountains and gorges? Do you see the beings that live in the trees? They are quite different from those at home. They seem old, ancient, hoary and cracked like the mountain-crevices; one might well fear them. But they are good, I know it."

"No, Li-Erl, I do not see them," admitted Lie-Tse, "but I know of them. They are servants of the great God Who has created us and all things. They will be helpers to you when you are permitted to fulfil your task."

"Will you tell me what my task is to be?" the youth asked diffidently.

But Lie-Tse declined.

"When the time comes, He Who gave you the charge, before your soul dwelt in this earthly body, will remind you of it. Then you will know again for what purpose you have come to the earth."

The servants had withdrawn to be able to talk more freely. Now one of them came rushing back with every sign of great terror. An evil demon had appeared not far from their fire; a horrid fellow with grotesque features. Surely their lives were all in danger.

Lie-Tse shook his head, while Li-Erl sprang up and sped towards the fire before anyone could stop him.

Horrified, the servant shouted:

"Run after him, it could be the death of him. You should not have let him go. He is entrusted to us!"

But Lie-Tse shook his head again.

"It is all right. He must get to know the evil ones."

And the old man remained calmly seated. But the servant dashed after his young master and found him standing motionless near the fire-place.

With wide-open eyes, Li-Erl looked at the scene that met his gaze. The other servant lay on the ground, and on him knelt a monster of repulsive appearance. Hairy and unkempt, it was suggestive of a wild beast, and even the bloodshot eyes coincided with that picture. Yet its movements and dress were quite human. The horrible creature looked up, grinning.

When no feature on Li-Erl's countenance changed, the attitude of the demon became unsure. Again it cast a quick glance at the youth, but immediately averted its eyes. At the same time it seemed to the young man as though it were growing smaller. Not for a moment was he afraid. A burning curiosity filled him, making him rivet his eyes on this apparition which was completely new to him. He had known of the existence of demons, had often heard about them, but as yet he had seen none.

He wanted to speak to it, to call upon it to let go of the sorely frightened servant, but to his own astonishment he could not utter a word. To him it seemed as though someone was preventing him from actively intervening. He simply had to watch, to watch unceasingly.

And now it became quite clear: the longer he looked with searching, penetrating gaze at the misshapen creature, the hazier its contours became. It seemed to grow steadily smaller. The burning eyes were extinguished, the clawed arms shrivelled, and thus released their victim. And all of a sudden the whole apparition had vanished. The servant lying on the ground rose to his feet, still terror-stricken.

Li-Erl turned to go, deeply preoccupied with what he had seen and experienced. The servants extinguished the fire and followed him. They felt safer near him.

The youth sat down silently opposite his teacher, who also said nothing. And yet Li-Erl perceived Lie-Tse's most vivid community of feeling. There was a wondrous swinging between them, which was better than the liveliest conversation.

Even during the days that followed neither of them referred to the experience that had left a deep impression in Li-Erl's soul. The longer he reflected on it, the greater became his certainty that his fearless gaze had worked destructively upon the demon. If, as promised, one would come who was to destroy the demons, he would surely have to fight with spiritual weapons, not with axe and sword.

If only the goodness of the gods would soon send another demon their way, to enable Li-Erl to put to the test what he had just learned. Countless times the youth made the wish; then it was granted.

This time it was he himself whom the demon approached, as he walked through a tall forest at dusk, some distance away from the others. Warrior-clad, the furry monster barred his way, brandishing a crude, iron-studded club.

For a brief moment terror arose in the youth's soul; the dreadful sight had come upon him too unexpectedly. But he composed himself at once. Taking a step back to lean against a tree, he rested his hands on his staff and regarded the ferocious monster, thinking the while:

"You are not a creature of God. The Sublime One cannot create such forms! But where do you come from?"

At that the demon roared with a deafening voice:

"From within you!"

It did not surprise Li-Erl that the demon responded to an unspoken question. His association with good spirits had accustomed him to that. But the manner in which the question was answered almost upset his inner composure.

"If such a thing can come from my inner being, what must it be like?" he thought, horrified.

In so thinking, however, his attention had been diverted; the demon had made use of this to draw menacingly closer.

Roused, Li-Erl called out loudly:

"Ah, so you think to make easy game of me by posing riddles about my inner being?"

Now he directed the intent gaze of his radiant eyes at the enemy. And the same thing happened as before: the figure slowly shrivelled until it disappeared.

Li-Erl shuddered. He had learned much. Not for one moment must he yield to reflection when in such danger. The object was to remain vigilant, if the demons were to be vanquished. He was convinced that he had within him the power to triumph. Hence it lay with him whether a demon could endanger him.

All this became a certainty for the youth. But he was unceasingly preoc-

29

cupied with something else. The demon had said that it came from Li-Erl's inner being. That could have been a blatant lie calculated to divert him from his vigilance. But somehow the young man sensed that there was some truth in it.

"Is that how my inner being appears?" he asked himself again and again.

For days he pondered over it, until finally he decided to ask his teacher. To this end, however, he must describe the two encounters with the demons, which he had hitherto kept to himself.

The aged man listened quietly. When Li-Erl finally put the question that occupied him so intensely about the origin of the demon, Lie-Tse smiled gently.

"The monster was right: it was a product of your own inner being. The first demon that you saw was also created by human beings. At that time it arose from the fear of the servants, which took on form in the creature and returned to them strengthened. With you it was not fear that caused the demon to manifest. Try to remember what it might have been."

"My own wish!" Li-Erl shouted, in utmost surprise. "Indeed, I had no thought but to see such a monster again and to test my strength upon it."

After that he relapsed into silence; for now the thoughts followed one another unceasingly. – –

Meanwhile they were approaching the capital of the province, their journey's end. Li-Erl had not imagined the city to be so extensive and so magnificent. Nearly all the buildings had two storeys. But there were also much higher ones.

Lie-Tse explained that these were the pagodas, the temples. They certainly looked different from the poor little temple of his home-village.

The way led them through a gate richly ornamented with carved dragons and closed by sliding beams artfully fitted together.

Before it sat a sentry, of military appearance and richly attired, with a curiously-shaped broad sword on his knees. He questioned the newcomers in detail about whence they had come and whither they were bound, also about the destination and purpose of their journey.

Lie-Tse gave particulars, but was extremely sparing of words. His manner was familiar to his pupil, who was nonetheless surprised that the sage did not depart from his habit in addressing this "distinguished" man.

However, his teacher's answer must have satisfied the sentry, for he rose to his feet ceremoniously, laid the sword on a table, and began to slide the beams apart. In doing so he paused repeatedly to scrutinise the travellers once again.

Finally there was an opening in the gate, wide enough for a man to slip through. But the bulky guard stepped in front of it, and asked yet another question.

"You have said, old father," he began, "that you are the teacher of this young man. Are you a Lama?"

"Yes."

"Then I greet you with redoubled reverence, wise man. Joy will blossom for me that I have been allowed to exchange words with you this day, and to behold your countenance which is blessed by the gods."

The man bowed low, and stepped aside respectfully. The two newcomers walked quickly through the gap in the gate. Li-Erl was glad that they could finally enter the city, which seemed mysterious and wonderful to him.

Lie-Tse directed his steps purposefully through a maze of narrow lanes and alleyways, and Li-Erl followed, although he was tempted to linger. Everything he saw seemed important and glorious to him.

Not far from one of the large pagodas, the travellers halted in front of a house lavishly decorated with red lacquer. At the old man's strangely rhythmical knock the door immediately opened.

It was a very simple middle-class house, although it seemed like a palace to the youth. At the back of the ante-room into which they were admitted stood an altar lit by colourful paper lanterns, and evidently used for ancestor-worship. Mats and sleeping rolls covered the floor; the walls were painted in bright colours.

An old man approached the sage and conversed with him in a language which Li-Erl did not understand. He then turned to Li-Erl, and addressed him kindly in his mother tongue:

"Welcome to my lowly house, Son of the Heavenly Gardens. It is at your disposal for as long as you may wish to tarry here. Your commands will be carried out before my own. Your presence will be an honour and a joy to me."

Although from childhood Li-Erl had been accustomed to the rather affected language, it had never yet seemed to him so overdone as here. He was at a loss for a reply. How could the stranger call him a Son of the Heavenly Gardens! That did not apply to him.

Uncertainly he directed his gaze to his teacher, who expressed thanks on his behalf. Then they were shown into a room where they could stretch out and rest from their arduous journey. A meal was brought to them by their own servants, who also attended to their comfort.

The youth had many questions, but fatigue overcame him; they had to wait until morning.

When he awoke the next day, he found Lie-Tse no longer by his side. On summoning the servants he learned that the venerable man had already gone to the temple, and would soon return. Li-Erl had an ample meal, and then prepared to go out. His host was not in evidence. When his teacher did not come, he began to look round the house.

Apart from the ante-room and his chamber, there were four similar rooms, all of which seemed to be occupied. A kitchen and bedrooms for the servants had been added at the back. Everything gave the impression of solid prosperity.

For a long time the youth regarded all that there was to see; then he was anxious for more. Yesterday he had observed that this house also had two storeys. Having inspected the first, he now also wished to see the second.

He looked round in vain for a flight of stairs. There was not even a ladder leading up. Perhaps he had to climb a rope. While Li-Erl was conducting his fruitless search, his teacher returned. The first question came immediately:

"How can I get up there?"

"You cannot," was Lie-Tse's calm reply.

The youth assumed that he alone was not to go upstairs, but that did not solve the riddle.

"How do others get up there?" he now asked.

And again the answer was:

"They do not."

"Do they not live upstairs as well? How do they get to their rooms?" Li-Erl's question was almost impatient.

"Nobody lives up there. That is the abode of the ancestors and good spirits. They must not be disturbed. No one goes up there."

Amazed, Li-Erl looked at the aged man, and in the flood of thoughts assailing him forgot the other questions which only that morning had seemed so important to him.

If the upper parts of all the two-storey houses were unoccupied, those in the pagodas could probably not be entered by human beings either. Did the gods dwell there, he wondered? And how were they accommodated? After all, every pagoda had many storeys.

Li-Erl was well pleased when his teacher urged that they should visit the nearby temple. There he would surely find out all that he wished to know.

Many steps led up to the pagoda. On either side of them stood small stone statues, between which visitors to the temple had to pass. Li-Erl seemed to hear a voice whispering:

"He who approaches the Deity must not fear the spirit-world."

Nor did he indeed fear the grotesque images; he looked boldly at them as he mounted step after step between them. But now, what was that?

Those were no longer stone statues, but mobile, transparent figures, grimacing at him, reaching for him with long, thin arms; figures that seemed to be convulsed with scornful laughter.

Li-Erl summoned all his courage. He refused to show any fear, but it began to take hold of him within. If he closed his eyes he did not have to see the forms; that might facilitate the ascent.

He tried, but soon stumbled. Involuntarily he reached for his teacher, but the usually-so-helpful man avoided his reach. He was to go alone! No sooner had he become conscious of this than his courage grew.

When the demons – for that was surely what they must be – approached him, he forcibly opened his eyes wide, and stared at them. With that their movements ceased; they assumed solid form, and after a few moments he again beheld stone figures on the steps.

Then it seemed to Li-Erl that a veil was rent asunder before his inner eye. He saw clearly the connection between the demons on the journey and these forms. And from his very own experience he knew that he had simply to look either one straight in the eye in order to dispel them.

He was overjoyed at the recognition gained and would have liked to give voice to his joy, had they not just then reached the topmost stair.

Before them was the entrance to the temple, consisting of a superbly carved portal. It gleamed in red and gold, with contrasting green and black between. Temple-servants in elaborately embroidered silken robes walked sedately up and down, their hands concealed within the wide sleeves.

Lie-Tse went up to a tradesman sitting apart, to bargain for offerings. He bought all kinds of fruit, a bowl of cooked rice, and a pigeon. Li-Erl looked on, amazed. At home they had only placed flowers upon the altar, flowers which his mother had grown herself.

Slowly, at his teacher's side, the youth entered the forehall of the temple. An intoxicating fragrance enveloped his senses. From open vessels rose smoke, weaving a bluish vapour around the carvings on the ceiling.

This seemed strangely mysterious to the visitor, who had never seen anything like it before. And it was this haze that exuded the scent – a mixture of fading flowers and a variety of smouldering resins. It almost took one's breath away.

Along the walls stood wooden sculptures, elaborately carved and painted. Some were also clothed in silken garments. But no matter how splendid, they all had grotesque, horrible features. Li-Erl shuddered involuntarily.

Then one of the statues began to advance slowly towards the two visitors. Cold fear gripped the young man's heart, but he remembered what he had so recently learned, and gazed as resolutely as possible at the presumed demon.

But the figure began to speak. It reproached him for staring so presumptuously.

Lie-Tse whispered to him that he should bow. But a firm command from the teacher was required before Li-Erl decided to show his respect to the demon. He did so awkwardly enough, but the gruesome one must have been satisfied, for he slowly moved on, letting the two visitors pass.

Hardly were they out of earshot than Lie-Tse whispered:

"That is one of the priests of this temple. You must not again fail to show due respect to such a person."

Li-Erl had a question ready, but he was silenced by a quick gesture, for as they walked on they had reached the splendidly embroidered silken curtain which separated the inside of the temple from the fore-hall.

A number of musical instruments resounded in an unusual rhythm; particularly dominant was a kind of small drum that emitted a high-pitched, clear tone, not unlike the cry of a water-fowl. Fragrances and smoke increased.

As if through a mist, Li-Erl walked into the interior of the temple. Statues made of wood, of white clay, of stone and of bronze stood everywhere. Lie-Tse slipped quickly past them. He was anxious to bring his pupil immediately before the main statue.

Again they ascended steps, and were suddenly standing in front of a richly decorated golden screen. As they came to a stop the youth raised his head and found himself face to face with a monumental sculpture.

A figure, larger than life, sat there in the most perfect repose. After all the grotesque images he had seen until now, it was a relief to behold such an embodiment of psychic harmony. Might the features be less repugnant than those of the others?

Almost timorously Li-Erl looked up, and a sound expressing the greatest delight escaped him involuntarily. The countenance of the figure was of perfect beauty. The harmonious features appeared to be animated by a smile, but even that accentuated the peace emanating from the image of the deity.

Absorbed in deep worship, Li-Erl stood for a long time, gazing up at the face. Then he turned to his teacher, and asked in a whisper:

"Who is this?"

Lie-Tse motioned to him to be quiet. Then both turned to leave. After this deep impression, neither of them wanted to see anything else.

Adjacent to the temple was a grove with all kinds of exquisite plants and shady trees. Thither the aged man took his pupil, and they seated themselves upon a grassy bank.

For a long time neither of them spoke. Finally Li-Erl began:

"Who is the god whom we have just seen? Is it an image of the Sublime One, about Whom you have told me?"

"No one can picture the Sublime One, Li-Erl; for nobody has ever seen Him, nor will anyone ever be permitted to see Him. However, this picture, which has moved you so deeply, is the embodiment of some of His attributes. Go there often, and seek out what it has to tell you. The image will reveal the Magnitude of the Sublime One, if you are able to see aright."

"How is it possible for the priests of this temple to have such grotesque features? After all, they serve the Sublime One, Whose attributes give rise to such a picture of repose!"

"They know not whom they worship. They regard the statue as one of their gods."

"But even so they should not look like that," the youth insisted, uncomprehending. "Their features are coarse, uncouth, as if carved in wood, lifeless ..."

Lie-Tse interrupted him.

"What you see are not the features of the priests, Li-Erl. They wear masks carved out of wood. Behind these they have human faces like you and me."

The teacher, who only then understood his pupil's indignation, said it almost with a smile. But Li-Erl grew all the more indignant.

"If those are masks, it accounts for the strangely rigid, contorted expression of all these features. But is it not a disgrace for priests to hide behind masks, especially as they are regularly in the holy temple?" ·

"You really do not understand, my son," the old man advised him kindly. "There is a deep meaning in this custom. With these masks the priests wish to express that they cease to be human beings the moment they serve the deity. No one must know them, no one is to know anything about their lives. Thereby they want to set themselves apart from the rest of humanity."

"In that case it is actually something beautiful, carefully thought out, which causes them to act as they do," Li-Erl admitted pensively. "But why do they choose such horrible, grotesque masks? Is it their purpose to call forth respect, or to spread fear and terror with them?"

"I believe that they do not want to be better looking than the images of their gods."

Li-Erl sighed. Suddenly he dreaded everything he would still have to learn.

After a prolonged silence, Lie-Tse began to speak again.

"When we requested entry to the city, you were about to ask a question. Do you still remember what it was? Now the time has come when I may answer you."

Without hesitation the pupil replied:

"Of course I still remember it, my father. The sentry asked whether you were a Lama, and you said that you were. What is a Lama?"

"In our country the priests are called Lamas."

Lie-Tse knew that the answer would not suffice, but he awaited further questions. Only when the pupil enquired further, eager to know, was he to be granted an explanation.

Swiftly the question followed:

"Which country did you come from?" And without waiting for the answer, Li-Erl pleaded:

"Tell me at last, why you came to us, who sent you, and if you will now remain with us always."

Slowly Lie-Tse began:

"My homeland lies far, far away from here amid mountains. We call it Tibet, the blessed land. There people live different lives from those in this Middle Kingdom. Their life is strictly regulated, and all of them serve the Supreme One, Whom they worship without picturing Him to themselves.

"Each of our young sons is brought up in such a way that he can serve in the temple at any time. We deem it the most exalted vocation for a man, and therefore only a few may practise it.

"Each year a small number are chosen, and ordained for the temple. The others must ply a trade or look after the cattle. A small number learn to use weapons, so that we are not undefended and powerless against our neighbours. We ourselves do not initiate wars, as we live in the Laws of the Eternal One.

"Those who are ordained for the temple continue to learn under the guidance of the older priests. We possess ancient writings which we are permitted to read, and from which we learn glorious things. But often one of the older Lamas is granted tidings from above, through which our knowledge develops further.

"Those on whom such a connection with the more luminous world is bestowed are held in great esteem by the other priests and Lamas. They are permitted to wear the Yellow Cap as a sign of their connection with the Light."

Impetuously Li-Erl interrupted him:

"And you are such a Lama, my father? Do you also wear a Yellow Cap? What does it look like?"

"Like this," Lie-Tse replied calmly, and drew forth a piece of yellow silk fabric from the breast-folds of his robe.

He unfolded it and put it on. The shape of the cap was unusual; it covered his ears and the back of his neck right down to his shoulders. The aged man looked indescribably venerable with this head covering.

A faint perception awakened in Li-Erl that it was surely a particular act of grace on the part of the Sublime One that had given him the aged man as a teacher. He gazed at him in devout wonder. But the sage concealed his cap again, and continued his tale:

"High in the mountains lay the monastery in which I held office. We preserved an ancient tradition, which said that only so long as we kept ourselves completely pure from any alien teaching could we remain in connection with the Eternal Gardens. Mankind would slowly head towards perdition, but the Sublime One would send them help. If we kept ourselves pure, such help would always be allowed to come from our people."

Lie-Tse paused with a sigh, and closed his eyes. Sad thoughts might be passing before his inner gaze. He turned very pale. But he put aside these thoughts forcibly, and continued:

"Even though we knew this, we could not prevent an alien spirit from taking hold of some of our brothers. We fortified the borders of our country, we prevented the neighbours from entering and yet new thoughts came to us as though borne on the air.

"Then the monasteries isolated themselves completely, so that there at least the old purity would be preserved. Mine too was like a citadel, in which the strictest regulations prevailed.

"I devised ever new plans for training the rising generation, and then sending them among the wavering ones in the lowlands. Surely it would still be possible to win them back to the true teaching. Then one night I received the Command from the Sublime One to leave everything behind and journey to a foreign country."

"Have you been permitted to speak with the Sublime One yourself?" Li-Erl wanted to know.

"No human being is able to do that," Lie-Tse rebuked him. "The Supreme One has countless servants, whom He sends out to make known His Will. One such luminous figure came also to me and announced that the Sublime, the Ineffable One wished to call forth a Truth-bringer in a great people of childlike human beings. He showed me the soul, which dwelt above in the Gardens of Eternity awaiting incarnation. And I saw that this soul was exceeding pure.

"'You are to be the teacher and guide of this soul on earth', proclaimed the Luminous One. 'Therefore set forth, and journey to the country to which this soul will be sent.'

"And I left everything behind in order to obey the Command of the Sublime One. It was many months before I reached your homeland, Li-Erl."

The youth had listened, deeply moved. Now he bowed his head and whispered softly:

"O Thou Sublime One, Whom I divine from afar, I thank Thee! I am not worthy of Thy Goodness, but I want to be Thy servant."

This conversation with the aged teacher had brought to life in Li-Erl many things which had lain as though covered with veils. Clear light fell on much that had hitherto seemed to the youth inexplicable. Above all, he had for a long time now concerned himself with the question:

How did his mother know of the Sublime One for Whom she had set up the altar? Why was his parents' home the only one in the whole district where the belief in the gods had been supplemented? They had not abandoned the old gods, but they worshipped a new, mightier One Who was above all others. Why?

As Li-Erl now reflected on these questions, the answer arose spontaneously within him:

"You are to become a Truth-bringer!"

How much was contained in these words! Undreamed-of vistas were revealed to the young spirit, who bowed jubilantly before something which he was not yet able to fathom. Truth-bringer! Servant of the Supreme One!

But he who was to bring the Truth must himself first have received it. When would that be? Did it require a special consecration?

Lie-Tse, whom he finally asked, shook his head.

"You are consecrated, Li-Erl. The moment the Sublime One singled out

39

your soul in the Light-Gardens and called it to His service, at that very moment the stream of consecration also flowed over you. Since then luminous hands have guided you from above. Here below I was chosen to impart to you what earthly knowledge you need."

After this answer the youth was silent for a long while. He had first to come to terms with it inwardly, before he could enquire further. Then he wanted to know:

"Why have you brought me here to the temple-city, where I cannot learn even a single word about the Sublime One? You could instruct me better at home, my father."

"I brought you here at the behest of the Divine Messenger who guides me in all things concerning you, so that you should learn to know from your own experience the false teachings of the priests.

"He who is to bring Light must know the Darkness he is called to illumine. From tomorrow onwards I shall bring you into direct contact with the priests and wise men, from whom you can learn infinitely much if you open the gates of your spirit. Not all that they say is wrong.

"Listen, absorb within yourself, and learn to distinguish. But above all, never let them perceive that you are a Called one."

And as Lie-Tse had said, so it came to pass. From the following morning, Li-Erl became a pupil of the priests. But they soon realised that they could teach him but little. As he had also mastered the third stage of the language in reading and writing, he was able to read everything that seemed important to him and to them. But the scribes, who would rather have kept such knowledge to themselves, were not pleased with that.

They did not even understand why the young man aspired to wisdom. When they asked if he wished to become a priest, he declined, without entering further into the question. But if he were not to become a priest, they felt no inclination to answer his numerous questions. In this dilemma they turned to Lie-Tse.

First they demanded of him that he should prove his identity. If he were the teacher of the youth, he must possess great knowledge. Why then did he go about so unobtrusively and modestly among the common people, instead of presenting himself with appropriate dignity?

He told them that he was a Lama, and that he belonged to the Yellow

Priesthood, but preferred to remain unrecognised. Above all, his pupil was not to know of his rank until he was able to understand what was spiritually associated with it. Although he had learned that the old man was a Lama, it had made no impression whatsoever on him. Things should continue in this way for some time yet.

The priests shook their heads. However, since Lie-Tse was far superior to them all in rank, they had to submit to his wishes. But now they wanted to know what the sage had in mind for his pupil.

"He is to learn what you can offer him; after that I shall take him to other masters," was the unsatisfactory reply.

Careful deliberation followed, in which tempers ran high, but there was no agreement. The majority of the priests were in favour of sending the youth and his Lama to another town, to other temples. Then they would be free of all responsibility.

Some, however, agreed that a definite term of instruction should be set, perhaps twelve months or so; but they should endeavour to tell the pupil as little as possible. Only a single elderly priest spoke against them all: he offered to instruct Li-Erl to the best of his ability. Should this anger the gods, he would take all the blame upon himself.

This offer settled the matter. Li-Erl was assigned to the aged Maru for an indefinite period of time.

For teacher and pupil much that was beautiful arose from the instruction, bringing benefit to both. Lie-Tse never took part in it. No one knew what he did during the many hours that Li-Erl spent in the temple. But when the youth returned home, full of all he had heard, his teacher appeared soon enough.

Maru answered the numerous questions of the inquisitive pupil to the best of his knowledge, although most of them took him by complete surprise. He recognised that deep thought, such as he had never seen anywhere before, had been given to everything.

One day they came to speak of the pagodas. Li-Erl enquired about the meaning of the several storeys; in reply he was told that those were the dwellings of the gods. Then both were silent for some time, for Li-Erl always reflected on each reply, until he knew whether it satisfied him. This one did not.

41

"Do the gods really live in the pagodas? Surely they cannot be in all of them at the same time, scattered all over the country. Or do they live there only from time to time, taking up residence now here, now there?" he wished to know.

Maru was at a loss. He had never given it a thought before. He pondered for quite a while; then he had a sudden idea that might be helpful.

"You must not picture it tangibly, Li-Erl," he said quite firmly. "The gods probably live up above. But we would like to have them near us; therefore we assign to them places in which we perceive them to be particularly close to us. The people however believe that they actually dwell in our pagodas, and they are happy with the idea."

Maru was quite pleased with this explanation, but it did not in the least satisfy his pupil.

"Do the people really accept such impossibilities as true?" he asked doubtfully. "Among the multitude of human beings there must surely be some who think, and do not simply repeat what others tell them!"

"That is just what is so good about it, that the people accept simply and easily what the priests tell them."

Maru said it quite conclusively, but then added with a little smile:

"What would become of us if all human beings were as thorough as you are, Li-Erl?"

"That is too terrible," the words burst from the younger man. "So you take advantage of the childlike credulity of the simple people, to make them believe all kinds of untruths! And you too have lent yourself to such things, Maru?"

The teacher gazed at him without understanding.

"What is so terrible about it? Each receives what is good for him. Believe me, Li-Erl, the people are happy in their delusion, which does no harm to anyone."

"But it does cause harm," interrupted Li-Erl vehemently.

Completely lost was the modest tone in which he usually addressed the teacher who was so much his senior. A great upheaval stirred his soul.

"It causes harm! It prevents the people from seeking further, from advancing to the Supreme One Who rules over the gods. The people must not be allowed to go on living in this way.

"If they believe that the gods dwell in the pagodas, thus that they are always within their reach, they obviously also assume that all the wrong perpetrated takes place in full view of the gods, without their preventing it.

"That is the reason why licentiousness and sin continue to spread. It is quite clear to me now. If you were to enlighten the people with the knowledge that the gods dwell high above them, and can only be reached through living a spotless life, mankind would be better served."

Maru had listened in amazement. In the impetuous words that penetrated to his soul he sensed the truth, and he did not close himself to it.

"Li-Erl, whoever may have taught you such things has acted aright," he said, deeply moved. "I am not too old to learn from and through you. Certainly I do not see how what has been perverted for centuries could be remedied. But perhaps, since you have discovered the fault, it may be granted to you to find the remedy."

"What do you think?" he added after a few moments, while Li-Erl was seeking to regain his composure. "The pagodas would have to be demolished. That would put a quick end to this belief."

But even as he spoke, he himself realised that this expedient was entirely inappropriate. He said so, and the younger man agreed.

"It would also be a pity," said the latter, "for the time-honoured buildings, whose sight always instils within me a singular feeling. Whoever first built them must have had in mind something more than to create the semblance of an abode for the gods."

For a long time these thoughts remained with Li-Erl. The next day he put them before Lie-Tse, after telling him about his talk with Maru.

"Do you know, my father," he asked, "why the pagodas were built in this unique manner? Do you know the significance of the many storeys rising heavenwards?"

"You are right, Li-Erl," replied Lie-Tse thoughtfully; "they rise heavenwards, and are meant to point us from what we call heaven to that which the heavens are in infinity. They are meant to indicate the path which the soul must tread as it approaches Eternity.

"Step after step must it climb, to reach the proximity of the gods. Human feet may not touch the upper storeys. He who created the first pagoda conceived of the higher sections as being inhabited by the more delicate

43

forms of human beings, by their finer bodies, their souls. From this may later have arisen the false belief that these storeys were the dwellings of the gods."

"I do not quite understand you, my father," said Li-Erl reflectively. "What do you mean by the finer bodies of human beings?"

"You know that, apart from the visible body, we bear with us an invisible one, in fact not just one but several bodies. That which lives in all these bodies is our spirit. You know all that. I have also taught you that when we depart from this earth we leave only the visible body behind.

"But we believe that all the invisible ones then enter the first of the upper floors of the pagodas, until they again succeed in releasing themselves from the outermost cloak. Then they move on to the second. And so it goes on. The lighter the body becomes, the higher will be the dwelling-place of the soul, until finally it is permitted to enter the gardens of the gods."

Li-Erl had listened, deeply moved.

"Is that really so?" he asked, only partly convinced. And Lie-Tse's answer was simple:

"I have no other explanation."

How much more beautiful was this interpretation than Maru's answer! Li-Erl occupied himself with it all day, and did not seek out Maru. But other thoughts assailed him as well: Where was he to find the Truth?

Lie-Tse knew other and better things than the priests, but it did not seem to be the whole Truth. Then the word "Truth-bringer" recurred to him. If he was destined for this, he must surely first find the Truth! There were the old, tormenting thoughts once more.

Again he turned to Lie-Tse, but he either could not or would not answer. Evasively he said:

"You will be told everything in good time. Now learn what is offered to you, and try to repress the questions arising within you."

Next day Li-Erl went to Maru, who did not ask the reason for his absence, nor did he refer to their last conversation. Instead, he suggested to his pupil a visit to the underground rooms of the temple.

It had been but a tentative offer; however when Maru observed the eagerness with which the youth accepted the suggestion, he too was overcome by the feeling that he was approaching some unforeseen experience.

In great suspense, both descended the steps, which were easy at first, but soon led into narrow winding passages.

"We must be careful here," said Maru slowly, "otherwise we shall get lost and be unable to find our way out again."

"Surely you know the way," said Li-Erl, unconcerned, but he was surprised when Maru replied:

"No one quite knows it."

"How is that possible?" was the pupil's prompt query. But he had to be satisfied with Maru's assurance that he would be told later. For the present Li-Erl should also keep his eyes open to take exact note of the way.

With the earnestness which he applied to everything, the youth did as he was told, and tried to impress on his mind the distinguishing features and turns along the way. This naturally put a stop to their conversation; and although Li-Erl felt tempted to ask about a number of remarkable things that he noticed on the way, it all had to wait until later.

Now they came to ladder-like steps leading still further down. They were slippery, as though covered with slime; Li-Erl shuddered involuntarily.

Must he really make this descent? he asked himself, but at the same moment he felt threatened by the grotesque forms which he had already seen several times before. Then he knew with absolute certainty that yielding only once to the fear of them would bring about his headlong fall. Hence he must face them boldly.

He wanted to do so, but – – he no longer found within him the courage which alone could be of help. He was beset on every side. He felt giddy, and began to lose consciousness. Now it had to come: the inevitable, awful plunge into the depths!

To call Maru was pointless; the old teacher had never stood at his side in such moments.

"Courage, courage," he implored inwardly. "After all, I am to be a Truth-bringer!"

And this one word "Truth-bringer" dispersed the mist that surrounded him. Now he knew whence he might draw the strength he lacked.

"Sublime One, I am nothing; strengthen Thou me!"

The words burst forth aloud from his choked throat. Then he felt a warm glow flooding through him, while at the same time he was fanned by a cool breeze. Beside him stood the Messenger of God with a shining sword, fending off the rabble so that it sank away trembling into nothingness.

Freely and easily Li-Erl descended until he stood on solid ground once more. Then his helper departed, but the strength remained with him and completely filled him.

Maru, who appeared not to have noticed any of this, turned sideways towards a greenish-covered gate, which he opened ceremoniously.

They entered a large hall filled with the glow of countless offertory vessels. By the flickering light of these flames, numerous shapes could be discerned leaning against the walls. They were images of gods and demons carved in wood or stone, used only at special festivities. The sight of all these grotesques was horrible; but they no longer distressed Li-Erl.

After passing through this hall, they entered vaults lavishly decorated with precious stones and ornate carvings.

Here Maru finally began to speak. He explained that this was the burial-place of priests and nobles, who waited here until the gods should again summon them on to the earth. Therefore costly robes and precious stones were bestowed on them, so that they need not appear poor and destitute, but could demonstrate at once that they were special personages.

Li-Erl did not understand.

"But our priests and nobles are cremated on tall pyres of sweet-scented wood," he said impatiently. "I have witnessed it myself."

"Have you actually seen the dead persons?" asked Maru. "You see, Li-Erl, when a man who was a blessing to his people dies, he is buried in these tombs, and an image is burned instead of him to satisfy the people."

"So deception again, even here!" cried Li-Erl, grievously agitated. "It is time to enlighten the misled people."

"And what do you hope to achieve by telling the people about the burial-place?" Maru wanted to know. "Hold your peace about everything that I show you, Li-Erl. Chaos would ensue if you spoke, chaos which no man could undo. The tradition of centuries is not altered by one man's hand."

Li-Erl fell silent, not out of conviction but because his heart was too full. And Maru was afraid to show more; so he turned to go back. He feared that Li-Erl would ask to be allowed to go on, but contrary to his enquiring nature, the youth was ready to leave the tombs at once.

In haste they traversed the vaults and the hall; even climbing the slippery stairs required little effort. But then they stood before a number of passages branching off in different directions, of which Maru identified now this, now that, as being right. A few steps sufficed, however, to show that he was wrong. His pace quickened, and he looked more and more alarmed.

Finally he turned to ask Li-Erl if he remembered the way. Directing a searching gaze about him, the pupil perceived a faint glimmer of light in one of the passages. That must be the right one.

Unhesitatingly he walked on towards it, and soon found features and signs which he had noticed before. Unhindered they reached the broad stairway leading up, and only then realised that the teacher had been walking behind the pupil. That was a grave offence against all traditions, and Li-Erl made haste to beseech the old man's pardon.

But the latter said solemnly:

"That was perfectly right, Li-Erl. Where the pupil knows better than the teacher, he should also be permitted to lead the way."

"What would have happened if we had missed it?" Li-Erl wanted to know.

Maru seated himself on one of the steps and explained. The burial-place must be protected from the prying and curiosity of bold intruders. For that reason a vast number of passages had been made, only half of which led to the goal. The others were false passages ending somewhere in the rock, along a watercourse, or in other passages. If you were to lose the way, you would run the risk of not coming to the surface again, and starving to death down below.

Before the great festivals every year, the remains of those who had had to pay with their lives for their curiosity would be found. Although he, Maru, knew the passages because as a young priest he had performed duties here, he had not used them for so long that he became afraid. Therefore it was good that Li-Erl had remembered everything.

The youth was about to speak of the light which had shown him the right way, when he felt a gentle pressure against his lips, and understood that Maru must know nothing of this. But once again the old priest entreated his pupil never to mention a word about the tombs to anyone. Li-Erl remained silent. Maru grew more insistent. Then the youth said kindly:

47

"I will speak with Lie-Tse, thereafter I will know whether at some later time I may disclose the secret."

Lie-Tse! That was a lifeline. The Lama would not permit the sacred customs to be made public! Maru sighed with relief, and agreed to the suggestion. But at the same time he decided to speak to the Lama himself, and ask him to entrust his pupil to someone else. Dear as Li-Erl had become to him, the fear and anxiety associated with the instruction of this very special person was too great. –

As was his wont, Li-Erl allowed a few days to pass, during which he himself tried to achieve clarity about the questions that beset him, before putting them to his venerable teacher.

But meanwhile Maru had gone to Lie-Tse, and handed back to the Lama the charge entrusted to him. He was too fearful of the consequences possibly arising from any further enlightenment of this thoughtful pupil.

With Lie-Tse he had hoped to find complete understanding for his concerns, but to his surprise the Lama took everything that was said as a matter of course.

"Do you think, Maru," he asked, "that the gods would demand such special instruction for Li-Erl if he himself were not a special human being? But the paths of such a one as this are concealed from ordinary human thinking. If, in accordance with the will of the gods, we teach our pupil all that we ourselves know, then we shall have done enough, and may calmly leave what may ensue from it to the gods."

For a moment Maru was alarmed: had he relinquished his duty too soon? But then the feeling of great relief triumphed, and he returned contentedly to his monotonous daily round.

Now Lie-Tse waited for Li-Erl to speak with him. When at first there were no questions, and the youth also kept away from the temple, the aged man suggested an excursion in the surrounding district.

Li-Erl accepted joyfully, and the very next morning the two walked out into the bright dawn, following a path taken by Lie-Tse that meandered up into the mountains. Li-Erl had for a long time wished to go there. He took delight in the route, but was amazed that his aged teacher could walk so nimbly beside him.

Lie-Tse smiled.

"The mountains of my homeland are much higher than these. I have been used to climbing ever since my childhood."

"Tell me about your country," begged Li-Erl in a childlike way, and the Lama acceded.

He knew that the youth was not interested in outward things. Warmly he told of life in the secluded monasteries, and the manner in which his account was received revealed to him what progress his pupil had made.

"Tell me about the Sublime One," begged Li-Erl, when Lie-Tse was silent. "You know about Him," replied the Lama. "Over the years I have told you all I know. Now others must instruct you further, and you will find the best in your own inner being."

"How could that be?" the pupil wished to know.

Lie-Tse shook his head, declining to answer.

"Wait and pray," said he, and lapsed into a long silence.

The path had become stonier and steeper, so the conversation had to stop in any case. Slowly they climbed uphill, each engrossed in his own thoughts, which unknown to them were similar.

After a few hours the path ended on a plateau of wild beauty. Round about lay great boulders; at this height there was no vegetation. A keen wind whistled across the vast plain. The distant view was enchanting. Li-Erl, who had never seen anything like it before, stood in silent devotion.

"Why do people pray in temples and pagodas?" he asked after a time. "Up here I feel a little closer to the Sublime One. I seem to sense the streams coming from On High. – I do not mean the rushing of the wind," he added almost with embarrassment, "I feel boundless power coursing through me."

"Not everyone can climb up here," replied Lie-Tse evasively; but this did not satisfy his pupil.

"That is only an outward reason, my father," he murmured. "May I not know the true reason?"

"As with everything earthly, the outer and the inner are so closely interwoven that they can hardly be separated," replied Lie-Tse. "Indeed it is true that man can worship God wherever he is. Man can also find Him everywhere. He who feels the urge to seek Him up here is not prevented from doing so."

They had seated themselves on a large boulder and were looking around. But while the eyes of the aged man rested peacefully on the plains below, the younger one's gaze sought eagerly to penetrate the rocky wilderness rising up behind them.

At last Li-Erl broke the silence:

"May I ask you something, my father?" he began.

This hesitant opening suggested to his teacher that Li-Erl's question was one which he himself was unable to resolve. He nodded his head in assent, and the youth now told him of the visit to the burial-place, which had ended so abruptly.

"Is it not a sin against the people to withhold truths from them time and time again?" he asked impetuously. "Why do the priests withhold the knowledge that many of them are not cremated?"

"Consider, Li-Erl: what would be the outcome if the people were to discover this?"

"They would no longer believe the priests."

Teacher and pupil were silent, then Li-Erl resumed: "I have pondered over it for a long time. It would not be a bad thing if that were to happen. But at the same time the people would have to be told that the priests have realised their wrongdoing, and henceforth will proclaim only the truth."

Lie-Tse suppressed a smile.

"The people would not be satisfied with that," he said. "This priestly intent they would also disbelieve; at the very least they would doubt that the priests had the strength to implement it. No, if we want to help the people, we must proceed differently."

Again there was a long silence. Then a luminous figure, seen also by Lie-Tse, stepped behind Li-Erl and laid its hand on his head. Glowing power penetrated the youth, and with it new knowledge flowed into him. He himself began to glow; unreservedly he yielded to the new.

When the luminous figure vanished, Li-Erl sprang up.

"Now I know what has to be done: Of course the people must be shown that they have hitherto been deceived; but then they must be led on to a completely new path. Everything, everything must change!"

Lie-Tse slowly nodded his head, and a warm ray shone out of his eyes. Li-Erl did not see it; he was too preoccupied with the new revelations.

From now on the people would have to be guided differently. But who was to do it? If he really was the Truth-bringer, this must surely be *his task?*

These and similar thoughts assailed the youth who, breathing heavily, stood leaning against one of the boulders. He – he was to do this? But he was still so young! What did he know of life?

When he reached this point in his reflections, the Lama answered as though he had read Li-Erl's thoughts.

"You know nothing at all or at least very little of life as it is, Li-Erl. Do you understand now why I was directed by the Sublime One to lead you into ever different circumstances, to let you become acquainted with new things, even if these new things are not in accord with His Holy Laws?"

"Yes, Father, I understand, and I thank Him and you!" the youth cried, overwhelmed. Then, however, he begged with a childlike impetuosity that had not yet given way to the maturity of manhood: "Show me more, let us depart from here so that I can learn more!"

"That was my intention. In the next few days we shall journey to the capital of our country to let you become acquainted with worldly life and its activity. You have become so strong that the glittering things you are about to see cannot divert you from the path of virtue."

Although Lie-Tse spoke these words with confidence, a peculiar, almost questioning tone rang through them, which touched the youth's heart.

"I am to fight the demons, so I must not fear temptations. If they approach me I will pray. Then I shall be invulnerable."

These two, who understood each other even without words, said little more. As they walked home it was firmly decided that they would set out on their travels the very next morning.

FOR SOME DAYS now they had been journeying on busy roads, again leading to a plain. At first Li-Erl still walked as though in a dream; his spirit was very active within him, closing itself to outer influences. But with increasing clarity he became aware that this was not so willed: he was to see with open eyes all that he encountered in life! He was to absorb what he saw, good and evil, in order to learn from it and to prepare himself for his task!

51

The Lama perceived what was taking place in his pupil's mind, but did not wish to influence him. He waited.

One hot midday they passed a beggar on the dusty, wide road they were travelling. There were many of them to be seen by the roadside everywhere, stretching out their hands imploringly to passers-by, reciting their woes in monotonously plaintive voices. It was such a common sight that they were hardly noticed any more.

But this man was different. He rose from his crouching position as the two travellers drew near. It was not easy for him, and he did so only with the aid of a kind of basket which he was in.

These movements caught Li-Erl's eye; he regarded the man more closely. For a beggar he was remarkably clean, even though he was dressed in rags. His face, wrinkled with age and privation, had nothing repugnant about it. But above all it was the radiant, expressive eyes fixed on Li-Erl that held his attention.

He could not pass by without offering alms to the poor man. But this he did not do in the way alms are usually given, by throwing them to the person like scraps to a dog; instead he went up to the beggar and addressed him kindly:

"You have a heavy burden to carry, my father," the words fell from the speaker's lips almost without his knowledge. "Permit me to make your life a little easier. The Sublime One, Who knows you too, will make of my small gift a blessing for you."

Deeply moved, Lie-Tse heard the words of the youth. He knew that henceforth Li-Erl would speak and act by listening within him, at first still unconsciously, but then, growing stronger in the spiritual guidance, with clear consideration.

While these thoughts filled the aged Lama, the beggar had bowed. Then in a pleasant, resonant voice, he spoke:

"I thank thee, who art blessed by the Supreme One. As thou dost offer me a gift today on His behalf, that it may assuage the distress of my body, so wilt thou one day bring to thy people that which they need. They are lame as I am, rags are their splendour, rags that barely cover their nakedness. However they do not yet know this. But I behold thee," – the man's voice turned almost to song, and his eyes seemed to gaze into far distances – "but

I behold thee surrounded by good spirits, tearing off the tatters so that men writhe in shame! Then, however, thou dost offer them exquisite things to envelop them, glorious things to fill their inner being and uplift them again. Thou treadest the paths of the Sublime One; His Blessing is with thee. I thank Him that I have been permitted to behold thee!"

The beggar was silent. The travellers had listened, deeply moved, and his words re-echoed within them. Li-Erl wished to address a question to the man, but he waved them on. He kept his eyes closed now, and his body slumped.

Lie-Tse grasped the youth's hand and led him away. He feared that Li-Erl would now lapse into day-dreaming again, but his silence was of a different kind. It was not long before he looked about him with bright eyes, giving attention to everything that came their way.

The clothing of those they met was quite different from that which was customary in Li-Erl's homeland. There the men wore wide blue garments without ornament, apart from the family crest on the front. This was made of a piece of fabric that varied in size according to the wealth of the bearer and the nobility of his lineage; on it his name was embroidered in coloured silk.

Besides the name, it might also display pictures of his ancestors' deeds. This family crest was extremely important to all inhabitants of Li-Erl's homeland. It was made for every boy when he attained manhood, and was so durable in quality that it could last all his life. People would rather dispense with silk for the garment, and be content with one made of plant fibre, than economise on the family crest. Li-Erl also wore one like it; a work of art elaborately embroidered by his mother's nimble fingers.

But here none of the natives displayed such a crest. They wore black robes of shiny stiff material which hardly shaped itself to the body. Under them they wore coloured trousers of a softer material. The black robes were adorned with embroidery, and over these the men wore necklaces of variously-shaped kaolin beads, or also of small pieces of coloured wood and stones.

And just as Li-Erl regarded the passers-by in order to absorb all the novel impressions, so the eyes of the others followed the two travellers, one of whom they readily identified as a Lama.

53

Hitherto Lie-Tse had avoided spending the nights in villages. So long as Li-Erl had travelled as a dreamer, his teacher wanted to avoid people. That had changed now. Already the following night, Lie-Tse directed his steps towards a larger settlement, and asked for a night's lodging in an imposing house.

Amazed, the youth looked about. Much was unusual to him. They were admitted and invited to share a meal of cooked rice and fruit; then they were provided with pillows and rugs, and shown a corner of the large entrance-hall where they could sleep. Not much was said; only the head of the family enquired briefly where they came from and what was their destination.

The weary travellers were even less inclined to talk. Li-Erl had glanced searchingly all around him. But nowhere did he find an altar at which to say his prayers. So he went outside to seek the Sublime One above the dark blue, starry sky.

The travellers woke in the morning refreshed. It was still early in the day, yet there was brisk activity around them. Everyone went about his business, and had neither the time nor the inclination to attend to the guests.

They were allowed to share in the morning meal, consisting of hot tea and a kind of flat bread; afterwards Lie-Tse offered the head of the family small flat kaolin discs, which were gladly accepted. Now the Lama turned to go, but something restrained Li-Erl. He could not journey on without asking about the altar. Almost meekly, he turned to the head of the family and asked:

"Would not my father care to show me where he worships? I feel impelled to pay my respects to his ancestors, after resting under their roof."

The man gazed at the speaker in astonishment. Never before had such a request been made to him. Without a word he turned and proceeded to the back of the house, beckoning the travellers to follow him.

Through a sliding door, concealed by a richly embroidered curtain, they entered a spacious room against whose broad wall stood an altar. Nothing required by ancestor worship even in Li-Erl's homeland was missing on it: vases with flowers, incense-bowls, portraits of ancestors, images of the gods, along with dishes of rice, bowls of tea and beautiful fruits, were arranged meaningfully on the table, over which was spread an embroidered blue silk cover.

Quietly the three went up to the altar to say a silent prayer. Then Lie-Tse laid a few of the small white discs beside a flower vase and said:

"We are travelling, and have nothing with which to give pleasure to your ancestors, dear host. We offer what we have."

The man gave him a friendly look, and responded: "Our ancestors thank you, and will not fail to ask for blessing on your future path."

Now Li-Erl began to observe the room more closely. This delighted the man, who was evidently proud of his beautiful hall of worship. For his part, he now directed the youth's attention to certain things that otherwise would have escaped his notice. Embroideries and watercolour drawings hung on the walls, telling of the deeds of his ancestors.

On the floor under the pictures stood large and small vases of kaolin or bronze on wooden plinths. It struck Li-Erl that alongside artistically painted vases of exquisite form stood others that were clumsy and scarcely decorated. This so preoccupied him that he had to ask.

Responding to the interest shown, the man had altogether cast off his reserve, and willingly informed Li-Erl.

"I must tell you that these vessels date from different times and generations. When one of our ancestors died, a vessel that he had particularly cherished, or liked to use, was placed here. Usually a vase was made for the purpose even during a person's lifetime; it was designed to suit the means and the taste of the individual who commissioned it.

"Here you see large and small, simple and costly vases. Mine too is ready, waiting to be put in place as soon as I follow my ancestors."

With that he indicated a corner where a massive vessel, draped in a silken cloth, stood ready for use. Li-Erl would have liked to look under the cloth, but did not dare.

With a few friendly words to the man about this beautiful room of worship, and an expression of thanks, Lie-Tse had turned to leave, but Li-Erl was still not satisfied:

"Do all the people in this region have such rooms of worship?" he enquired, and was told that only the poor were without them. As a rule, every house had a room for ancestors added to it at ground floor level.

"I saw yesterday that you have two-storey houses also," commented Li-Erl. "Do your ancestors never live on the upper floor?"

The man shook his head.

"No, the living dwell there. When a family grows too large, then as many rooms as they require are built on top of the house; the married son moves into them with his family. In your homeland, do you have sufficient space in the house for everyone to live on the ground floor?"

Li-Erl explained that only small houses were built in the place of his birth. When a son married, a small house was built for him on his father's land. The man could not conceive of this at all. In that case his guest's friends must be immensely wealthy to own so much land!

All at once the man wished to hear still more about Li-Erl's home. He who until then had seemed not to have a moment to spare for his guests, now wanted to devote all his attention to them. He begged them to stay at least another day, and the travellers agreed happily.

Now it was Li-Erl's turn to speak. With the exuberance of youth he described his parents' home and garden. Suddenly he knew that he must also speak about the altar which his mother had set up before his birth.

Lie-Tse looked at him amazed. Hitherto that had been so sacred to the youth that he never spoke of it! But now the pupil was talking freely about the sanctuary; moreover, he began to speak of the Supreme One in such a way that the people listened with rapt attention.

The man had been joined by his adult sons, who eagerly absorbed what Li-Erl had to offer them. Then they began to ask questions, and wondrous to hear: the youth had the complete answer to everything.

Blissful in giving, he did not ask the source of the answers that came to him. But when he lay down on his bed, tired after a glorious day, he was overcome with amazement. Now even Lie-Tse asked: "Tell me, Li-Erl, who imparted to you this knowledge about the Sublime One?"

"Until today I myself hardly knew half of what I was allowed to tell," Li-Erl replied thoughtfully. "It was as if I was quietly told what to answer." – –

"Oh," he exulted suddenly, "this is how I am to find the Truth! By helping others to recognise the Supreme One, I myself will discover Him ever more readily and completely; I will find the Truth in all things."

Deeply happy, he gazed at Lie-Tse, who rejoiced with him. Even as he was falling asleep Li-Erl murmured:

"So I have learned something important today: Give of the power granted to you by the Supreme One as much as you are able to pour forth, and it will flow into you in greater measure!"

NEXT MORNING it was the Lama who insisted that they must leave. The host regretted the departure of these travellers whom he had been less than ready to receive. He thanked Li-Erl, and invited him to come again some day. He must see whether his teaching had borne fruit!

The day's journey was less arduous, thanks to their rest, and Li-Erl still felt elated by his experience. Towards noon they came to a great river, such as Li-Erl had never seen before. He stood for a long time on the bridge that arched over it, and gazed at the yellowish waves racing turbulently beneath it.

"Our life is like that," said Lie-Tse. "It streams unceasingly from eternal sources towards the longed-for goal, often bearing with it things that cloud its purity."

"But look," cried Li-Erl, "now the waves deposit the rubbish along the banks, and flow on liberated. That is reassuring!"

He was happy when Lie-Tse told him that their route would now lead along the banks of this river for days.

In the evening they asked for a night's lodging in a fair-sized village, but at several houses they were turned away unkindly.

"We have no public shelter here," they were told. "Go on to the next village, there you will find what you seek."

The two did as they were advised, and reached the very dirty village at nightfall. The inn was no exception to the prevailing condition. Had they not been so weary they would have walked on.

An ugly old woman admitted them, served them with rice and tea, and allocated them a corner in which to sleep. Lie-Tse enquired about the master of the house, and was told that he was travelling across country with his sons.

Despite their disgust at the accommodation the wanderers eventually lay down to rest. Exhausted, they soon fell asleep.

In the middle of the night Lie-Tse was awakened by a faint noise. He looked across to Li-Erl, and perceived that the youth too was awake and listening.

Whispering voices could be clearly heard, but Li-Erl was unable to understand what was being said, the language was unfamiliar to him. Lie-Tse, however, started up from his bed. The people were speaking Tibetan. He understood every word, but every word also aroused his indignation! The man intended to kill the strangers, because he assumed that they had money.

Quietly the old man got up, brought from the folds of his robe the yellow cap which Li-Erl had been permitted to see once before, and put it on his head. Then he pulled out an embroidered band which he placed round his shoulders, with the ends of it almost touching the ground in front. He looked indescribably dignified. Li-Erl was so amazed that the voices became all but inaudible to him.

At that very moment, however, two male figures entered the room. They carried a paper lantern, whose light fell fully on Lie-Tse. Horror-stricken, the men recoiled.

"A Lama!" cried both as with one voice. They dropped to their knees, touching the floor repeatedly with their foreheads. But Lie-Tse addressed them imperiously, reproaching them for their wrongdoing, so that they trembled with fear.

Li-Erl watched in astonishment. Was the aged man given such authority over human beings?

Lie-Tse had finished speaking, and the men staggered from the room. But now Li-Erl wanted to know what had happened. His teacher told him, but the young man was not satisfied.

"Tell me, my father," he asked insistently, "how is it that the men are afraid of you? Can you punish them? What actually is a Lama? You must be more than a priest of God, otherwise you would not have such authority."

"Tomorrow, when we are on our way, I will answer your questions, my son," the old man promised, "for the present suffice it to say that no harm will befall us. The men have sworn to protect our lives."

The night passed without further incident. In the morning an ample meal was prepared for the guests. None of the men appeared; the old woman went out of her way to be obsequious and render service.

58

As soon as possible the travellers set forth, striding out into the fresh morning. Li-Erl could hardly wait for Lie-Tse to speak. But they had already been journeying for some hours before the venerable man decided to do so.

"Last night, my son," he began almost hesitantly, "you asked me what a Lama is. I told you some time ago that in our country the priests are called Lamas. Every Lama is held in high esteem, for he has learned more than anyone else, and he has dedicated his life to God, Who in our country is the Ruler of all thoughts and deeds – at least that is how it used to be."

He interrupted himself with a sigh, and Li-Erl made use of the pause to interject promptly:

"You say 'that is how it used to be', my father; is it now no longer so? Why has it changed? If a people know of the Supreme One, then surely they must cling to Him with all their might?"

"Many questions all at once, Li-Erl," said the Lama good-naturedly. "Let us defer the answers until I have dealt with the question of the Lama. Perhaps certain other matters will then also become clear to you.

"Well, as I said: a Lama is held in great esteem in our country, and wherever Tibetans have settled in foreign countries.

"The Lamas, who strive to live their lives according to the Will of God, live solely in the thought of Him. This determines all their actions, whether they make offerings in the temple, speak to the people, visit the sick, succour the poor or comfort the bereaved: To them human beings as such are nothing but creatures of their Lord, Whom they serve by serving them.

"But owing to this being-wholly-immersed-in-God, most priests see and hear more than other people. Their inner connection with the more luminous realms evokes a greater sensitivity to all that takes place outside gross matter. That is why such Lamas, sent to outposts where no earthly command can reach them, need only listen within them to know exactly what to do at any moment. Just how am I to express it so that you can fully comprehend …?"

Li-Erl, who had been listening with radiant eyes, interrupted eagerly:

"I well understand, my father! The Lamas lead a completely secluded life in the midst of their activity for others. Their souls belong to God, their knowledge and their powers to their fellow-men. Is that not so?"

"That indeed is how it should be," Lie-Tse said, and regarded his pupil with pleasure.

'I knew it because *you* are like that, my father!'

"But now among the Lamas," continued the venerable man, "there are those who are deemed worthy to see even further than the others. They are permitted to speak with the Messengers of God, and to receive the commands sent to them by God for all. They convey these messages, and see to their execution. Now and then God also makes use of such a Yellow Lama for some special mission on earth ..."

Again Li-Erl interposed impetuously:

"As with you, exactly as with you! You had to come to me, so that I may become a Truth-bringer. O, Lie-Tse, how inconceivably great and exalted it all is! In His Infinity the Supreme One is mindful of us puny human beings; He considers what is of benefit to us, and ensures hundreds of years in advance that someone is there to take up a particular task! It should be called out to all people, until all, all of them hear and perceive it! O, Lie-Tse."

Deeply moved, the youth lapsed into silence. But after a few moments he turned to his teacher, who walked beside him in quiet contemplation:

"Forgive me, Father, I interrupted you again. When will I learn not to speak at the wrong moment?"

"I said," continued Lie-Tse calmly, "that God sometimes makes use of the Yellow Lamas for special tasks. Our Tibetans know this, and for that reason they revere the Yellow Lamas above all. It must be so," the speaker said without any presumption, "otherwise we could not carry out God's Commandments. Often enough God has lent emphasis to our words through some event, so that retribution overtook the disobedient without our intervention.

"This also explains to you why the wicked men trembled before me last night. They feared God's Judgment, which will certainly overtake them sooner or later; for they are great evildoers."

"Are they from your country?" asked Li-Erl. "You spoke in a tongue different from ours here."

"Unfortunately they are Tibetans, who fled the country because of their misdeeds," Lie-Tse replied.

"Oh, and I believed all people in Tibet to be righteous," sighed Li-Erl, disappointed.

"So they still were about a hundred years ago," responded Lie-Tse. "I believe I have told you before that we tried to maintain the old discipline in the monasteries at least. But the spirit of evil has even invaded the monasteries, at least in the lowlands. Those in the mountains have still been spared. There the Brothers serve God with all their heart, and even the inhabitants of the surrounding villages, who are closely linked with the monasteries, know of nothing better than to be allowed to serve God."

The Lama lapsed into wistful silence, but Li-Erl took up his words and asked:

"For days now you have spoken always of God, and I believe you mean the Supreme One. Why do you do this? Shang-Ti is also called 'god'."

"Yes, he is one god among many; the Supreme One is God. In former times He alone was called by this Name; then when men had lost the connection with Him, they became accustomed to regarding His servants as gods and calling them so. There will come a time when only the Supreme One will bear the name 'God'."

"Would it not be better to stop calling Him by this misused name until that time?" asked Li-Erl. "It pains me when you, my father, use it in addressing the Supreme One."

"It shall be as you wish," replied Lie-Tse earnestly. He knew that it was right.

Now they were quiet again for a long time, and Li-Erl's gaze roamed over the gently-sloping hills. But always it returned to the river, enchanted. Suddenly a thought came to him, which he had to voice at once:

"Look at all that water, my father. How good it would be if people were to wash themselves in it several times a year. It would have to be decreed by law to ensure compliance!"

The thought filled him with enthusiasm, and he enlarged on it.

"It seems to me that a human being who refuses to tolerate anything unclean about his body will also keep his soul pure. Just think how dirty the majority of my people look! If I were to have a say in it one day, I would demand that all people should wash themselves in the river."

"Fortunately this is not the only river in your country, Li-Erl, otherwise people would have to undertake long journeys to obey your decree," said the Lama, smiling.

But he too found it a good idea. New thoughts of all kinds arose in the youth. The old man observed it with joy. If only the time when they might be realised would come soon!

But Li-Erl still had much to see and to become acquainted with before then. They had been travelling for quite a long time, and were now approaching the capital.

The traffic in the streets increased. Riders on shaggy little horses, two-wheeled carts drawn by white oxen, came towards them or passed them. Porters hurried along at a steady quick pace, carrying burdens on their head or back.

The clothing of all these people was different again from that worn by those in the province they had just traversed. The dress clearly reflected the rank of its wearer. The working men wore long trousers made of dyed, mostly faded, blue cotton, and short jackets with wide sleeves of the same colour. Their feet, tanned by all weathers, were like leather.

The riders wore tight-fitting long leather breeches, and a similar sleeveless tabard, actually consisting of only two square pieces. They covered the chest and back, and were laced up at the sides. Apparently made of tanned hide, long strands of animal hair hung from their edges.

Underneath this tabard the men wore a short garment with long, tight sleeves, which according to the wearer's rank was made of cotton or silk. The nobler the rider, the more beautifully ornamented was the leather on his chest. Most of them carried weapons: short swords and long, lance-like spears.

Lie-Tse indicated to his pupil that these riders belonged to the Guard. They probably had to ride round the city and its environs at certain intervals, in order to watch over its security.

"Does the Emperor then live in the city we are now approaching?" asked Li-Erl. "Shall we be allowed to see him? Have you ever seen him? Is he young? What is his name?"

"I will try to answer all these impetuous questions at once," said Lie-Tse in gentle rebuke.

"We are now coming to the capital of the whole vast Middle Kingdom. It is situated here on the banks of this river, and its name is Kiang-ning. The river is called Yang-tse-kiang. The city is many hundreds of years old and strongly fortified, as you will see. One of the six solidly-built towers will soon appear in the distance.

"The ruler of the whole empire with its twenty provinces lives in Kiang-ning. His name is Hou, and he is descended from the mighty line of the Tshou, which has borne the country its Emperors for more than five centuries.

"You will probably see the Emperor, who allows himself to be called 'Son of Heaven', at one of his receptions, at which rich and poor are permitted to bow before him; but I cannot say whether you will come in contact with him. That lies in the Will of the Supreme One, and will be made known to you at the right time."

They had been walking briskly on a comfortable road, and suddenly one of the towers described by Lie-Tse appeared on the horizon. Li-Erl had imagined it to be something like an immense pagoda, and was now surprised to see a very wide stone building. It was rectangular, with sloping walls, the rectangle at floor level being far larger than the one on top.

In reply to Li-Erl's question, Lie-Tse explained that these towers had to serve as quarters for innumerable soldiers in case of an enemy attack, hence the size of the buildings. But the slanting walls had been deliberately constructed to present a minimal surface for attack by a shower of stones.

"When we come closer, you will see that each of these towers supports another like it, but smaller, on top."

Li-Erl shuddered.

"Why must such things be?" he asked. "Men should live in peace. If they serve the Supreme One aright, there can be no disagreement."

But he had no time to indulge in these thoughts; there were too many new impressions besieging him. The city was surrounded by a belt of lush orchards, alive with the brisk activity of women and children, as well as numerous small dogs frolicking among them, and reminding him of his own little dog at home.

It was next morning before they entered the gate at the east side of the city. Like the towers, it was built of solid rock, with no ornamentation whatsoever. Li-Erl, who had seen so many beautiful things, was disappointed. But when they had proved their identity, and were permitted to enter the city, Lie-Tse invited his companion to look behind him.

The bare stone gate was as though transformed. The whole of the side facing the city was covered with the most exquisite wood-carving, which shone in a blaze of colour.

But there was no time to stop and marvel. Li-Erl was almost knocked over by hurrying pedestrians, and had to make a determined effort to follow Lie-Tse, who had walked briskly on, and turned into a maze of narrow lanes filled with all kinds of smells.

The newcomers had virtually to struggle through a medley of people, animals and implements. It seemed as though the people's whole life here took place in the street.

At last an unusually narrow lane led unexpectedly on to an open square. Here rose a large, beautiful temple with a yellow roof and tall pagoda. Numerous steps led up to its portal.

"This is the Temple of Heaven," explained Lie-Tse. "Since the Emperors call themselves 'Sons of Heaven', its roof has the Imperial yellow colour. We shall soon enter the temple. For the present, let us call on our host, who has offered to accommodate us for the time being.

"He is a very learned Lama from Tibet, who has lived in Kiang-ning for a long time, and is occupied with cataloguing the manuscripts in the Imperial Palace. You can learn a great deal from him, once you succeed in drawing his attention to yourself. He is usually so engrossed in his work that he takes no heed of his surroundings."

For a moment the Lama was silent, then he continued cheerfully:

"You are surprised that I did not tell you this before. You were not to be distracted by anything on the journey, and now it is time enough for your thoughts to turn to our host."

Again they walked through a maze of lanes until finally they stopped before a house which, though inconspicuous, was distinguished from the others by being cleaner and of a slightly different style.

Li-Erl had already noticed that most of the houses were carelessly built. The walls were uneven in length; as a result the small houses stood lopsided in the lanes. Not even the doors were rectangular in form, but seemed to have been cut haphazardly into the front wall.

The very small house that they now entered was constructed with remarkable care. Although the material was no better than that of the neighbouring houses – a few stones, wood and straw – these had been put to more effective use. The inside too was distinguished by its pleasant cleanliness.

An old man approached the travellers; but when he caught sight of Lie-Tse, he burst into a stream of jubilant words which Li-Erl did not understand. Then he drew the hem of Lie-Tse's robe to his lips, bowed before Li-Erl, and disappeared behind an exquisite curtain on which a single large dragon was embroidered.

Soon afterwards the master of the house appeared, – a white-haired, venerable man with equally radiant eyes under bushy eyebrows like Lie-Tse's.

Li-Erl's countrymen trimmed their eyebrows, so that they lay completely flat on their faces. He had already observed that all people from Tibet whom they had met allowed this hair to grow naturally.

But the heightened radiance of his eyes certainly could not be due to that? It must come from the soul. And Li-Erl's soul flew in great joy to meet that of the host.

The latter, however, bowed low and said:

"Welcome to my house. It shall be yours for as long as you wish to sojourn here."

Li-Erl at once assumed that these words were addressed to Lie-Tse, but to his great surprise the old man continued:

"Li-Erl, Son of the Heavenly Gardens, great grace has God granted that I may behold you. You have kept yourself pure, as when you were sent. Pure shall you go among mankind to rekindle the expiring Light, to bring the Truth again to the world suffocating in sin."

Li-Erl knew not what to say. What he had just heard was too overwhelming. While he knew that he was chosen to be a Truth-bringer, no one had spoken of it, apart from Lie-Tse, and the time of his work still seemed to him incredibly far off.

He had no idea that this work had already begun quietly, and that he was marked as a Messenger of God with a sign invisible to normal human eyes.

But Lie-Tse was also taken aback. He, who had always been near Li-Erl, had not perceived the sign. Now that the host had discerned it, he too saw it, and pure joy filled him.

Thus their arrival in the home of Pe-Yang proved to be entirely different from what the travellers had expected. Happy and free, the youth now stood between the two scholarly elders, learning from them, benefiting from their great wisdom, and yet at the same time being the giver!

Unconsciously he passed on powers that flowed to him from above. He strengthened their souls, which had grown old and weary, so that they regarded life with fresh confidence, envisaging new tasks to come.

Li-Erl would have preferred to turn at once for instruction to Pe-Yang, whose simplest words seemed to him fraught with meaning. But the two Lamas had other things in mind.

First the youth should become familiar with the capital, which would take time. Although initially Li-Erl was reluctant to submit to this arrangement, he soon enjoyed it; each day he took fresh delight in all that presented itself to him. The numerous temples were lavishly decorated; there were many things of real beauty, together with countless others that were repulsive and grotesque.

He did not attract the attention of the priests whom he encountered. They could not see the sign, and regarded him as an immature, inquisitive student from the country. But since he was accompanied by a Lama they tolerated him. Pe-Yang never took part in these excursions, but he bade Li-Erl give him an account of them in the evening; and Li-Erl learned from the way in which his descriptions were received.

Ever more clearly he perceived that the fight against the demons, against the dark, destructive belief in these man-made forms, must be his first task.

He tried to speak about it also with Pe-Yang, but found no response. The old Lama gave a friendly ear to his words, but made no comment. It was obvious to Li-Erl, who turned to Lie-Tse to discover the reason.

"You must ask him yourself, Li-Erl," came the unsatisfactory reply.

Some time passed before Li-Erl ventured to put the question. But one day, when the youth had been deeply disturbed by terrible events in the temple, it burst forth from him:

"I am telling you such dreadful things, my father. I would like to hear from you when the time will come for a change to be brought about. I would like to know what you think about it, for your thoughts are deeper than those of others, but you are silent! Why? Am I too childish to share in your wisdom?"

"Li-Erl," said the aged man in a deep voice that betrayed his emotion. "Li-Erl, you are not too childish. But consider: You have been sent from Heavenly Gardens to be a Truth-bringer. Should not He Who elected you show you the ways which you are to tread? No human word may seek to guide you, no human knowledge may approach you! I may only listen to what wells forth from your soul, so that you may become still within ere you set about your task. None of us can do more. Any more than that would be a sin against God."

Deeply moved, all three were silent. But it was as if a blessing descended upon the youth. From that hour he viewed his life differently, and had a completely new approach to everything that came his way. He had matured, had become conscious of the Divine Guidance.

THEN SOMETHING NEW ENTERED his life. The very next morning Pe-Yang introduced to him a young dignitary who often came to his house as a student. He arranged that from now on Hai-Tan should accompany Li-Erl, and show him other things besides the temples.

Hai-Tan was older than Li-Erl, but he had an unaffected, cheerful nature, and was happy to be able to acquaint Li-Erl with all the beautiful things Kiang-ning had to offer, and thus to be of service to his old teacher.

A completely new life unfolded before Li-Erl. At first he ventured somewhat hesitantly into the magnificent bazaars where exquisite merchandise was offered for sale. Then, however, he took pleasure in the beautiful things for which he had always had a receptive mind.

Hai-Tan also took him to the workshops where kaolin and silk were produced. He had access everywhere, and enjoyed being with the enquiring youth. Even to him everything seemed more important now that he perceived Li-Erl's interest.

They never spoke of deeper things. Li-Erl was reluctant to approach Hai-Tan's jovial nature with that which moved his soul, nor did the young mandarin seem to desire anything else.

One day Hai-Tan promised his companion a very special pleasure. He would be allowed to accompany him to a public house in the evening. This meant nothing to Li-Erl, but since the older man spoke so mysteriously about it, he agreed. In any case walking through the streets of Kiang-ning in the evening was quite a novelty.

Hai-Tan never sought out narrow alley-ways or back lanes, but always led his companion along splendid avenues. Long since, he had insisted that Li-Erl exchange his plain native garment for silken clothes that did not contrast too markedly with the apparel of other young men.

That evening they entered a brightly-lit room in which many people were dining. There seemed to be unusual dishes which Li-Erl had never seen before. Hai-Tan urged him to sample some; but he could not be moved to do so, asking for rice and fruit instead. Hai-Tan was amused.

"You will learn to enjoy it. At least you must drink something, that is the proper thing to do."

But even after the first sip of the intoxicating drink, he flatly rejected the cup, ordering his usual tea. The waiter who had served the drinks grinned openly, but Li-Erl pretended not to notice. When they had finished eating, he wanted to go home, but Hai-Tan indicated that the pleasure was just beginning.

They went towards another room, from which music was heard. The peculiar sounds had a definite rhythm which struck Li-Erl as unpleasant. He could not account for their effect on him, and would have much preferred to go home. Just then he felt that someone was speaking to him quietly:

"You should see as much as you can, even if what you are shown does not swing in the Laws of God."

Of course! He also had to become acquainted with unpleasant things.

Resolutely he entered a fairly large room, laid with carpets and hung with tapestries. Little consideration had been given to value or beauty; what seemed to matter was comfort.

Standing or sitting against the back wall were showily-dressed women with stringed instruments. Swaying their hips, they brought forth monotonous sounds from their instruments, apparently without joy. The effect on Li-Erl was also joyless.

On soft cushions scattered about the floor sat the few visitors; no joy emanated from them either.

"Why do people come here?" asked Li-Erl in surprise. Hai-Tan laughed.

"You will soon see," he replied mysteriously. Then they also sat down, after Hai-Tan had carefully chosen their places.

The music began a new strain. In the background curtains parted, and seven quaintly-attired girls emerged. Li-Erl looked at them aghast.

"How can maidens be allowed to expose themselves to men?" he cried out almost aloud. "Even in the theatre men take the roles of women; for the gods have forbidden girls to display themselves!"

Hai-Tan shrugged his shoulders.

"My young saint, you will yet see many things that your secluded life has failed to teach you. That is exactly why you are to go about with me. Believe me, if all men did only what the gods permit, it would be a dull life indeed. The very things that are forbidden make life agreeable."

Again Li-Erl needed all his strength to remain. Unwholesome currents surged about and seemed to constrict him. He breathed with difficulty. Then, from deep within, he called to God:

"O Thou Sublime One, at Whose behest I must be here, let me come to no harm, and let this terrible spectacle not be in vain."

Then he leaned back in his cushions, and tried to regard as calmly as possible what there was to be seen. Hai-Tan smiled; the young man would get used to it in due course!

Now the girls began dancing towards the audience. They bowed to the sound of the instruments, they turned and twisted their limbs. Truly, what they were doing was not beautiful, thought Li-Erl. But he could not deny that the figures were lovely. One young girl in particular, of slender build, caught everyone's eye. Her limbs were graceful and delicate.

Suddenly she broke off in the middle of the dance, and rushed back towards the curtains through which she had emerged. An older girl barred her way, calling a few hasty words to her, to which the younger responded.

The dancing ceased; all the girls gathered round the two. The guests looked at the group in astonishment. Nothing like this had ever happened before. From the background there came first an old woman and then an old man, who joined the agitated dancers. The excitement mounted.

After a lengthy discussion, the man approached the two visitors who had been the last to arrive. He turned to Li-Erl:

"Sir, we ask you to leave the room. Ta-Li will not dance before you."

Everyone looked aghast, or in spiteful glee, at the person who was being expelled, but Hai-Tan cried:

"This is an outrage that cannot be inflicted on my friend with impunity. You will regret what you have done, for he is under my protection."

At that Li-Erl rose. Without further consideration he said in a ringing voice:

"You are mistaken, Hai-Tan. It is not an outrage, but an honour for me if a girl realises that she is acting against the will of the gods. Woman is to stand in the life of men like a flower: pure and happy. But girls like these have stepped into the mire of the street, no one can have delight in them any longer."

The visitors looked in amazement at the eccentric who dared to preach in this place. He was a handsome youth, with radiant eyes. A glow emanated from him.

There was a stir among the girls. The youngest lay weeping on the floor, her face covered. But one of the older girls approached Li-Erl with greater propriety than he had expected, and said:

"Sir, I thank you! From this day on my sister and I will seek other ways of earning a living. No one has spoken to us as you have done; everyone has urged us to undertake this work, and praised us for doing it. But you must be a messenger of the gods, that you have so captivated our hearts. I have never been to the temple, but from tomorrow onwards I will seek out the priests. I thank you!"

She bowed gracefully and quickly retreated. Gently she helped her sister from the floor to her feet, and left the room with her. Then the other girls, who until now had stood irresolute, hurried to follow. The festivities were over! The visitors departed slowly. Li-Erl also was about to leave, when the old man barred his way.

"You have ruined my business, stranger. What will you give me in return?"

He had relied on Li-Erl's inexperience, but had forgotten about Hai-Tan. In a sharp voice the latter reminded him that he might well fear being reported to the priests, and that the best thing he could do was to move to another city without delay.

Wide-eyed, Li-Erl gazed at the two; then he said: "You surely know that the gods are not pleased with what you do. Give up your wrongful business."

The man laughed maliciously, and showered him with abuse. But Li-Erl turned and left the house with Hai-Tan.

In silence they walked the long way back to Pe-Yang's dwelling. Li-Erl was in a state of intense inner activity and struggle. Hai-Tan, however, began to sense that this inexperienced young man, whom he had regarded with a somewhat derisive smile, was purer and better than other human beings. He would not disturb Li-Erl's childlike knowledge with his philosophy of life.

The two companions stayed awake all night. Li-Erl strove to find a way of helping such unfortunate girls, a way of preventing such wicked men from carrying on their evil practices. As was his wont, he wished to clarify his thoughts before speaking with the Lamas.

Hai-Tan, however, was deeply affected by Li-Erl's nature, without realising it. A longing for purity, for connection with the gods, arose in him, and grew with the advancing night.

The next day he did not go to Li-Erl who, engrossed in his own thoughts, did not miss him. But in the evening he appeared, a changed person.

"I can show you nothing more, Li-Erl," he began almost humbly. "All that I know would drag you down. Now it is your turn to teach me. You know things that lead upwards. Show them to me."

Great joy filled Li-Erl's soul. If Hai-Tan freed himself from his earthly preoccupations he could become the friend, the helper, for whom Li-Erl longed.

They spent the whole night in discussion. In the morning they went together to Lie-Tse to tell him that Hai-Tan was willing henceforth to accompany Li-Erl as helper and protector, but that it was no longer possible for him to show his friend anything other than what he himself would wish to see.

Lie-Tse seemed not at all surprised by what had happened. He had foreseen it. He told Li-Erl that his time had come to an end. He, Lie-Tse, was

71

now allowed to return to his monastery in Tibet, since Li-Erl had found an earthly protector, and Pe-Yang would support him as teacher.

Li-Erl was shocked. Lie-Tse had been by his side for as long as he could remember; he was henceforth to do without him! He loved his teacher, and knew of no one in whom he could place his trust to the same degree. Pe-Yang he revered and admired, but he could not replace his fatherly friend. He begged the Lama to stay with him for yet a while, until he could become accustomed to the thought of their separation. But Lie-Tse shook his head calmly.

"The mission entrusted to me by God was to accompany you until you yourself should choose a worldly companion. That has taken place. Now my duties call me back to my monastery."

"May I go with you?" asked Li-Erl, who was completely dazed by the sudden turn of events. "I have long wished to know Tibet, and life in the monasteries, from personal experience."

He had hoped that Lie-Tse would grant his request, for the Lama had often pointed out how useful a knowledge of Tibet's customs might be to the young Truth-bringer. But even then the venerable man refused.

"The time has not yet come. We shall meet again when you are older and more mature. I too have learned many things in these years, by which I hope to benefit my monastery. Then I shall live in anticipation of your coming, Li-Erl."

He prevailed upon the youth to go with him to the Temple of Heaven, where in a hidden niche it had been their particular joy to call upon the Supreme One. Together they prayed, and the aged teacher blessed his pupil, to whom he had given of his best for years. And while Li-Erl was still on his knees, absorbed in devotion, Lie-Tse walked slowly out of the Temple. During the days that followed Li-Erl moved about as though in a dream. He could not come to terms with Lie-Tse's absence, although he had to admit that his teacher had left him very much to himself during recent months. But he had still been available in the evenings, and had often helped to bring order into Li-Erl's thoughts.

Hai-Tan was concerned that his request to be allowed to accompany Li-Erl had prompted the Lama's departure. He did not understand the connections, and assumed that jealousy had motivated the old man.

When Li-Erl perceived this, he tried to explain how every action, indeed nearly every word of the venerable teacher had been determined by God, so that his pupil's life might be shaped in an absolutely defined manner. And while explaining, he himself became aware of the Lama's selflessness, and the overwhelming nature of Divine guidance, so that, marvelling and worshipping, he grew inwardly calm.

Now he re-entered Pe-Yang's study, where he found the sage bent over his manuscripts as if it had not been days since their last conversation. Pe-Yang warmly granted Li-Erl's request for regular instruction from now on.

"I will do so with pleasure, Li-Erl," said the Lama kindly. "But I must tell you one thing in advance: Until now Lie-Tse arranged your life as directed by the gods. He has left. But I receive no instructions from above concerning you. I have only been charged with teaching you whatever you may desire. Henceforth the organising of your life will lie in your own hands."

"How can I know what I am to do!" exclaimed Li-Erl, perplexed.

"By listening within you, my son," replied the old man earnestly. "You receive guidance; pay attention to it. Every day you should ask that your ears may be open to the voices from above, which will sometimes sound only faintly and gently. They will direct you. Then leave everything else aside and do what the voices demand of you, and your life will be guided in exactly the same way as before, until the time when you are sufficiently mature to guide yourself and then your people. Make every effort, for this time is drawing near."

Indeed, it was hardly necessary to remind him of the voices. Li-Erl was accustomed to hearing them. But it gave him strength that the Lama spoke of them so naturally, and yet so solemnly. He had not yet concluded these thoughts when Pe-Yang asked:

"How have you envisaged your studies with me, Li-Erl?"

And when the latter, bewildered, remained silent for want of an answer, Pe-Yang enquired further:

"Do you wish to come only whenever you feel urged to hear something new, or shall we set aside specific hours each day for work?"

"May I come to you every morning, like today?" asked Li-Erl. "I know

73

that from you I can receive an explanation with regard to the nature of the world which we do not see."

He said it without thought, entirely from within, and was himself amazed at his words. But Pe-Yang smiled kindly.

"So you are on the right path, my pupil. I cannot teach you much, but what I myself know shall be yours."

Then he grew serious and said:

"You know that one Invisible, Sublime God reigns over us all. You know that we have many names for Him. He has created everything we see, and everything we do not see. But just as on earth a great man only issues commands, and has servants to carry them out, so He has only seen to the beginning of all things, leaving the rest to His creatures.

"With the exception of men, all living things on earth were created by the sun, into which the Supreme One poured His heat. Animals and plants, clouds and waves are creatures of the sun, and are dependent upon it. At the behest of the Sublime One, it regulates their life, their well-being, their decay. It is golden-yellow, hence yellow is our sacred colour."

Li-Erl listened attentively. He could not imagine how the sun created animals and plants. He had only observed how it caused the buds to sprout; but these buds must first have been in existence. He knew that it had sustaining and destructive power, but could it have creative power?

That then was already the first thing which, uncomprehended and incomprehensible, stirred his soul. Who would provide the answer? The longing for his old teacher welled up fervently within him. Lie-Tse had never said anything to occasion conflict. But probably it must be so now.

He did not dare to ask; for without interruption, the old man expounded his knowledge of the Invisible. Much of it was wonderful; Li-Erl could readily believe it. But other things settled like a grey cloud on the youth's senses. At that moment Pe-Yang declared: "I will tell you a secret, Li-Erl. The Sublime One has many children, sons as well as daughters. He sends them to the earth at certain intervals to ensure that the knowledge of Him does not die out and to bring Him tidings of the activities of men."

Now Li-Erl really had to interrupt him.

"Lie-Tse said, my father, that the Sublime One has only two Sons, Who would not set foot on earth until the far distant future. What do you mean by the other children? Is that merely a human name for Truth-bringers? In that case, I would find it presumptuous and wicked."

Li-Erl had talked himself into a state of excitement, his eyes sparkled. Pe-Yang gazed at him with satisfaction.

"That pleases me, Li-Erl. Continue so modest. It can only benefit you."

Thereupon he lapsed into silence, and after a few moments he returned to his book as though his work had never been interrupted. Apparently he intended to say no more this day.

In great dismay Li-Erl went to his own narrow room, and paced it impetuously. Obviously he had come to Pe-Yang at the behest of the Supreme One. But what if the old man taught him things that were not true? He still remembered Lie-Tse's teachings, but what would happen when he penetrated more deeply into the knowledge of the Lama? Would he then himself be able to distinguish?

He was overcome by great inner distress, feeling utterly forsaken. And while grappling and struggling, he became conscious that this also was meant to strengthen him inwardly. Nor was he alone. As before, he could see a Luminous Messenger of God approaching to bring him clarity.

The voice seemed to him as lovely as song, although he realised that it only resounded within him.

"Li-Erl," the voice rang out, "do not despair. You are to become a Herald of the Supreme One. Many invisible helpers surround you. Be aware of this in every situation of your life, and you will perceive the help."

"Messenger of God, I thank thee!" exclaimed Li-Erl, who was beginning to be filled with great confidence. "I thought myself alone, and still so unworthy of the lofty task. Help me! Tell me what I am to make of Pe-Yang's knowledge, which is no truth after all."

"Li-Erl, you are to become acquainted with the wisdom of the world. You are to experience what people believe, who still actually occupy themselves with thoughts of the Supreme One. The others can readily be recognised for what they are: they live from day to day as they please, far from anything spiritual. They will stretch out their tentacles for you in vain.

"But wise, learned and pious men – and Pe-Yang is a pious sage – have partly replaced the knowledge about the Divine with thoughts of their own. These are the people who could become dangerous to those who seek God.

"You carry within you the Truth from above. Let it awaken, Li-Erl! Whatever you may hear, listen within you and compare. If it does not stand the test of that which lives deep within you, it is wrong, however good it may sound.

"But mark my words: Whatever you experience in that way is thrust into your hand as the weapon for battle against all Darkness! You are to become a Luminous Herald of God, Li-Erl. Do not forget that. There shall be Light in you and around you. Therefore cast away all brooding and faint-heartedness. It is unmanly and wrong."

The Messenger was just turning to depart, when his voice rang out once more:

"Do not forget to seek connection with the Supreme One every day. Although no human being can ever reach Him, yet many threads, bridges, rays lead close to Him. Every seeker of God has a different name for what he has found, but it is always the same: that which draws the soul, which came from above, upwards again." -

Refreshing sleep enveloped Li-Erl, who awakened late in the day, reinvigorated and joyful. He stepped before the small altar that he had set up for himself in a corner of his room, similar to his mother's at home. Fervent prayers of thanksgiving rose up to the Supreme One, Who had deemed him, the young Li-Erl, worthy of so great an office.

And while he prayed, he felt as though here and there a little door opened in his spirit, allowing him to see into undreamed-of expanses of future activity and spiritual knowledge. –

Hai-Tan had enquired after him several times, the old servant reported. Now he was expecting his call. But Li-Erl wanted to wait until the following day. He loved being alone with his thoughts.

Next morning at the usual hour he went to Pe-Yang, who turned towards him amicably. Had he not noticed his absence yesterday? Nothing could be inferred from his behaviour; he was of the same even good-heartedness.

Hardly had Li-Erl seated himself than the old Lama continued where he had left off before the pupil's exclamation cut the thread of his discourse.

"God, the Supreme One, sends His sons and daughters to the earth. You must not imagine this as occurring with a great display of pomp. No, Li-Erl, they are no different from you and me."

For a moment Pe-Yang hesitated, and gazed penetratingly at the youth sitting before him, but the latter's face remained impassive.

"They are born on to the earth like other human beings, mostly two at the same time to make it easier for them. But they have to live in different places and are only allowed to meet occasionally. Our learned men have calculated that now the time for a son of God has come again."

Once more the old man was silent for a moment. In Li-Erl, however, the inner voice spoke quite clearly, so that he was able to remain outwardly calm.

Pe-Yang resumed:

"Old prophecies refer to this time, and our greatest scholars confirm them. A son of God will come to tell mankind about God, to bring tidings of the Light and to disperse the demons. He will grow up in humble and simple circumstances, but then he will show forth great splendour. He will become sovereign of the vast Middle Kingdom. All the great ones will be subject to him. Just picture it to yourself aright, Li-Erl," the old man cried enraptured.

But his pupil said in an utterly matter-of-fact, though pleasant manner:

"Would you not rather say 'Messenger of the Supreme One' instead of 'Son of God', Pe-Yang? I think that it would be more correct."

The Lama stared at the youth as though unable to grasp what he had heard.

"Messenger of the Supreme One?" he asked in a low voice. "Do you command me to say so?"

Li-Erl's intellect wanted to object that he, the younger one, could not command his older master; but something within him was stronger, and triumphed.

"Yes, Pe-Yang, it is my wish," said Li-Erl calmly. And Pe-Yang bowed, and simply said:

"It shall be as you will, Messenger of God."

And then he turned again to his big book, and the conversation was over for that day.

This time Li-Erl had learned a great deal. He perceived that Pe-Yang regarded him as a son of God. Therefore it was high time to set him right. But had the Lama realised that his thoughts were wrong? Li-Erl's inner voice maintained the contrary. He had to be satisfied that his teacher at least no longer used the wrong expression. The rest must be left to time.

Moreover Li-Erl felt that in a sense Pe-Yang's statements were to test him. He was to demonstrate the extent to which he would allow himself to be tempted by thoughts of earthly power and pomp. Well, such things did not dazzle him; he seemed to be certain of that.

But his teacher could suffer no interruption. Whenever Li-Erl made some comment in his usual impetuous way, Pe-Yang was silent. How patient Lie-Tse had been! Would it ever be possible to develop such teaching into the kind of dialogue that Li-Erl loved?

At that moment Hai-Tan entered the room, greatly delighted to see his friend hale and hearty. But Li-Erl, lost in thought, forgot that they had not seen each other for two days, and called to him:

"Tell me, Hai-Tan, does Pe-Yang always become silent when he is interrupted?"

Hai-Tan laughed.

"Certainly. He is like a great spindle, from which you can reel off as much silk thread as you like so long as you pull gently. But if you interrupt him with questions or comments the thread breaks, and the spindle comes to a standstill.

"Pe-Yang then does not trouble to pick up the thread again, but apparently considers the measure of his wisdom for that day to be fulfilled. He becomes submerged again in his own world of ideas. It is a splendid way to silence him when you have had enough, or if his talk annoys you, which also happens occasionally."

When Hai-Tan learned that Li-Erl had not yet thought at all about what his friend should show him, he showered him with reproaches.

"All my possessions, my servants, my money are at your disposal, Li-Erl. I can acquaint you with all the beautiful things Kiang-ning has to offer, with everything worth knowing, but you disregard my endeavour to serve you!"

"You are mistaken, Hai-Tan. I value your help so highly that I even had to give up Lie-Tse for it," said Li-Erl a little wistfully.

That placated his friend, but he almost flared up again when Li-Erl expressed the wish to see the streets of the poor.

"Surely you do not need me for that!" he cried. "Any beggar can show them to you."

But Li-Erl remained firm. On Hai-Tan's advice the two friends put on servants' clothing and went to the east of the city, primarily to call on the 'priest of the poor'.

The latter, an old, rather ignorant man, officiated in an almost tumbledown temple, the 'Temple of the Poor'. For those who were no longer able to dress well were denied entrance to the other temples of the city. They had their separate place of worship.

"Are not all men equal before the Supreme One?" asked Li-Erl, disgusted with this way of accentuating the misery.

"Not all," was the calm reply. "The young gentleman surely knows that we are not on earth for the first time. He who was righteous in his previous life will have a pleasant existence in prosperity and comfort this time. But he who has sinned must return as a beggar. Would the young gentleman answer for the distinguished of the realm worshipping together with sinners?"

Li-Erl was still not content.

"Why do the sinners come as beggars? Surely only so that they can atone for their sins. And if a sinner has made amends he will certainly be worth as much as any other devout person in the sight of the Supreme One?"

"Yes, some time later on. When he enters the Eternal Gardens all the expiated guilt will drop away from him; but until then he must regard himself as standing below all other human beings. The young gentleman should look at me. Would I be a priest in this temple of misery if I had spent my first life without sin? I too am atoning with the others, but my trespasses cannot have been quite so bad, otherwise I would not be a priest now."

Although Li-Erl was not satisfied with this explanation, he felt inclined to continue talking with the childlike old man. He could not question Pe-Yang without causing him to take refuge in silence. And as he had no one else, he asked:

"Does my father think that with these two lives all is over? And what if a person still remains wicked even as a beggar? What then?"

"He will certainly remain wicked, young sir," replied the old man serenely. "There are very few good beggars; most of them are good for

79

nothing. But it matters not. With this wretched life of theirs they have atoned for all sins of the previous one, and the wrong they have committed in this life will not be charged to them. After all, they did not choose this base environment."

Li-Erl shuddered. How much ignorance! How much false belief! At his request the priest gave him a few names of poor people who seemed to be deserving of support. Li-Erl would have much preferred to know those whom the priest regarded as lost, but he refused to answer. So Li-Erl had to entrust himself to his guidance here.

The priest's description of the first hut they visited was so accurate that they could not miss it. It hardly deserved to be called a dwelling; for it was given over to decay and filth.

As they entered, a surly voice asked what they wanted.

Li-Erl replied pleasantly that they were servants of a wealthy man who would like to do good to a number of poor people; they had come to see about his needs.

The disagreeable voice was transformed as it glibly provided particulars. He lacked everything; people had forgotten him, and no one cared.

"If that were the case, old man," said Li-Erl firmly, although he could not see in the dark whether the pauper was really old, "if that were the case, we should never have heard about you. The priest of the poor does many good things for you. Do not forget that!"

"Well yes, the priest of the poor sometimes comes to see me. But his prayers do not help me; and he hardly ever brings me gifts; he is poor himself."

"Why do his prayers not help; after all, he is a devout man?" Li-Erl's question was asked in earnest.

"His prayers will help me only in the beyond, but I suffer want in this world," said the man.

"You have not starved to death yet," Hai-Tan interrupted the conversation.

From Hai-Tan's remark the poor man inferred that he was not likely to receive a gift. He leapt up from his bed, and berated the visitors. With that they perceived him to be a big, strong man who was still young.

Hai-Tan walked to the door, but Li-Erl still did not want to give up.

"You seem to be in good health," he said kindly. "Why do you remain a beggar? Work, and earn your living. I will be glad to help you to do so."

The man stopped short, and examined his visitor from head to foot.

"No one has ever spoken to me like that. Must I not remain a beggar, since I was born as such? Prove to me that I can change my life, and I will do it!"

"Have you ever seen one of the large blue butterflies that flutter round the tea bushes?" Li-Erl asked the man.

Curious to know what was coming next, he said that he had.

"Do you know that this beautiful creature developed from a voracious, discontented caterpillar?"

"Yes," was the reply. "I have often seen such caterpillars."

"Well, if everyone had to remain what he was born to be," explained Li-Erl, "then the caterpillar would have to remain a caterpillar throughout its life, and we would have no blue butterflies."

Hai-Tan was at least as astonished as the beggar by this metaphor, but he remained silent and mused. Even the poor man did so. Suddenly he raised his bowed head.

"Master, the poor caterpillar would like to become a butterfly," he said in a low voice. "May I be your servant?"

Li-Erl hesitated for a moment. Could he bring such a person to the house of his host? But his inner voice answered yes, and he said kindly:

"Let us see how we get on together. Go to the nearest water, and cleanse yourself from top to toe. I will see to your clothing."

"What shall I cover myself with when I am clean, if you are not yet back?" the man asked modestly.

Li-Erl reflected. Then he promised the man that he would bring him clean clothing before he went to bathe.

"Can you be at the Temple of the Poor by sunset?" asked Li-Erl.

The man agreed, and the friends walked on. Trying to suppress the emotion rising within him, Hai-Tan said with feigned ridicule:

"If we visit many more of the poor today, Li-Erl, you will arrive home with a whole retinue of servants!"

"Do not mock," requested Li-Erl, "this man is different from the others. I had to accept him. He will be very useful to me."

Then Hai-Tan was silent; he was gradually beginning to understand that his friend possessed a knowledge greater than that of other human beings.

The next poor man whom they visited was really ill, and lived in desolation like the other. He was grateful for the kind enquiries, and answered them willingly. Li-Erl gave him a packet of tea and a small coin of kaolin. But then he asked:

"Why do you think you have to suffer so, my brother?"

The poor man looked at him in astonishment. No one had ever called him "brother", but the answer was obvious:

"I have sinned in my first life, Master," he said frankly.

"When you return, will you be rich and happy again?"

Once more Li-Erl had asked a question that perplexed the poor man.

"Master, do not scoff," he said, "no one comes back more than once. Every human being has two lives, after which he is permitted to live in the Eternal Gardens."

"That I did not know," admitted Li-Erl. "I come from another province, where this is not known."

The poor man was alarmed. Where could this questioner have come from? Perhaps he was a demon in human form who had come to destroy him altogether. His features took on an expression of pitiable fear.

"Master, take your tea and leave my miserable room. I would rather have nothing at all than consort with demons," he whimpered.

Li-Erl tried to reassure him. He spoke to him of the gods, to make the poor man realise that he also knew about them. He dared not speak of the Supreme One; the wretched figure lying there on the miserable bed was too intimidated.

After a long time Li-Erl succeeded in persuading the poor man that he was neither a demon nor an unbeliever. Then the sick man accepted the gift, but this time without joy.

When the friends were back in the street, Li-Erl admitted ruefully:

"I have bungled this completely. I should have waited until the third or fourth visit, when I had gained the man's trust, before asking questions as I did."

"Do you intend to continue these visits then?" asked Hai-Tan, alarmed. "I had hoped that today would have given you your fill of it."

"No, Hai-Tan," said Li-Erl. "I must go repeatedly to each of these people, so that I may know all about every one of them. Believe me, I need this for my life. But now tell me, Hai-Tan: Do you also believe that the poor must atone for their past transgressions, and that thereafter they are allowed to enter the Eternal Gardens with all their pleasures?"

Hai-Tan shrugged his shoulders.

"That is what they teach here," he said indifferently. "I have not yet thought about it, because I am not poor. But since I do not know whether this is my first or already my second life, I try to keep myself as honourable as possible, so that next time I do not have to come as a beggar, or perhaps be cast out into the pits of despair."

"What kind of a teaching is that!" exclaimed Li-Erl, horrified. "Who teaches you such things? With us people have quite different beliefs."

"I do not know who brought the teaching," admitted Hai-Tan. "Even our forefathers thought in that way, but it is not discussed. We go to the temples and believe what we like. Each can think what he pleases, nobody cares."

"But Hai-Tan, can you be happy and contented with that?" Li-Erl asked his friend urgently.

"You can see that I am," laughed Hai-Tan. "Don't trouble yourself with such things. Enjoy your life. And if you can only be happy in your way, no one will stop you."

They had reached another miserable lane, and asked for the man whose name Li-Erl had remembered. They were told that he had just died. Without any sympathy poor people were carrying the body, wrapped in vile rags, out of a nearby house. Seeing that, Li-Erl turned away with loathing, and abandoned any further visits.

The friends returned to Li-Erl's dwelling, and became absorbed in a writing which Pe-Yang had recently given them to study. Li-Erl seemed intent upon drowning all thoughts within him. He had almost forgotten the poor man who was waiting for him at the temple.

"He will be up and away when he has received the good clothes you sent," predicted Hai-Tan.

But he was mistaken. On the steps of the temple a decently-dressed, clean man, whose black hair had been cut neatly round his head, awaited them.

He sprang up when he saw the friends, and walked towards them. Still young, the man had almost noble features, and quick, vigorous movements.

"What is your name?" Li-Erl asked kindly.

"I am called Wu-Fu, Master," the new servant replied, "but, you may call me by whatever name you please."

"Then you shall be called Wai from this day on," responded Li-Erl almost involuntarily.

And the servant who had once been a despised pauper was called Wai for a long time. He was the most loyal of the loyal, a protection to Li-Erl in every situation of his life. He never left him, and repaid him for his goodness with joyful service.

In Pe-Yang's house it was hardly noticed that Li-Erl had brought a servant with him. For the first few days the Lama's old helper tolerated Wai beside him; then he withdrew, leaving Li-Erl's personal attendance to Wai.

Li-Erl now resumed his visits to the city of the poor in Wai's company.. Although these outcasts scarcely knew one another, since none of them troubled about anyone else, some did stand out from the extraordinary mass, in a good or a bad way, so that Wai remembered them.

First he took his master to a house of beggars of whose existence even Hai-Tan had no idea. Those beggars who still owned a dilapidated hut, a room in which they could do as they pleased, constituted the upper social stratum of the poor.

Far greater, however, was the number of those who owned nothing. Even this group was again divided into those who earned enough by begging to be able to pay a small amount each day for their night's lodging, and those who, disabled by illness or through inveterate sloth, would beg for nothing any more. Only those were the really poor in the eyes of the others.

Wai took his enquiring master first to a beggar-house where the lodging was paid for. It lay amid the maze of the dirtiest lanes, differing only in size from the other huts. The two visitors – Hai-Tan had remained, shuddering, at home – came at a time when the occupants of this house were out.

At the entrance a raggedly-dressed but very strong man was lounging. He did not know Wai, and could not understand what the two decently-dressed strangers wanted here.

He spoke of his "master", who might be angry with him if eyes other than those of its occupants were to see the shelter; even a few coins did not make him any more amenable.

"My master has placed me here to prevent unauthorised persons from entering," he growled. "How am I to know that you do not intend to spend the night here without paying?"

"But you have received more than the price of a night's lodging," said Wai, trying to mollify him. With a sly grin the man asserted:

"You have given me the money; however, I must hand over the sum for the night's lodgings to my master."

"Very well, we will pay you for the night's lodging in any case," suggested Li-Erl.

The man could think of no objection to that. The sound of Li-Erl's voice had a compelling effect on him. Sullenly he stepped aside, and indicated one of the paper lamps hanging by the entrance.

It was necessary to make use of the light. Without it the travellers would have stumbled; there was so much mess in the actually spacious dormitory. All available space seemed to be utilised – hard sleeping-rolls were everywhere. The ceiling was low, the atmosphere unbearable. After only a few moments the two left the house, which was thickly covered in filth.

The bad-tempered doorkeeper seemed quite relieved when the two were outside again. What he feared from them was difficult to tell; but he sensed some kind of danger for his master. Li-Erl began a conversation by slipping a packet of tea to him:

"If you do not need it yourself, pass it on to someone else!" he said kindly. But the man retorted:

"I come first, then the others. I have not seen any real tea for a long time. I am not so stupid as to give this away."

"Does your master not pay you enough for your services?" asked Li-Erl, to which the man grunted in reply:

"I get nothing but the permanent accommodation in this house, and the food which I may take twice a day in the eating-house over there. If the young gentleman needs to know such things for his studies, he may look round the eating-house. He will then realise that we do not get any tea there."

"How many people can sleep here?"

"As many as are able to pay," was the answer. "I do not count them."

"But must you not hand over the money to your master?"

"Of course I must do so. Every day in the early morning his messenger comes and takes from me what I received."

Wai laughed.

"Naturally you put some of it aside for yourself," he said in a questioning tone.

"Oh no, I never do that. My master expects to receive a definite sum every day. If my takings do not come up to the mark, I am beaten. But if they exceed the specified sum, I am allowed to ask for rice in the eating-house. That is better than having money."

"Who is your master?" Li-Erl wanted to know. The voice of the keeper became mysterious.

"Oh, he is a very exalted and powerful man. He lives in the Imperial city; that was disclosed to me by his messenger. But no one may know his name, not even his messenger. Besides this one, he has many such houses in the city of the poor. The messenger goes from one to another and collects the takings."

Even though the man had now become quite trusting, Li-Erl was eager to leave. Too many heavy thoughts assailed him; he wanted to come to terms with them first in the peace of his own dwelling. Yet Wai suggested that they should still go and see the eating-house, since they were in the neighbourhood in any case.

Li-Erl acquiesced, and in silence they walked the few steps to the indicated house. It appeared to be a little less dilapidated than its surroundings, but was equally dirty.

Here too as everywhere the interior was moderately lit by paper lamps. Here and there on the bare floor people in rags sat eating their meal. Each had before him a small bowl with a strange mixture, and beside some stood a cup of tea.

The new visitors chose a place that appeared to be a little cleaner than the rest. Immediately a thickset, slovenly-attired man appeared, and stretched out his dirty hand towards them.

"Will you bring us some tea, my friend?" Li-Erl asked pleasantly.

The man did not stir, but held out his hand emphatically before Wai's eyes, thus showing respect to the elder. Now the latter understood.

"Oh, you want your payment first? How much is the tea?"

"For seven kaolin you can have enough to eat and drink for yourself. Your companion must pay the same."

"You are overcharging, old boy," croaked a voice that seemed to belong to a ragamuffin nearby. "If you want only tea, one kaolin is enough. But a bowl of food costs three."

"But I said that for seven they could eat their fill," the stout man argued.

"I will give you seven for myself," Wai promised. "My companion is unwell, and only requires tea."

With these words he slipped eight coins into the man's hand. He shuffled off, and after a short interval returned with two cups of steaming tea and a small bowl containing the same substance as all the others. At close quarters it looked most unappetising. Li-Erl reached hastily for the hot drink, and put it to his lips. But he thrust the cup away in disgust. It did not taste like tea, but rather like dish-water.

Using chopsticks, Wai took a few mouthfuls from the bowl. A little while ago he would have been glad to have warm food; even now it seemed bearable to him. But one look at his master made him terminate the meal abruptly. Deathly pale, and with all the signs of nausea, Li-Erl had collapsed.

Without a word, Wai put his arm round the youth and carried him out of the house, in which no one paid any more heed to the two. At a brisk pace he carried Li-Erl through the maze of alleys until they finally reached a kind of spacious garden.

Here he carefully set him down on a large flat stone, and supported him until he was able to look freely about him again.

Then they walked home at a slow pace and in silence. While Li-Erl went to bed, Wai, under the direction of the old servant, prepared exquisitely fragrant tea.

Not until next morning was Li-Erl able to speak. He was ashamed that he could have been so overcome with disgust, but Wai would not let him speak of it. With an air of importance he reported that he had visited the eating-house again in the evening, but less well-dressed.

"First I went to my hut, which I found still unoccupied. There I covered myself in rags ... you need have no fear, Master," he added with a smile, "I have had a bath! Then I went into the eating-house and asked for a small bowl of food, which tasted horrible, but I praised it nevertheless.

"Since I did so deliberately in a loud voice, the others paid attention. They laughed at me, and shouted that the food was cooked from what some of them obtained by begging. For a few coins, certain beggars deliver the contents of their sacks at the eating-house every evening.

"On hearing that I too shuddered, Master," said Wai almost apologetically, when he observed the effect of his words on Li-Erl. "But you, Master, no longer need to go to such places yourself. I am now here for that. I also went to the alms-house, the one where you need pay nothing. The people there are not cold," he said, shuddering himself, "they lie on top of each other all in a heap. I was told that not a night passes without brawls, indeed even stabbings. It is so terrible that I would rather die in the open air than spend the night in such a house," concluded Wai.

Later, when Hai-Tan came to enquire how the day had gone, Li-Erl said little, but expressed horror that wealthy men owned such alms-houses. Hai-Tan had not heard of this before, but promised to make discreet enquiries.

"Oh, Hai-Tan," said Li-Erl plaintively, "wherever one turns there is evil and misery!"

"Would a Truth-bringer have to come if things were different?" Hai-Tan asked reassuringly. "It is only because our poor realm is choking in its own mire that the gods must send help. Rejoice, Li-Erl, that the time approaches when we shall behold the Messenger of God."

Hai-Tan had not yet grasped who this Helper was. He considered Li-Erl to be a forerunner. But Wai had listened with bated breath and gazed wide-eyed at his master. Then he quietly left the room.

A few weeks passed without any special events. In the mornings Li-Erl listened to Pe-Yang's wise teachings, which did not always arouse conflict in him. Frequently they were of rare depth and truth. Once the Lama spoke of the way in which man could adapt himself to fit in with the world.

"There are two ways," he said emphatically, "of living with the world around us, if by 'living' we understand more than merely breathing and eating. Either you are inwardly indignant about everything that seems to you wrong, and you let this indignation find a way to the outside. Then you are a fighter who, if strong enough, can enforce improvement by wielding a weapon.

"But what is gained *in that way*, Li-Erl, is of short duration, for it is imposed from without. Or else you leave the others to their own devices while you live your inner life with great intensity, until this too breaks through to the outside. Then, however, it floods the souls and brings about change. I believe, Li-Erl, that that will be *your* path, you blessed one of our God."

"Tell me more about the Supreme One," implored Li-Erl, who had completely forgotten how unsatisfactorily this question had been dealt with previously.

Contrary to his wont, Pe-Yang did not allow himself to be silenced by the request, but only gazed at Li-Erl for a while with a kindly, searching glance.

"I can tell you nothing of Him. Look within you. There you will find all the knowledge of Him which you need. But in order to do so you must go into solitude. Take your friend and your servant with you, and withdraw from human beings.

"Your guide will show you where you are to go, how long you are to remain there. I have fulfilled my task with you, Li-Erl. I send you to the better teacher: to the Spirit from above, Which will take hold of you once you have been prepared. May the Supreme One bless you, my son. I thank Him that my eyes have been allowed to behold His Messenger!"

Pe-Yang had risen to his feet, and spread out both arms in blessing. At that moment Li-Erl's soul was filled with fervent gratitude. He clearly saw how all that Pe-Yang had taught him was guided from above. He sensed that the Lama had really given him of his best. He found no words to express his gratitude, but bowed down, and drew the hem of Pe-Yang's robe to his lips. Then he left the room, never to enter it again.

When Hai-Tan heard of Li-Erl's decision to withdraw into solitude, he ardently requested to accompany him. That had been Li-Erl's hope, but the decision had to come from Hai-Tan himself, uninfluenced. While the latter went to make preparations, Li-Erl surrendered himself to his thoughts, which became prayers.

And the Luminous Messenger of God appeared and spoke to him:

"Li-Erl, your training is now drawing to its close. In solitude you shall learn what you still need to know. Wai will tell you where you are to go without your asking him about it. Wai has been placed at your side not only as a servant – that is the outward form of his being with you – but as a guide through the streets of men. Unconsciously he will lead your earthly steps, follow him.

"Hai-Tan, however, will protect you whenever you have need of that, and with his wealth he will pave the ways for you. Make use of him. But I myself will be near you and instruct you, as soon as you can listen to my words in complete quiet and seclusion."

The Messenger disappeared. Gratefully Li-Erl recognised the Goodness of the Supreme One, in Whose Almighty Hand lay the threads of his destiny and of his mission.

Then Wai entered.

"Master, I have been thinking about what you told Hai-Tan and me. I think I know a place you would like. A few days' journey from here, in the mountains, is a stone hut, once occupied by a wise man. It is so far from human habitation that no one would disturb you, and yet near enough for me to supply the few provisions that we require."

"Then let us set out for it early tomorrow morning," Li-Erl decided without hesitation.

The next day Wai led the friends into the mountains by very easy paths. Hai-Tan, who had witnessed the first encounter with the servant, could not cease to marvel at the way in which he carried out his self-chosen duties.

The sullen, angry beggar had become a discreet, devoted companion, never lacking in due tact. Hai-Tan would have loved to know whether Wai had really been born into poverty of poor parents, but Li-Erl asked him to refrain from questions.

After several days' journey, which at this cool season was not arduous, the three travellers arrived one midday at the place described by Wai. Halfway up a mountain which appeared inaccessible, there stood on a small, grass-grown plateau a stone hut which was still in excellent repair. It had also been kept clean, so that the friends took possession of it happily.

Inside were two sound rooms, and a side-room that seemed to have served the previous occupant as kitchen and stable. Without further ado Wai prepared for his master the larger of the rooms, which even had a window-opening.

Hai-Tan was given the room which was first entered on coming in from outside, and which received light and air through the door. The latter was made of solid beams, so that it offered protection from the cold. Wai made himself at home in the side-room.

Immediately he began to gather a supply of wood, so that quite soon the friends could have hot tea. It now became apparent that in his very large bundle Wai had brought almost exclusively things that were to ensure his master's comfort. For himself he was indescribably frugal.

On one of the following days he sought out human habitation, and returned with a long-haired goat, which he called Wu. It lived with him in his room, and together with its kid, Fu, which soon made its appearance, it became his friend and playmate. But his master, and his friend Hai-Tan, were fed with Wu's milk.

In the meantime Li-Erl had set up an altar in his room. He had brought the altar equipment with him in his bundle.

Hai-Tan, on the other hand, had carried up a great variety of things, without considering whether he would be able to make use of them in their complete seclusion. Now he laughed at himself, and regretted that he had not brought even a single object with which to adorn his altar.

In the time that followed he made long journeys of several days' duration in order to obtain altar equipment, and also because he enjoyed being among people again.

But Li-Erl, who retired completely into himself, was always glad when Hai-Tan was away.

Wai, who was a keen observer, could not fail to notice this. For a long time he considered how he should set about discreetly removing Hai-Tan. Often he appealed to the gods for help, and then it was granted to him.

A boy found the way to the stone house with difficulty; he reported that Hai-Tan had broken his leg, and was lying under good care down in the valley. Wai was to come from time to time to obtain money and advice from him; for Hai-Tan himself would hardly be able to climb up the mountain again.

Wai was so happy that it did not occur to him to send the victim a single thought of pity. Only now would his master be granted complete quiet. He himself kept so aloof that Li-Erl did not see him for days, even for weeks eventually. Only his faithful solicitude could be felt.

And as the months passed, Li-Erl's connection with his Luminous Home grew. Truth upon truth was revealed to him in the silence. All his questions were answered, and his impetuous nature was stilled. A wondrous peace filled his heart, and made him long to bestow this peace upon all human beings.

A YEAR HAD gone by like a dream; yet it was rich in inner experiencing. This time had left its mark on Wai too. He had deepened and matured. Above all, however, he had become certain of what he had only divined in the last days in Kiang-ning: he knew that Li-Erl was the promised Truth-bringer.

Supreme bliss filled him at having been chosen to serve this exalted one. He did not ask "why". Unassumingly he accepted the great grace as completely undeserved, but therefore also as all the more overwhelming and binding.

Hai-Tan, however, was tired of being with the simple folk who had nursed him, and with whom he spent his days reading and idling away his time. The loyalty he had pledged to Li-Erl forbade his returning to Kiang-ning. He wanted to remain near his friend, but wished impatiently for this seclusion to end.

He did not ask what would happen then. He had linked his fate to that of the youth, sensing that thereby his path must also lead upwards; but the rest he left to Li-Erl.

And even Li-Erl did not ask what was to be done next. He was blissfully happy in this final stage of his apprenticeship, whose end he felt was approaching.

One morning he walked far into the rocky mountain crevices which led upwards and downwards apparently in an inextricable tangle, and yet meaningful when looked at from the top of the mountain. Often they had served him as symbolic of human life.

On this day too such thoughts preoccupied him, and he climbed until he reached a large boulder that barred his way. There he sat down, and surveyed his surroundings attentively. How all kinds of little plants struggled to take root in the crevices! How did the seed get there? Had it been carried in a bird's beak? Impossible! Only large birds of prey lived here, and they did not concern themselves with seed-grains.

Good spirits must have done it. He knew there were good spirits, just as there were demons. The demons originated in the brains of men. Who had created the good spirits? Within him came the answer: "Can you still ask, when you use the word 'created'?"

"O Supreme One, then Thou hast also formed the good beings who help all that lives!" he cried, overjoyed. "I might have known; for all that is good and beautiful has its origin in Thee!"

Now it seemed to him as though new eyes were opened within him, so that he could see all the beings inhabiting the air and the earth. He conversed with them, and learned many new things about mountain and valley, river and wind. During the night too he remained in the open air to hear about the stars. Not until dawn did he return to his room, where the solicitous Wai awaited him with hot tea.

Li-Erl had these visions of friendly helpers a few more times, then apparently he knew enough about them, for he no longer saw them.

Some days later Li-Erl was again among the rocks of the cliff when he heard the voice of the Messenger of God, addressing him solemnly:

"Your time of apprenticeship is over, Li-Erl. You bear this name today for the last time. From now on you will be called Li-Pe-Tan, as a sign that you are sent by the Supreme One. Go back among the people, and bring them the Truth. You are not to fight with the sword, but with the weapons of patience and peace.

"You will accomplish great things if you always draw your strength from above, and remain faithful to the Commands of the Most High. The colour of your robes is to be deep violet. If you wish them to be embroidered, choose pure white and shining gold for the purpose. There must be no other colours in your clothing.

"On your feet you shall wear soft leather bound with straps, lest they become unsightly in the dust of the streets. The Supreme One has marked your brow with a sign, which will identify you as His Messenger to all who are pure in heart. It is a star formed of two intersecting triangles. Use the same sign as your new escutcheon.

"Return to Kiang-ning, and let Hai-Tan attend to all these things. After that, when you are wearing the new raiment, you will appear before the Emperor. Do not ponder over what you are to say; at the right time it will be given to you from above. Do not reflect either on how you shall come before his countenance. Your guide will see to that.

"Always follow the promptings of your inner voice, and you will do what is right, so long as you maintain the connection with the Supreme One. But if you do not know what is to be done, call on me. I am always near you."

Li-Pe-Tan thought he could hear the ringing voice and see the shining rays, even long after the Messenger had disappeared. Deeply moved, and yet infinitely happy, he then set out for the stone house, where he found Wai awaiting him.

"Master, just look what has happened!" the servant called to him. "More than half the roof of our house has caved in, without any outward cause! Is that to signify that we should move on?"

Delighted, Li-Pe-Tan looked at the speaker.

"Yes, that is what it means, Wai," he answered in a cheerful voice. "For a short time we will return to Kiang-ning, where I must attend to all kinds of business. But then we will go out into the world. Are you looking forward to it, Wai?"

"Wai will go anywhere with his master, but is also happy to stay at home, if his master does so," was the servant's reply.

Then the man set about packing their few belongings into a large bundle. Only the altar equipment was left for Li-Pe-Tan to carry.

Sooner than the latter had expected, they were ready to set out. Li-Pe-Tan had not envisaged his departure as being so sudden, but he remembered that he was to follow Wai in such things. So he bade farewell in thought to the place where he had spent invaluable months.

After a few hours on the road they found themselves face to face with a startled Hai-Tan.

"How fortunate that you have come today," he called to them. "I am returning to Kiang-ning tomorrow. My father has sent for me; I must obey

94

his call. Now you can accompany me. Tomorrow you would no longer have found me!"

Li-Pe-Tan realised how well advised he was to follow Wai. But his friend was glad that the time of seclusion was over.

"You have changed considerably," he said suddenly, scrutinising Li-Pe-Tan. "You have become more manly, your features are strangely illumined, and a radiance emanates from your forehead."

Then Li-Pe-Tan told him about his change of name; this set Hai-Tan thinking.

"Did you choose the name yourself?" he asked eagerly.

Li-Pe-Tan said that he had not. Then Hai-Tan bowed down to the ground and pressed the hem of Li-Pe-Tan's robe to his lips.

"So you are not the forerunner of the Messenger of God, but the Messenger himself! Some priests would say that you are the Son of the Most High. Li-Pe-Tan, let me be your servant henceforth."

"You are my friend and protector," replied the Truth-bringer earnestly. "That you shall remain as long as you yourself wish to accompany me."

The following day they arrived in Kiang-ning, and were joyfully received by Hai-Tan's father in his palace.

In contrast to the wretched huts of the beggars and the small houses of the scholars, the palaces of the wealthy and the nobility were sumptuous. They were surrounded by large gardens arranged like a belt round the magnificent Imperial Palace.

It appeared quite unreal to Li-Pe-Tan that he was to live in the most exclusive district of the capital, the so-called Imperial City. But he was received everywhere with the greatest respect.

While his robes were being made, Li-Pe-Tan remained in his beautifully-appointed room. After that he visited first the Temple of the "Son of Heaven".

There were many mandarins and dignitaries present, in far more resplendent raiment; but Li-Pe-Tan stood out among them, so that the Emperor became aware of him and enquired about him. However there was little information to be had.

The man in the violet robe was a wise man who was staying in the house of Tsong-Tan, and probably came from far away. That was all they knew.

But this did not satisfy the Emperor, and in the afternoon he sent a message to Tsong-Tan, bidding him come to the Imperial Court with his guest.

Li-Pe-Tan was amazed. Although he had already often perceived how the guidance from above intervened in his life, it seemed miraculous to him every time. And again, with what unspeakable ease the acquaintance with the Emperor was now unfolding! He would certainly not be concerned either about what to say.

At the appointed hour attendants bore the two men in carrying-chairs to the Imperial Palace, where they were received by numerous splendidly-attired servants.

Tsong, a worthy general of the Emperor, was greeted respectfully; but when Li-Pe-Tan alighted from his chair everyone bowed to the ground. Something intensely awe-inspiring emanated from him, making people forget his age and youthful appearance.

Led by a marshal in a richly-embroidered robe, the visitors moved through rooms of indescribable beauty. Every object was inlaid with shimmering mother-of-pearl, from which the sunlight elicited a blaze of colours. Their feet trod on thick rugs woven of colourful wool.

Everywhere the eye fell upon flowers in exquisite vases. Li-Pe-Tan was so fascinated by it all that he completely forgot the purpose of his visit, and was only reminded of it when he noticed that his attendants had prostrated themselves on the floor.

Amazed, he looked at Tsong-Tan, who was sliding forward on his knees ahead of him. Must he also do that? Probably. After all, he did not wish to make himself conspicuous.

It went better than he feared. Suddenly the attendants stopped moving forward. As Li-Pe-Tan looked up, he found himself before a golden throne, behind which was spread yellow silk embroidered with huge dragons.

Sitting on the throne was a man, still young, wearing an exquisitely-embroidered yellow silk robe trimmed with fur. On his head he wore a narrow golden crown studded with precious stones. From its sides strings of priceless white pearls hung down to his breast. A golden chain was fastened about his shoulders, with a dragon in bright colours hanging in front. The Emperor's features were pleasing and noble.

But a look of infinite pain, which arrested Li-Pe-Tan's attention, seemed to be engraved upon them. Li-Pe-Tan could not take his eyes from him. And Hou-Chou perceived the ray from the clear eyes of his visitor, and directed his own upon him. For a few moments the two pairs of eyes rested in one another, the sad eyes of the Emperor, sick at heart in all his splendour, and the shining eyes of the wise man. Only slowly did they release one another.

Then, however, Hou-Chou called in a clear ringing voice, which betrayed the youth of the supreme dignitary:

"Rise from your knees; and you, wise stranger, come to the steps of my throne that I may question you."

The visitors complied with the request, and while Tsong, making the numerous prescribed obeisances, stepped to one side where many gorgeously-attired courtiers stood, Li-Pe-Tan went forward unconcernedly, bowed slightly, rested one foot on the lowest step of the throne and looked up at the Ruler.

Piercing looks were directed at him, attempting to draw his attention to the impropriety of his conduct. But he did not understand their intent, and simply looked round him for their source. His gaze fell on an elderly, sinister man, with a moustache whose thin ends hung down to his breast.

In contrast to all others present, he was dressed in black. Over his heavy silk robe he wore a black-painted coat of chain-mail which in no way impeded his movements. His right fist clasped a huge sword. His features were coarse. In every respect he seemed to be the very opposite of his Ruler.

Li-Pe-Tan turned away with a slight shudder. The Emperor began to ask questions. Where the stranger came from, what was his name, from what lineage he was descended, and what he intended to do here in Kiang-ning.

Li-Pe-Tan's answers were guarded. Quite contrary to his usual openness, he gave evasive answers, thereby unintentionally surrounding himself with the fascination of the mysterious. In addition to this there was his unreserved behaviour, which was unusual here at court.

The courtiers looked at one another. They had the impression that the stranger must be an emperor's son from a distant land, who wished to live among them incognito. That was the reason for the fairy tale he told of his birth in the Middle Kingdom.

The Emperor too believed something similar. The unaffected nature of the guest gave him a sense of well-being, and he wished that he could meet him more often. But that depended on so many things! So thought Hou-Chou with a gentle sigh, as he listened to the words of the stranger.

"What do you propose to do now?" he asked.

The usual answer to this question would have been: "What my illustrious master commands." The Emperor almost held his breath with suspense to see whether the guest would make use of these words, and a faint smile flitted across his features when Li-Pe-Tan said without further reflection:

"I do not know yet, illustrious Emperor. In any case, I shall not remain here long. I am awaiting a call that will direct me to other regions of your Realm."

The courtiers listened with bated breath. What would the Ruler say now? For a moment he was silent, then he replied:

"Let me know when the call reaches you. But I would like to speak to you before then," he added after a brief hesitation.

It seemed to Li-Pe-Tan as though the Emperor cast a quick glance at the black-clad man by his side. At this point the latter took up the conversation by saying in a gruff voice:

"There will hardly be time for that, Ruler of the Realm. You have other things to do than to receive foreign sages, who would do well to leave our city soon."

Then he clapped his hands to indicate that the audience was over. Courtiers approached the guests, and led them out of the hall, hardly allowing them time to bow.

As though in a daze, Li-Pe-Tan walked at Tsong's side through an endless array of rooms and corridors until they reached their carrying-chairs again. At a brisk trot, the attendants bore them back to the home of the general. There Hai-Tan eagerly awaited what news his father and his friend would have to convey.

"Wen is angry," said Tsong emphatically.

"He often is," said his son, unconcernedly, while Li-Pe-Tan asked:

"Is that the name of the black one who was standing beside the throne?"

Instead of replying, the general said gravely:

"You do not know what you have said with these words, Li-Pe-Tan. The black one beside the throne, the dark cloud that overshadows our exalted

Ruler. The evil in the life of the good one! You are right, Li-Pe-Tan. He is the one."

"How can he end a reception given by the Emperor, while the Emperor is still speaking?" asked Li-Pe-Tan indignantly, but was given the answer:

"Wen can do whatever he likes."

"Is he all-powerful?" asked the stranger.

"All-powerful?" Hai-Tan scoffed. "He thinks he is, but one day he will see the end of his power. He deposed Hou-Chou's father Siang many years ago; afterwards, when he realised that the people would not be without an Emperor, and refused to acknowledge Wen's rule, he reinstated Siang.

"Siang was Emperor in name only. Wen ruled. And his rule is harsh, capricious and unjust. Then Siang died, and Hou-Chou came to the throne. But he too is unable to assert himself against the sinister Wen. He must do his gaoler's bidding. 'Gaoler', that is what the black one is called by the people, who murmur against him. If only they would find the strength to revolt!"

Li-Pe-Tan had listened with rising indignation. How was such a thing possible! And out in the provinces nothing was known about it? Or had he alone not known, because he lived for nothing but his studies?

Hai-Tan's thoughts, however, had moved on, and were preoccupied with Wen's displeasure towards his friend.

"Do you think, Father, that Li-Pe-Tan is in danger?" he asked anxiously. "Should we depart this very day?"

Tsong looked up.

"In my house my guest is safe," he replied with dignity. "Let us wait and see whether Wen will take any action."

The meeting with the Emperor, who was actually held captive, had affected Li-Pe-Tan deeply. His thoughts were constantly occupied with the Ruler. Who could help him? Suddenly he realised that the Messenger of the Supreme One had promised him this audience. Hence it was the Will of the Most High that he should speak with the Emperor. And nothing ever happened without good reason. Having spoken with the Emperor, he would be granted further contact with him. Consequently he, as the Truth-bringer, might also be a helper to the sorrowful Ruler!

When his reflections had reached this conclusion, he fell on his knees before his small altar, and implored the Supreme One to let him know how he could serve the Emperor. He faltered at the word "serve". He was God's servant, and must serve no human being, but surely help.

The following day, one of the priests at the Temple of the "Son of Heaven" sent a manuscript which no one could decipher. Li-Pe-Tan was asked to try his hand at it. Although he had never even seen such characters, it was not difficult for him to convey the meaning of the words. It seemed that someone was quietly telling him sentence upon sentence, he only needed to write. It was a song of praise to the Highest of gods, portraying in glowing words His Might and Sublimity.

Li-Pe-Tan accomplished the task with great joy, but kept the script for a while, as Hai-Tan pointed out that the priests would be suspicious if what none of them was able to do was so quickly completed.

In the evening a veiled messenger brought a note for Li-Pe-Tan. He was asked to open the back door of Tsong's house at the onset of total darkness, and there to expect a guest. Since the messenger did not wait for an answer, Li-Pe-Tan was unable to find out who had sent him.

He avoided Hai-Tan, and went to see Tsong. He wished to know if he could comply with the request. After all, a criminal might seek to gain access to the general's palace in this way. Tsong thought it over briefly.

"Do what is asked, Li-Pe-Tan," he then said. "I shall remain hidden in the background to protect you and my house if need be. It is as well that you did not tell Hai-Tan any of this, for he would suspect Wen behind it, whereas I believe something quite different."

At the appointed hour Li-Pe-Tan stood by the opened door. He did not have long to wait. The guest, veiled in silken cloths, arrived in a carrying-chair. He stepped hastily into the house while the bearers retired into the garden with the chair.

"Take me to a room where we can speak alone," sounded a voice that seemed familiar to Li-Pe-Tan.

He tried to recall where he had heard it before, as he conducted the guest to his own room. There the stranger promptly cast aside the cloths, and stood in simple attire, yet distinguished and regal, before the astonished sage. It was the Emperor who had come to him!

Li-Pe-Tan prostrated himself before him, not because custom decreed it, but out of a deeply-felt urge. The Ruler, however, bade him rise and be seated with him.

"Let us say and do nothing unnecessary, Li-Pe-Tan," he said sadly. "My time is short. You must know that I am held as a prisoner. I am only the cloak which Wen dons to remain the unrecognised ruler. As long as his rule was to some extent just, I endured in silence what my father took upon himself before me. But now I am to protect misdeeds, injustices and villainy with my name. That I can no longer do.

"I have prayed to the gods, and have been promised that a man in a violet robe with the six-pointed star on his breast would be my teacher and helper. You are the man, Li-Pe-Tan. Help me!"

Li-Pe-Tan knew not what to answer. Then he said simply:

"I have entreated the Supreme One to allow me to help you, Emperor. This is His response. I obey."

To both men it seemed that something immense had entered their lives. For Li-Pe-Tan the Emperor's request signified the beginning of his task. Hou-Chou, however, stood that very moment at the decisive turning-point of his whole existence. Deeply moved, both remained silent, while their thoughts rose upwards as prayers.

Then the Emperor resumed:

"Today I had to come to you in secret, Li-Pe-Tan. But that is odious to me. Yet if I summon you publicly, thereby defying Wen's designs, even my most loyal servants could not protect you."

"But God can protect me. He will do so, I am not afraid," was Li-Pe-Tan's unruffled reply.

"If you were afraid of men, you would not be the one who was promised to me. But I can see no peaceful progress so long as I have not completely freed myself from Wen. Let us both pray to the gods this night. They will answer our prayers, I am sure of that. Then I will come to you secretly for the last time tomorrow at the same hour, so that we can make further decisions in accordance with the answers we are given."

Quickly the Emperor covered himself with the silken cloths, and stepped out of the room. Li-Pe-Tan walked silently ahead, leading him unseen into the open, where the bearers were already awaiting him. The chair arrived at the Imperial Palace unchallenged.

But the two who had found each other today spent the night in fervent prayer. However ardently Li-Pe-Tan implored, he received no answer except:

"Await what is to come!"

Though unable to understand the meaning of the words, he became confused if he tried to ponder over it. This made him clearly realise that he must simply await whatever was to come, whether a human being, as he assumed, or some event.

The Emperor, who was completely absorbed in meditation in the manner that he had been taught, was told that the way in which he was to associate with Li-Pe-Tan would only be made known to him in two days' time, and that he should wait patiently.

So the next evening he sent a secret message to the sage, saying that he should not be expected until the following evening.

Neither Li-Pe-Tan nor Hai-Tan left Tsong's palace during these days; they had enough to do with the deciphering of more manuscripts sent to them by the priests.

Towards evening, however, they were roused from their work by a tremendous uproar. A steadily increasing tumult and screaming appeared to fill the streets around the palaces.

Wai entered the room in great distress, and begged the friends not to venture outside. Something terrible must have taken place. Anyone who did not find himself on public roads at this time would be fortunate. Whatever could have happened?

Li-Pe-Tan unconsciously linked the unknown happening with the answer from above. Was this what he was to await? Praying, he compelled his senses to be still. At the right time he would learn what he must know.

Suddenly Tsong rushed into the room, showing every sign of the greatest alarm. He who was normally so calm was trembling all over.

"Something dreadful has happened!" he cried. "Wen has been murdered in the Imperial Palace. If the assassin is not found, suspicion may fall on all of us who were his opponents. My life is no longer safe, and you too would do well to flee!"

"Wen dead!"

This was the promised happening. At the thought, Li-Pe-Tan felt gratitude and joy; but then with impressive calm he turned to the agitated general.

"Think for a moment, Tsong," he urged. "The Emperor will be relieved to be rid of Wen. For the sake of appearances he will make enquiries to find the murderer, but no one will hurt a hair of your head. You are not to flee; on the contrary, you must rededicate your life to the service of the Ruler, who needs you now. Hasten to the Palace, stand at Hou-Chou's side. That is what is worthy of you. But Wai and I will await what this evening has in store for us."

His quiet composure had a wonderful effect on the others. Without questioning, Tsong followed the advice of his guest, while Hai-Tan asked a little ruefully:

"And you make no mention of me! What am I to do?"

"You must decide that yourself, Hai-Tan," was Li-Pe-Tan's friendly reply. "I do not yet know whether I am to remain here in Kiang-ning, or whether I will set out on my travels even tomorrow. If you wish to remain my companion and protector, I shall be grateful to you."

That evening Li-Pe-Tan waited in vain for his visitor. But in the night God's Messenger appeared before him, and requested him to undertake the journey to Tibet the following day. The time had come to visit the monastery of Lie-Tse. He would still hear from the Emperor before his departure.

More joyful tidings could hardly have been given him! If he had ardently wished for anything, it was to be permitted to visit Lie-Tse, and to experience life in the Tibetan monasteries. Now this would come about sooner than he had anticipated.

He wakened Wai, and instructed him to prepare everything for the journey. But it turned out that Wai had already quietly made arrangements. He had bought riding-horses and a pack-horse; he had obtained rugs and leathern bottles; in short, everything was perfectly arranged for a ride high up into the mountains.

Amazed, Li-Pe-Tan enquired how all this had occurred to the servant.

"Master," said Wai simply: "You have an invisible guardian who gives me the necessary instructions. I am blessed to be able to hear them."

Early in the morning Hai-Tan rushed into his friend's room.

"The murderer has been found," he cried joyfully, "he is a porter, who frankly acknowledges his guilt, even though he knows that the Emperor must pass sentence on him. He says the people would no longer endure Wen's rule. It fell to his lot to carry out the deed which thousands would have been willing to do. I hope that in time he will be set free," added Hai-Tan.

A little later a servant came to summon Li-Pe-Tan to the presence of the Emperor.

The young Ruler received him in a sombre mood.

"The need for secrecy is past, Li-Pe-Tan," were his words of greeting. "My fetters have been burst through the love of my people. May they never regret having made me their sole Ruler."

Li-Pe-Tan was about to speak, but the Emperor did not give him an opening.

"There is now a great deal for me to do in the immediate future. I must gain insight into all the administrative branches, must examine and direct. May the gods help me to do it in the right way. But after that the time will come when I can have you to live with me as my teacher.

"I have a favour to ask of you, Li-Pe-Tan," said Hou-Chou hesitantly. "Would it be possible for you to attain the rank of a Lama? Perhaps I am interfering with your plans by this request, but it is important to me to be justified before the people by your rank when I summon you to my side."

"I am on my way to Tibet," said Li-Pe-Tan almost solemnly.

He was deeply moved that even this was preordained by his guidance. He told Hou-Chou of his charge, and the young Ruler was truly happy.

"I have one more request to make," the Emperor then announced. "I would like you to take with you on your journey an additional servant whom I will appoint. He is accustomed to carrying loads, and doing the most menial work. I know that he will serve you loyally just as he demonstrated loyalty to me. Do not ask his name, or where he comes from. You may give him a new name."

A suspicion of who the servant might be arose in Li-Pe-Tan, and his heart was filled with joy over this token of delicate consideration. Truly Hou-Chou deserved all the help bestowed on him!

The parting was brief, for they expected to meet again, even if years were to pass until then.

At the gate of the Palace Wai awaited him, conversing with a simply-clad man whose face was shaded by a broad, flat wicker-hat. This man joined Li-Pe-Tan on the short way home. No sooner had they arrived at Tsong's palace than he announced that he was the porter appointed by Hou-Chou. Li-Pe-Tan nodded in agreement, and then asked Wai:

"What shall we call the man?"

A smile spread across the earnest features of the trusted servant.

"It seems that those around you are somehow related to poverty, since our names end with 'ai'. Prince Hai; I, Wai ... well then, let us call this man Lai."

Li-Pe-Tan had to laugh.

"Very well," he consented, "but make sure that no confusion arises."

Then he went to see Hai-Tan, whom he found eagerly making preparations for the journey.

"Of course I am going with you!" he called to his friend. "Tibet has for some time been the object of my longing. But you must allow me to take my servant Dai with me."

Loud, hearty laughter interrupted him.

"The number of the poor grows steadily," cried Li-Pe-Tan, "how many more 'ais' will join me?"

Then he explained to Hai-Tan, who had looked on in total bewilderment, what had made him laugh so much, and now Hai-Tan in turn joined in the merriment.

Towards evening the little band set out. Li-Pe-Tan was anxious to leave the city as inconspicuously as possible; therefore they rode out through different gates, and met only a good distance away outside the city.

Li-Pe-Tan had chosen Lai as his companion, but he abandoned the idea instantly when Wai advised against it. He knew only too well that he was to follow Wai in everything pertaining to journeys and such matters.

Again the advice proved to be sound. It had been observed that Li-Pe-Tan was joined at the Palace by a man unknown to the imperial servants. And the escape of Wen's murderer from custody was discovered. Immediately Li-Pe-Tan came under suspicion.

When he reached the gate he found there friends of Wen, who stopped and questioned him. But he could truthfully say that he had never seen the man, nor did he know his name. Also he was unable to indicate the man's present whereabouts. So the mandarins had to let him go.

But as he rode on, Li-Pe-Tan reflected on what he had just experienced. "How simple it is to obey," he thought, "and how seldom it is done. Usually we think that our own ideas are the best."

And now began a journey that lasted over three months. Wai seemed to know the way well. It led through remote regions and past rocky slopes, up rugged mountain paths and downhill again. Often wide detours had to be made to get from desolate regions back to human habitations, where they could rest and replenish their supplies.

Garments of fur had to be purchased, for the higher the riders advanced, the colder it became. Shuddering, Li-Pe-Tan thought of Lie-Tse making this journey on foot. How he must have suffered on the way! Would he still be alive?

Finally one midday the riders approached a village built close into the rocks. The huts resembled piled-up boulders, and seemed completely unsuited for human habitation.

Only when the travellers were granted a night's lodging in one of these disdained huts did they perceive how practical the building was. Biting winds howled across it without causing damage, and the heavy boulders kept out the cold.

Inside, the walls were lined with furs and hides. The air was stale, but warm. The food offered was extremely frugal: hard, flat bread, whose ingredients Li-Pe-Tan was unable to identify, and milk from the mountain goats which shared the hut.

The members of the family offering hospitality were as happy as children when Li-Pe-Tan served them with some of the tea prepared by Wai for the travellers. With a little smile, Wai added some fat which he considered no longer good enough for Li-Pe-Tan to use.

With shouts of joy the people fell upon the welcome gift, and stirred it into their tea. The travellers observed it with a shudder; only Wai appeared not to be surprised.

"What are the people doing? They are spoiling their tea," cried Li-Pe-Tan, horrified.

"Master, to them it seems better that way. Leave them to their pleasure," said Wai gently. To his master's surprise he spoke to the people in their language.

From these hut-dwellers Wai learned the approximate position of Lie-Tse's monastery, so that the following day they were able to advance further into the mountains, making straight for their destination. Nevertheless it took over a week before the monastery appeared at the top of a sheer cliff.

What presented itself to their searching gaze looked like a fortress. Thick walls surrounded the monastery and all its adjacent buildings. In these walls were apertures, evidently providing a look-out for guards.

By a winding path the riders reached a gate. It was not the kind of gate familiar to them, made of intricately interlocking beams, but the beams formed a flat surface held together with iron braces. On this surface strange signs were painted in red.

Wai gazed at the door, his eyes beaming with joy. He looked completely transfigured; his master had to look at him again and again, but forbore to ask the reason for his joy.

The gate was closed, nor did it open when the riders – not knowing how else they should draw attention to themselves – threw stones at it. Should they attempt to ride round the wall, perhaps to discover an open gate? They all turned questioningly to Wai, who suddenly seemed to have an idea – or was it a recollection?

He sprang from his horse, and walked up to the gate. There he eagerly inspected every stone in the framework within his reach. Then he seemed to have found what he was looking for. He reached with both hands into a cleft in the rock, and tugged at something with all his might. But nothing appeared, instead a tremendous noise began, like the pealing of a very large bell. And the more eagerly Wai pulled, the louder became the pealing.

With a sigh of relief the servant finally ceased. At that very moment the sections of the door opened, and the riders beheld several venerable-looking priests stepping aside to make way for the most venerable of all, whom Li-Pe-Tan recognised as his teacher.

"Welcome, my son," Lie-Tse greeted him. "I have been expecting you for days. I am happy that you have arrived safely."

Then the Lama turned also to greet Hai-Tan, and nodded graciously to the servants, who had dropped to their knees before him.

Lost in wonder, Li-Pe-Tan gazed at the faithful guardian of his childhood. Here he looked completely transformed. His robe was more costly than anything Li-Pe-Tan had ever seen. Precious stones gleamed at the borders. On his head he was wearing the Yellow Cap, on his right forefinger a ring with a large yellow stone.

The aged man looked both venerable and imposing. Li-Pe-Tan's head swam at the thought of how simply this High Lama had lived in his parents' home. But Lie-Tse allowed him little time to marvel. Servants conducted the newcomers to their appointed rooms, and informed them that the exalted father, the highest Lama of all, expected Li-Pe-Tan and Hai-Tan to join him for a meal a few hours hence.

The servants came punctually to fetch the friends and lead them into a small room where they met Lie-Tse. Today he wished to take the meal with them quite alone, to make arrangements for their further stay in the monastery.

The profound dignity emanating from the former teacher silenced Hai-Tan, and even Li-Pe-Tan hardly dared to address his fatherly friend.

After the servants had brought in the few but carefully prepared dishes and withdrawn, Lie-Tse uttered a prayer, thanking God for His Goodness.

During the meal the Lama asked Li-Pe-Tan about his plans.

He was overjoyed to hear that his pupil wished to continue his studies. It was what he had expected.

"From tomorrow morning you will join the monastery as a Learning Brother, Li-Pe-Tan. It depends on you how many years will pass before you can leave it as a Lama. Naturally you are free to leave at any time, but then without the rank to which you aspire.

"Wai will be admitted as a Serving Brother; this corresponds with his wishes. For Hai-Tan and his servant there is a pleasant house outside the monastery, where he can live and spend the time of his sojourn as he pleases. But what about Lai?"

Lie-Tse asked the question very thoughtfully. Li-Pe-Tan had imagined it to be a simple matter to hide the fugitive in the seclusion of the monastery – for he had become increasingly aware that Lai was a fugitive. Now he realised that not everyone could find ready acceptance. Lie-Tse was quite emphatic about that.

"Only very seldom do we admit members of another race here, Li-Pe-Tan. That you are welcome is something you owe to the guidance of God, which announced your coming to us beforehand. Wai is a Tibetan, as you may have observed. I see that he has kept his word, and told you nothing of his life. Later on you will be given precise information about it.

"But you, Hai-Tan, do not actually wish to comply with the strict rules of the monastery. Solely the desire to serve your friend has brought you here. We will make your stay as pleasant as possible. Your servant may look after you. But Lai?"

The Lama sank into deep reflection, but then he raised his head resolutely.

"I will appoint him to help the gardener. There he will be associated with our life, without having to share in it more than he himself would wish. This will automatically decide what road he will choose later on."

Hai-Tan was rather taken aback at being pushed aside without further consideration. But he had to admit to himself that a life of abiding by the strict statutes of an order, in a faith alien to him, would have been uncomfortable indeed. The separation from Li-Pe-Tan, however, did upset him.

He had to set out directly after the meal in order to reach the house intended for him before nightfall.

"When may I come back to see Li-Pe-Tan?" he asked, expecting that the answer would be: "Whenever you wish." But instead Lie-Tse said kindly:

"That cannot be decided yet. First of all the student must become familiar with his surroundings and with the language of our country. For this he will have to make the most of every free minute in the day. You will be told when your visit is convenient. Farewell."

Servants came, Dai too made his appearance, and before Hai-Tan had considered everything, he found himself already on the way to life outside the monastery walls.

"Do you know why your friend was removed so promptly, Li-Pe-Tan?" asked Lie-Tse kindly.

The student looked at him questioningly.

"He still bears no longing for God in his soul. His thoughts and intuitive perceptions would obtrude on all of us here, and make it difficult especially for you to accustom yourself to the life here. His only desire is to be with you. For this very reason I must deny him that. It is not possible for a soul to attempt to approach God, if the actual motive is to be near a human being.

"If Hai-Tan's inner life is of the right kind, he will cast off his superficiality, and long ardently for God. With that he will have been helped for all eternity. But if he is satisfied with the comfortable life awaiting him on his return to the lowlands, he is not the person to continue as your protector. Do you understand me, Li-Pe-Tan?"

"Yes, my father, I understand you, and deeply respect your wisdom."

The answer came in a ringing voice from the student, who was happy to be permitted to learn once more under this benevolent guidance.

"Then let me take you now to the room intended for you, since you wish to live among us as a Brother and no longer as a guest. And one thing more, my son: here we are all equal as human beings; there is no princely rank. Only the degree of knowledge about God confers rank. Therefore you will henceforth be called Li-Pe, just as you were once called Li-Erl."

With these words, Lie-Tse walked through a long narrow corridor, into which light fell from outside through small windows. This corridor was intersected by a wider one, with openings on either side, high enough to admit a man.

The openings led into very small rooms, hewn into the rock or built of stone. Apart from a large stone slab, which apparently served as a bed, there was nothing in them. Each of these small cells had a window at the top of the outside wall; but it was impossible to see out. Only fresh, rather cold air poured in.

"Behold your future dwelling, Li-Pe," said Lie-Tse pleasantly to his student. "You are accustomed to better things, but you must learn that he who seeks God can dispense with all else. Here you will spend your free time and the nights. For your studies you will go to a hall, where you will be assigned a place. The meals are taken by the students together.

"Remember your cell, the seventh from the corner; for it is forbidden to enter other cells. And now come, that I may introduce you to your teacher."

Li-Pe looked up in alarm. He had firmly believed that Lie-Tse himself would instruct him. It was a hard blow that this was not to be, but no word

110

of objection escaped him; he even repressed any thought of it. He would obey; only thus could he show God his gratitude.

As if he could read his thoughts, the Lama cast a happy glance at the student. Li-Pe would surpass all expectations, he was sure of that.

They walked through several corridors, all of them alike. How would he ever find his way about in them? No sooner had he thought this than his teacher said warmly:

"It is easier than you think, Li-Pe, and to begin with an older student will fetch you for the studies and the meals. He will also show you where to wash and dress. But do not try to talk to him. The monastic rule forbids unnecessary words."

Then Lie-Tse opened the door of a large hall, with many low tables arranged in rows. They were the kind at which Li-Pe was accustomed to eating. Many old and young monastery-students were bent over them, reading and writing, all in dark, plain loose-fitting robes of various colours.

Had these colours any significance? Li-Pe quickly looked about to see if he could find a violet robe. But before he had ascertained that there was none of the kind, an old silver-haired man with a long white beard approached the newcomers, bowing low before Lie-Tse. The students continued their work, apparently taking no notice of the interruption.

"Mi-Yang, this is the new student of whom I have already spoken to you," said Lie-Tse to the old man, making use of Li-Pe's mother tongue.

Mi-Yang answered fluently in the same language, and bade Li-Pe welcome.

"You will first of all have to learn our language, so that you can follow the divine worship in the chapel," said the teacher. "I shall assign to you an older student, with whom you can walk up and down in the garden for an hour each day for four weeks, and learn your lessons. After that you will be able to speak our language."

He said this so positively that Li-Pe had no doubt about it either.

While Mi-Yang showed him his seat, near a large, bright though closed window, Lie-Tse left the room without addressing another word to Li-Pe.

The latter sat down before his small table like the others, and Mi-Yang brought him an elaborately written manuscript in his own language, to which the student directed his eager attention.

111

He must have been reading continuously for three hours, when wonderful singing filled the room. Enraptured, Li-Pe raised his head, but could not discover the source of the sounds. It was a solemn melody, and the words, which he did not yet understand, seemed to be equally solemn and uplifting.

All the students quietly gathered their things together and threw themselves down before their small tables; so did Li-Pe, who in this solemn moment felt a real need for it.

When the sounds had ceased, all rose to their feet, arranged themselves in pairs, and walked out of the hall. A young man with a noble, attractive face had stepped beside Li-Pe; he seemed to be his helper.

Just then Mi-Yang came up to them.

"This is Tshai-Su, who will assist you this year. You may ask him about everything you need to know, but the less you ask, the better for both of you."

With every fibre of his being, Li-Pe longed to find out the meaning of the wonderful singing, where it came from and who performed it. But he contained himself, and it was easier than he expected.

Through a few corridors, which looked like all the others, the Learning Brothers now came to the dining hall, where they were allowed to sit down comfortably in front of low tables. Seven venerable Lamas were seated at a separate table. Probably all teachers, thought Li-Pe, for he saw that Mi-Yang too was among them.

One of the aged men rose, uncovered his head and said a short prayer, which Li-Pe could not understand. Yet he was moved by the heartfelt tone in which the words were spoken.

Then bowls of rice and cups of tea were served. In addition each student received a delicious slice of bread, and as much fruit as he wished to have. During the meal one of the teachers read slowly and clearly from a book. No one spoke.

After the meal the students walked again in pairs into a courtyard, where clear water gushed from a beautiful fountain into a superbly ornamented basin. There they all washed their faces and hands, and then strolled through the extensive, beautifully laid-out garden, in a corner of which Lai was working.

The garden was separated from other gardens by a quickset hedge. Li-Pe was quite surprised that such beautiful plants could thrive at this altitude and in this cold air. They were evidently tended with the utmost care.

A bell rang; the silent band returned immediately to the monastery and the working hall, where one of the other teachers seemed to be giving a lecture.

The students listened attentively; Li-Pe, though not understanding a word, dared not devote himself to his manuscript. At the end of the address, which must have lasted about two hours, the teacher went up to the new student, and spoke to him in his native tongue:

"I am surprised to see that you are one of those who do not appreciate the value of time. I had expected you to attend to your task, since my lecture could tell you nothing. But you have idled away the precious time. Tonight you will make up for what you have neglected."

Li-Pe was deeply dismayed. He had not dared to disturb. He would much rather have read than listen to the words which he did not understand. But he was diffident about replying. He stood up and bowed. The teacher looked at him searchingly before leaving the hall.

A younger Lama entered, and distributed manuscripts to the students. Li-Pe was given one in his own language. It presented the following passage for contemplation:

"God is the Unity.
The Unity becomes Trinity.
From the Trinity come all beings."

As soon as the student believed that he had understood the meaning of the passage he was to write the explanation below it in his own words.

Li-Pe was aglow. This was glorious! It was unspeakably beautiful and exalted! It seemed to him that he had always known what these words signified. It was the greatest mystery of God!

He looked about desperately for something to write with. The other students took brush and ink from a breast pocket under their robe. Only he had nothing yet. He did not dare to ask. And yet precious minutes were slipping by!

Finally he made up his mind. He got up, went to his helpmate, and without a word, but with a friendly look, took from him his writing materials.

Tshai-Su looked at him horrified. Then he began to laugh, and his laughter also infected those sitting nearby. All of a sudden the newcomer was no longer a stranger to them. He was able to take care of himself. With an effort Tshai-Su restrained his laughter; he nodded kindly at the thief, and went to a niche in the wall, from which he fetched brush and ink for Li-Pe.

The latter set to work eagerly. He wanted to paint the symbols as beautifully as possible, but the words kept flowing to him, so that his hand could hardly follow. He had come to the end of his parchment.

Again he cast a searching look about him. What did the others do in that case? They were writing slowly, and with many pauses for reflection; not even half of their sheets were filled. So he had to help himself again. He went to the niche, and actually found parchment, of which he took two sheets. No one paid any attention to him, therefore what he did was probably right.

Just as he had made the last brush-stroke, the wonderful music of men's voices sounded again. It seemed to come from the wall, in which there were two rows of openings. Then a student collected the sheets, and when he had to take three from Li-Pe, he raised them up high for all to see, and everyone smiled kindly at the newcomer.

Now everything took place just as at midday, except that after the meal and the ablution in the courtyard the students proceeded to the chapel. To Li-Pe it seemed impossible that there could be anything on earth so sublime.

On tall pillars arranged in a semicircle along the back wall, flames burned in brightly-coloured bowls. All these colour-radiations were magically interwoven. In front of the pillars was an altar covered with white silk, on which glowed a single ruby-red chalice. At the foot of the pillars, colourful vessels and bronze vases were filled with bright flowers from the garden.

The students filed into the space specifically marked out for them, and went down on their knees. Lie-Tse said a prayer in front of the altar, first in Tibetan; then he repeated it in Li-Pe's language.

He thanked God, the Most High, for allowing the seeker to find, and for bestowing on His Messenger the ultimate consecration.

The worshippers rose to their feet, and listened to a solemn hymn sung by male voices. Then they left the chapel in pairs and went out into the garden. But after a few minutes they returned to their cells.

Li-Pe also was about to enter his cell, but Tshai-Su restrained him. Kindly the helper led him back to the working hall, and placed on his table the manuscript which Li-Pe should have completed in the afternoon. Then he left him.

Actually, Li-Pe was too full of the sublimity of the short devotion to be able to absorb a treatise on the connection between space and time; but he wanted to obey! So he became absorbed in the paper, and tried to understand it.

He read page after page, always aware that he understood nothing of it. The sentences were so complex that they admitted of varying interpretations. At first he was about to lose heart, but then he told himself that after all he was still a student. Some teacher would come to his aid, and help him to understand. After that the reading progressed swiftly. Even before the flickering wick of his little oil lamp expired he had completed the task.

But he dared not leave the hall, fearing too that he would not be able to find his cell unaided. The light of the full moon streamed through the window: Li-Pe climbed on to his little desk and opened it. How the stars spoke to his soul! He was completely lost in contemplation of them.

What at first had seemed to him unjust punishment he now deemed a great joy. And then voices sounded around him.

"You were right, Li-Pe, to obey implicitly. Only he who has learned that can also make demands on others. Learn by day what your teachers can offer you, but look within you at night. Within you lies the Truth, lies all the knowledge about God which you need. Look around you, and you will find there the confirmation of all that you awaken in yourself."

Li-Pe spent the night praying and listening, and was astonished when in the morning the teacher entered the hall to look for him.

With harsh words he fell upon the student, saying that never before had a Learning Brother spent all night in the working hall. He should not imagine that with his stubborn attitude he would be tolerated here for long. As a punishment for his misdemeanour he would not be allowed to partake of the morning meal.

Li-Pe could easily forgo the light meal, but missing the morning devotion was hard for him.

When later all the students appeared for work, he met with many a sympathetic glance. The Brothers were on his side, no doubt. But nothing was said. Each was allocated his task, which he carried out in silence.

It was nearly midday when Mi-Yang came in, holding a number of sheets in his hand. They all stopped their work, and looked at the teacher.

The latter now delivered an address in which Li-Pe thought he heard his name mentioned from time to time, but he still understood not a word of it. Then Mi-Yang read out something from one of the sheets. All heads turned towards the newcomer. Li-Pe was anxious: Had he once more infringed some regulation?

Then Mi-Yang came over to him, and addressed him in his own language.

"What you wrote yesterday, Li-Pe, is so mature that I can teach you nothing more. Our father has decreed that you be admitted among the Helping Brothers. But first you must learn our language. That will now be your sole task. You will be assigned a young teacher of your own, who will help you with it. The sooner you reach your goal, the better you will be able to enter into the spirit of our monastery. Follow me."

Confused, Li-Pe rose to his feet and followed the venerable man, who led him to another wing of the monastery. There were cells here also, but they were larger, and contained all that was necessary for work and sleep.

The windows were placed so that he could see through them into the garden. There was plenty of writing equipment and parchment on a small table. No sooner had Li-Pe entered than a young Brother arrived, wearing a robe of blue silk. His name was Ya-Mi, and he began at once to instruct Li-Pe.

Here the uplifting singing which had called the students to the meals was not heard. Instead a Serving Brother came to the doorway, called out something, and offered Li-Pe a bronze basin of water and a cloth. He held the basin while Li-Pe cleansed his face and hands; then he disappeared. Ya-Mi told him that the Brother had announced that the meal was ready.

The hall in which Li-Pe took his meal today was far more spacious. It was also beautifully decorated. The Helping Brothers sat on their heels at long low tables. They wore robes of different colours; each colour had its own table. Here too seven venerable men were present; here too a prayer was spoken; this was followed by a reading. The meal seemed no different from that of the students.

After the meal Li-Pe, by Ya-Mi's side, entered a large beautiful garden, where they walked up and down for a short time. Then they returned to Li-Pe's cell and resumed their work.

Many days passed for Li-Pe in the same way, without a glimpse of his old teacher. Every day he understood more of the prayers and the devotions, which in their brevity and fervour seemed to him inconceivably beautiful. Each day a different Lama officiated.

Li-Pe did not see the teachers and students from the first hall either. After eager application to his studies during the day, he yielded at night to complete absorption in that which had awakened within him.

He was filled with ever new recognitions. It was as though the regular life in the ancient monastery furthered the swinging around and within him.

One morning he had found in his cell a lilac robe of exquisite silk, made in the same style as those worn by the Helping Brothers. But at the meal he sought in vain for lilac robes which he could have joined. He looked about perplexed. Then one of the older men came to him, and addressed him in Tibetan:

"Apart from you, we have no Brother who may wear this colour. Sit with the Yellow Brothers. Later you will find another place."

For a moment the old man's eyes rested penetratingly on Li-Pe. But he had understood everything; he bowed, and walked to the table of the Yellow Brothers, who willingly made room for him. He was now separated from Ya-Mi, but only at meals, when in any case there was no conversation.

AGAIN SOME TIME went by in the same way. Then one morning Li-Pe was summoned to Fu-Yang, the Lama who led the Helping Brothers. He found him in a magnificent room, splendidly dressed in yellow silk.

Li-Pe, who was accustomed to seeing yellow, as the heavenly colour, solely in connection with the Imperial House, at once assumed that Fu-Yang was a prince, just as he regarded all the Yellow Brothers at his table as princes.

He bowed low, but the Lama appeared not to notice. After looking silently for a few moments at the person standing before him, he began:

"You have gained sufficient knowledge of our language, Li-Pe, to be able to work now as a Helping Brother among us. The more mature Learning Brothers will be assigned to you, that you may help them to prepare for their task. They are to journey through our country, renewing and deepening the knowledge of God everywhere. It will be your duty to investigate how much they themselves know of what they are meant to bring to others.

"Therefore you will give an address to them every day, assign work to them, and through an exchange of ideas make their spirits ever more active."

Fu-Yang looked at the Helping Brother, expecting a reply, but Li-Pe asked quietly:

"Shall I be able to do that, my father? I came here to learn!"

He was given a friendly reply.

"You can do whatever you have to do. Lie-Tse himself has ordained your task."

And that very same morning Li-Pe had to take up his office, which he approached with great inner trepidation. But what a surprise! As soon as he stood before the small band of Learning Brothers whose eager eyes were directed towards him, the words he needed came to him. He was unaware that he was using the foreign language; he was quite conversant with it.

He told of God, Who existed before the beginning of all the World, of Him Who created and sustains everything, of Him Who can wait until men find Him, for He does not need them. They need Him.

No one had spoken to the students like this before, and they perceived that he who taught them was an exalted man. And while Li-Pe attended to his duties with joyful enthusiasm, hoping to grow into them steadily over the years in which they would be entrusted to him, everyone who was more familiar with the rules of the monastery knew that their good fortune would be only of short duration.

A few months later, Fu-Yang entered Li-Pe's cell to inform him that he had been raised to the rank of Teaching Brother. His task now was to assist the Helping Brothers who would be trained as teachers.

Once again there was a change of cell and dining hall, of garden, and above all of students. He became teacher of the Yellow Brothers, who received him with joy.

But here too, as everywhere, silence reigned. Only the absolute minimum was spoken. Li-Pe had not yet been able to ask anyone about the meaning and purpose of the monastic rules, with which he was slowly acquainting himself; but it no longer seemed important to him.

Just as he intuitively regarded the silence as a precious gift, so he began to understand why the complete separation of all the inhabitants of the monastery was so rigorously enforced, why he himself was always moved on as soon as he began to settle in one place.

"Everything flows," the inner voices said. "You human souls must never stand still, otherwise you will wither away. You must strive upwards, further, ever further, there is no end for you."

And Li-Pe strove and learned, taught and helped the weaker ones by his example. Then again he advanced. From the Teaching Brothers he moved to the Seeking Brothers, and thereby to the proximity of Lie-Tse for the first time since entering the monastery.

The Seeking Brothers constituted only a small circle of about thirty Brothers, who were instructed by Lie-Tse himself. Each day, after the morning's devotion, he gave them a theme on which to reflect, and comment in writing before evening. Once every seven days the papers, all of which showed a high degree of maturity, were discussed in detail.

Lie-Tse's kind and understanding spirit was over them all, helping them to penetrate still more deeply into the Eternal Truths. Filled with admiration, Li-Pe looked up reverently to his former teacher, only now understanding the sacrifice Lie-Tse had made for him at God's Command. Not however for him, the human being, was it made, but for the Truth-bringer. This realisation always filled Li-Pe with new strength.

The first theme which Li-Pe was allowed to work on was:

"He who seeks knowledge increases day by day;
He who seeks the spirit, decreases day by day."

Li-Pe sat before his parchment thinking for only a little while; then he wrote:

"He who seeks only knowledge attains to what he sought; he becomes learned and self-important.

"He who seeks the spirit from above must decrease ever more and more, until there is nothing left of the self. Only then can the spirit permeate him, and lead him upwards to the place whence he came.

"He who is afraid to give himself up should give up the search for the spirit."

A few days later the theme read:

"Where the spirit rules, no spirits have access."

This sentence also was easy for Li-Pe to understand. But he could still learn from Lie-Tse's explanations, and in the evening, when he looked back on his day, he felt immeasurably rich and blessed.

Then this too came to an end. Lie-Tse sent for him and announced that he was deemed sufficiently mature to be given the rank of Lama. He should prepare himself for seven days in the quiet of his cell. The meals would be brought to him there. Afterwards Lie-Tse, with great joy, would bless his one-time pupil in the sacred chapel which until now Li-Pe had not entered.

Again a new phase in his life! Li-Pe's head swam. How long had he been here in the monastery? In retrospect he thought it must be almost two years; in terms of experiencing the time appeared much shorter.

And now he was to be blessed with the high rank to which he had aspired. He knew that it was the guidance of the Supreme One which had enabled him to accomplish it, since it was needed for his task.

If he was to bring the Divine Truth to his people, he must present himself in a superior style, otherwise no one would listen to him. But why think about it now? The seven days had been bestowed so that he could listen deep within himself, and be totally open to the Light. He was to prepare himself! Prepare himself to be capable of receiving a new, great Power.

"O Supreme One," he implored, "Thou hast deemed me worthy to be Thy herald on earth. Take from me all that is mine, let me be wholly Thy servant and messenger. I desire naught for myself, for I am blissful to be allowed to serve Thee."

On the morning of the first day he resolved to spend these seven days fasting. Therefore when the meal was brought he did not look up at all.

But a gust of wind blew a small sheet of parchment, apparently placed beside the food, to his feet. He picked it up and read:

"The Supreme One is not served by imposing privations on the body. No strong spirit can enter a weak body. Take and eat."

Li-Pe obeyed, and reflected on what he had just learned; he realised that all the priests, venerated as holy, who rendered themselves unfit for life among men through fasting or mortification of the flesh, were doing wrong. He had heard about an old Lama who tied himself to a tree, his body leaning against the trunk, his arms wrapped round two branches of different height. He was said to have spent half his life in this position, until he became completely rigid. People who went to worship him pushed morsels of food into his always slightly opened mouth.

Li-Pe had only been able to think of this old man with abhorrence. Today he knew why. No, he wanted to take care of his body, he wanted to keep himself clean outwardly and inwardly.

These thoughts brought to mind his own people who to some extent were degenerating in filth. How immaculate everything was here in the monastery, how clean every individual. The whole people should be like that, then diseases of many kinds could not occur.

This he gained on the first day. This one aspect of his work, hitherto ignored by him as concerning only externals, became clear to him.

In the night, however, he was allowed to converse with God's Luminous Messenger, who implanted the joyousness of his task deeply into his soul.

In a state of exaltation never before experienced, Li-Pe began the second day. What would it bring? He wanted to surrender completely to his guidance.

A Serving Brother entered and brought a small parchment, folded several times and painted with dragons and demons. On an enclosed strip of parchment, written in Lie-Tse's hand, were the words: "Do you know them?"

They were terrible forms. And Li-Pe thought about how he himself had once seen such entities, but had also learned to master them. Was not the promise received by his mother:

"He shall fight and exterminate demons, and prepare the ways for the luminous spirits to mankind."

Now it was time for him to enter upon this task! Many years of his life had already passed. But the Supreme One had provided for his preparation; as yet nothing had been neglected. He considered how he was to make contact with the demons.

Since he had been in the monastery he had seen no trace of them. Would he therefore have to seek out bad people in order to drive away the monsters? All day he was engrossed in this second aspect of his task, until it too filled him with a joy that was further heightened in the night through the Luminous Messenger.

Now Li-Pe looked forward expectantly to what the next day would bring. With the morning meal, Lie-Tse sent him a small precious oil lamp, but not a drop of fuel for it. Li-Pe took delight in the gift, inspected it from every angle, but had no idea what to do with it.

"If only I had oil!" he cried aloud. "This lamp is so beautiful. How wonderful it must look when it is lit."

No sooner had he uttered these words than the meaning of the gift became clear to him. His people were like a precious lamp. But it lacked what was required to make it shine. He was to bring his people this oil: the knowledge of the Supreme One. How blessed indeed he was above all men!

Within him rang the words: "This is the most beautiful part of my task."

But in the night the Luminous Messenger showed him that no part could be rightly accomplished without the other. First he should improve the state of the bodies, then free the minds from fear and terror and show them better things, and only then bring the Knowledge of God to the purified souls.

The next four days passed all too quickly in contemplation of this threefold task, in praying for strength, and in glorification and thanksgiving.

On the last evening servants commissioned by Lie-Tse entered the room, bringing with them sumptuous robes of lilac silk, embroidered in gold. With these came a lilac cap of the same shape as the yellow one worn by his teacher. He was conducted to a bath hollowed into the rocky floor of one of the cells; into it servants poured warm, scented water. Then a man trimmed his hair and beard, after which he was escorted back to his room, where a little bronze figure stood beside a bowl of tea.

With a cry of delight Li-Pe took it in his hand. It was a replica of the god-like statue which he had once beheld. Wonderful was the peace reflected on the features of the deity. And Li-Pe remembered Lie-Tse telling him that attributes of the Supreme One had been portrayed, since human beings are unable to portray God Himself.

"Thank you for this reminder, my father," cried Li-Pe. "More and more like unto this peace and serenity must I become when I am allowed to work among men as God's servant."

The day dawned that was to bring the new distinction to Li-Pe. Early in the morning Lie-Tse entered his room. Such peace emanated from the aged man that the ardent longing arose in Li-Pe:

"If only I could become like him!"

After a short, fervent prayer the Lama invited his former pupil to follow him. He looked with pleasure at the young man, who had donned the costly robes as naturally as if he had been accustomed from his earliest youth to wearing such apparel. He held the lilac cap in his hand, and Lie-Tse took it from him, to return it only later in the chapel.

After a short walk through rooms hitherto unknown to Li-Pe, they reached the chapel, which they entered together.

The magnificence displayed here surpassed all that Li-Pe had ever seen. The side walls were covered with golden, leafy vines, from which shone blossoms made of jewels.

Some of the blossoms served as lamps, in which scented oil was burning, diffusing the colours of the jewels about the immediate surroundings. A huge golden-red lamp was suspended from the ceiling.

On the Altar stood the ruby-red Chalice, surrounded by lamps and bronze vases of flowers. Soft mats covered the floor.

About forty Lamas were assembled, of whom half wore cloaks of the same colour as their robes. Here too the colours determined the seating arrangement. Li-Pe was directed to a cushion centrally placed among the Lamas. Here he was allowed to kneel while Lie-Tse went to the Altar.

The music of wonderful male choirs rang out. The fragrance of precious oils rose from the lamps; a light, hazy mist enveloped the senses. It seemed to Li-Pe that he was no longer on earth, but far removed from it.

Lie-Tse raised his voice in prayer. When he ended, a solemn silence prevailed for several minutes.

Then he called:

"Li-Pe, from today Li-Yang, step forward, that I may bless you!"

Almost faltering, the young man rose to his feet and stepped before the Altar, bending his knee before the Holiness which was about to be made manifest to him. He saw the Luminous Servants of God standing around Lie-Tse, he saw rays coming from above, and as his eyes followed these rays it seemed to him that a Countenance, sublime and full of Divine Goodness, looked down upon him. And he knew this Countenance. He must have beheld it in ages long past. Then Lie-Tse spoke:

"Infinitely long ago you were chosen by God through His Sublime Son to bear witness to Him. As you stand before me today, so you stood then before the Most Holy Countenance, and as you bend your knee today to receive through me the Blessing from above, so the Most High then laid His Blessing upon your head through His Eternal Son.

"You are blessed, twice blessed. You bear the Light of the Supreme One within you, and you are permitted to bring this treasure to your people.

"At God's Behest you have been prepared for your lofty task. Nothing has been neglected in your preparation, but you yourself have also done all that God demanded of you.

"As today you receive the rank of Lama, never before attained by one of your people, we are acting at God's Command. This distinction is to be your letter of safe-conduct on earth. It is to separate you from other human beings.

"As a token of this we invest you with the mantle of spiritual solitude."

At a signal from Lie-Tse two Lamas came forward, and placed a lilac mantle of a heavy material about Li-Yang's shoulders.

The venerable man's hands rested in blessing upon the youthful head, which was bowed in true humility.

Soft singing was heard, while from each group one Lama stepped to the Altar. Seven colours, seven Lamas surrounded Li-Yang.

The Yellow Lama approached him, fastened an intricately embroidered yellow ribbon to the inside of the mantle, and said:

"Brother, may the Light of Heaven never depart from you."

The Blue Lama came, fixed his blue ribbon beside the yellow one, and spoke:

"May the Truth be in you and around you."

The Green Lama brought his ribbon with the words:

"Be the longed-for Helper of your people, and you will be helped."

Next came the Brown Lama:

"Do not forget that on earth you are to work for the earth, and you will work aright in spirit."

"And do not forget the love for all creatures," admonished the red ribbon.

Silvern shone the ribbon given to him with the words:

"May purity guide you."

Finally a Lama in a black robe approached Li-Yang, and said:

"Live in such a way that you need not fear the homeward journey to the Eternal Realms."

With that the ceremony came to an end. The festal voices of the choristers sounded anew, and the Lamas moved out two by two into the flowering, fragrant garden. Lie-Tse joined Li-Yang, and led him to a bench by a small pool, in which little gold fish with gossamer-like tails swam merrily to and fro.

"You will remain with us in the monastery for a little while yet, my son," began the old man, who was almost overcome with emotion. "I shall always thank God for deeming me worthy to teach and guide His Messenger. We will now be in close communion, and you may ask me anything that is not clear to you with regard to our rules."

Without a moment's hesitation, Li-Yang exclaimed:

"Father, tell me, what is the meaning of the ruby Chalice on the Altar? I feel that it has to be there, yet I know not why."

Lie-Tse gazed into the distance.

"I cannot really explain it to you either, my son. But I will tell you about the Founder of all our monasteries; perhaps you will then gain a better understanding of many things."

There was silence for a little while. Lie-Tse seemed to be concentrating his thoughts on the one point, and Li-Yang prepared himself to receive his words.

Then the High Lama began slowly:

"In far distant times a sage came to our country. We believe that he was a

Light-bringer sent by God. At that time no one yet knew about God, nor about the gods. People worshipped the demons, feared them and made sacrifices to them. How terrible these were you cannot imagine.

"While the people in general were ignorant, and their manners uncultivated, a few particularly clever ones stood out from the rest. They claimed to have an invisible ruler, for whom they had all kinds of names and descriptions. On his behalf they began to rule over the others.

"They called themselves priests, and determined the sacrifices that were to be made to the demons. Parents had to slay their newborn children, men their wives, if the priests ordained it. Whoever had incurred the wrath of the priests had his eyes put out, and thus mutilated he was abandoned somewhere in the mountains.

"People suffered under this oppression. All joy died away. They passed their lives in fear and trembling.

"Then the Sage came. Countless are the tales among our people of how he appeared among them, encouraging and comforting them, how he finally defied the priests, and snatched their victims from them. He must verily have acted in God's Power, otherwise he could not have accomplished what he did.

"Around him gathered those who owed him their lives, or those of their loved ones. In the course of time they were joined by others, who recognised him in his deeds as an Envoy of the Light; for he brought Light into their darkness.

"From these followers he chose a group with whom he settled in the mountains, thus laying the foundation for the first monastery here in the country. He did not intend to cut these people off from their fellow-men for ever, but he wanted to transform them in the quiet and seclusion. Then he would send them out to bear witness to others.

"His plans were successful, like everything he undertook. Even during his lifetime he was able to found ten more monasteries, ours among them. But in the course of time it changed completely through alterations and extensions. The chapels too are more beautiful and more elaborate than they were at the time of the Sage. But the nature of our Divine worship and the arrangement of the Altar have been faithfully retained just as they were transmitted to us.

"'You cannot make an image of God', so our spiritual father is said to have taught, 'therefore never put a statue on the Altar as other peoples do. In the Realm of the Eternal Gardens the blessed spirits have a ruby Chalice in their most holy Temple. From it they draw all the strength they need. Do as they do. If your belief is pure and genuine, God will also fill your Chalice with His Power.'"

Li-Yang listened, deeply moved.

"Father, I thank you. Your words gave me more than just the answer to my question. You have shown me what my path will be as well. Like this Sage, I too am sent to fight demons and unbelief, and to pave the way for the pure spirits. How glorious that is!"

After brief reflection, Li-Yang had more questions:

"Did the Sage also determine the hierarchy among the Brothers, my father?"

"No, Li-Yang," replied Lie-Tse. "Subsequent High Priests have developed everything into the firm structure which you have now come to know.

"Where the Brotherhood of a monastery continued firm in their belief, God's Spirit and His Help were always visibly with them. There one of the Lamas was always given the grace to see and hear more than other human beings. He could turn to God with his questions, and God's Messengers brought him the answer. God Himself raised such a Lama above the others. He received the rank of High Lama, and with it the Yellow Cap."

"Was there always only one Yellow Lama in each monastery?" Li-Yang wanted to know. Lie-Tse answered readily:

"It did happen that a second or even a third Lama emerged almost simultaneously from the same Brotherhood; but then the additional ones were needed in some other monastery that was without a Head. In good time a message came from God indicating who was to leave, and whither he was to direct his steps."

"While you were with me those many years, Lie-Tse, was your monastery then without a head?"

"No, Li-Yang, shortly before I set out on the journey to you, a second Yellow Lama arose from our midst, to whom I could entrust my monastery. I believed that he would always lead this monastery in my stead, and that when my task with you was fulfilled I would have to go to a different Brotherhood. Instead, God's Grace led me back here. A few days before my arrival, my deputy had moved to another place at God's Behest."

"Is it true that the High Lama of this monastery is at the same time the highest of all the Yellow Lamas?" enquired Li-Yang.

"Whence do you know that, my son?" Lie-Tse asked in reply, but Li-Yang could only say that was how it seemed to him.

"You are right, this monastery is the leading one in the country. Should a dispute ever arise, the High Lama of our Brotherhood would have to settle it. In addition, all kinds of other offices and positions of honour are linked with our monastery, so long as the Brotherhood walks in the ways of God."

Lie-Tse fell silent. But Li-Yang reflected: How much had the venerable man given up in order to follow God's Command. How naturally he would have stepped into the position of subordinate Lama if God had demanded it of him. Would he, Li-Yang, be capable of a similar sacrifice?

"Tell me, my father," the younger one resumed, "why are only the Learning Brothers summoned to the meals by the wonderful choirs? Surely that is preferential treatment."

"Can you not understand that?" Lie-Tse smiled. "You see, the Blessing of God that can be present in the meals still needs to be demonstrated to the students. With the help of these prayers which are sung to them, they are to collect their thoughts inwardly, so that they will approach the meal with praise and gratitude to God. Later they will do so without these reminders."

"I have never heard anything so exalted as the singing of these male voices," reflected Li-Yang. "Are the singers specially trained?"

"Yes, the voices of all young students are tested. If God has endowed them with a melodious voice, they are given special training, so that they can join the choir once they are admitted among the Helping Brothers. They then remain members throughout all the further stages, so long as their voices are still able to praise God."

"My voice was not tested," Li-Yang said, "I would indeed like to know whether I can sing."

Again Lie-Tse smiled.

"What use would it have been to test you? Consider how fleeting was your time among the Learning Brothers! God did not send you to us to augment our choir."

A Serving Brother appeared in the distance; it was time for Lie-Tse to return to the monastery. But he took the young Lama with him.

In the time that followed they were inseparable. Lie-Tse was anxious to introduce his former pupil to everything that might be helpful to him in his task, and Li-Yang rejoiced in the opportunity to ask freely of his teacher the many questions that he had so long had to defer.

"What does it mean that I am the only one to wear a lilac robe?" he asked one day, when the wealth of colours in the chapel had again made a deep impression on him.

"Your colour was determined from above, Li-Yang," was the ancient man's evasive answer.

But that did not satisfy the enquirer. He wanted to know more.

"Have you never had a Lilac Lama?"

"We have, Li-Yang, several of them, but their robe was always worn at the express Command of God. It is said that the Sage also was dressed in lilac. Be content with that, my son." –

Numerous were the tasks entrusted to Li-Yang. There were manuscripts to be deciphered, and translated from Tibetan into the language of the Middle Kingdom. He was permitted to give lectures, now to one, now to another group of Brothers. Lie-Tse also walked with him through all the rooms and corridors of the very extensive monastery, so that he might come to know everything, and clearly picture the overall plan.

During these walks he repeatedly came upon Wai, who bowed low to him. In the gardens he found Lai busily working. Lie-Tse said that they were very pleased with both, but that it would be left to their own discretion whether they wished to go with Li-Yang when he left the monastery in the near future.

It was the first intimation of his impending departure. Li-Yang himself perceived that it was not far off. Then it came even sooner than he expected. One day it was announced that a magnificent retinue of riders with carrying-chairs and pack-animals was approaching the monastery.

"It is for you, Li-Yang," said Lie-Tse, with solemn kindliness. "The Emperor sends for his Adviser with all the splendour befitting his dignity."

"The Emperor?" Li-Yang asked, in surprise. "How can he know that I am ready?"

"I sent Hai-Tan to him, requesting a worthy escort for you," was the unexpected reply.

For two days men and beasts were allowed to rest near the monastery. But meanwhile preparations were made for a great celebration: the departure of the new Lama. To Li-Yang it seemed even more solemn than the preceding one.

Lie-Tse spoke to all the Brothers, proclaiming that Li-Yang was a Truthbringer sent to his people by God Himself. He besought God's Blessing on all his paths. Now Li-Yang was asked to speak to the Brothers.

He prayed God for the right words, and then he spoke from his deeply-moved inner being. He thanked them all for the support they had given him, for the kindness with which they had received him, the stranger.

And now the words flowed unceasingly: He set forth before them his task as it had been revealed to him during night-vigils, and also the way in which he intended to fulfil it. They all felt that a very exalted personage was speaking to them.

The parting itself was brief. Lie-Tse urged him to set out, and together with all the Lamas he escorted the departing one to the gate in the wall. Once more he blessed his former pupil, then the gate opened through which he, the Messenger of God, stepped out to a new life and work. Childhood, youth and apprenticeship were behind him, now came the time of the mature deed!

OUTSIDE HE FOUND Hai-Tan awaiting him. The friend fell back when he caught sight of Li-Yang, but then he bowed low before him.

"You have become a Lama, a wise man of God," he exclaimed, overcome with surprise. "But you have also changed outwardly. No one will recognise you any more!"

Wai, Lai and Dai came forward to pay their respects, and only then were the messengers of the Emperor permitted to approach.

Li-Yang declined the luxurious carrying-chair, and mounted a splendid steed richly caparisoned in gold.

Many times during the journey they stopped for the night in silken tents pitched by the servants. It was like a fairy-tale, and yet the mode of travelling seemed so unimportant to Li-Yang that he quickly accustomed himself to it all.

His thoughts were partly in the monastery, following the daily routine, whose uplifting devotions he sorely missed; but partly they moved ahead of him, seeking to gain clarity about what needed to be done in the immediate future.

Finally they arrived in Kiang-ning. How different his entrance had once been! How much he had been allowed to experience and absorb within him since then! His retinue escorted him to the Imperial Palace, whereas Hai-Tan went to his father's palace, asking that he be sent for when Li-Yang had time for him. During the journey the former friends had hardly spoken, for Li-Yang was used to silence, and Hai-Tan's reverence was too great for him to break the barrier.

Servants conducted the Lama into several beautiful rooms prepared for him. He was to spend a few days recovering from the journey, and then appear before the Emperor. Li-Yang was able to absorb the new impressions completely undisturbed.

First of all he arranged for an altar to be set up in one of the rooms, which he designated as his chapel and appointed accordingly. Towards evening he asked Wai to bring him servant's clothing, and together they scoured the bazaars and the workshops of the craftsmen, looking for a chalice made of ruby glass that seemed to him sufficiently worthy.

But he found none. The glass-workers shook their heads: it was impossible to make red glass. They showed him green and blue, even yellow glass, but that could not satisfy Li-Yang.

Wai, however, knew what to do. He told Li-Yang that a number of Tibetans lived in one of the remote parts of the city. Perhaps they could procure such a chalice from Tibet.

The following evening Li-Yang went there. He found poor but clean huts, and serious people whose features became transfigured when Li-Yang spoke with them in their language. But they claimed to know nothing about a red chalice.

Li-Yang perceived that they did not wish to reveal to a stranger what was sacred to them, and he took his leave without insisting further. The following evening, however, he only put on a dark cloak over his Lama attire, and went again to the Tibetan quarter.

The people grew uneasy when he appeared yet again, but they calmed down immediately once he had handed over his cloak to Wai. Now they became as trusting as children. He spoke with them of God. With that any lingering doubt left them, and they led him to a small, simple chapel hidden among the huts. Upon its Altar stood a wonderful ruby Chalice.

"It is the work of Kuang-Fong," they said, pointing to an older man who kept in the background.

"This is a magnificent piece of work," said the Lama in praise. "Will you make a similar chalice for my Altar? You will not regret it."

"Father," stammered Kuang-Fong, "if you want to have the chalice in order to serve God, I will not take a single kaolin for it. But you should give us something else in return: You should sometimes hold a Divine Hour of Worship for us here in this chapel. We have neither Lama nor priest."

With great joy Li-Yang promised to do so. He returned the very next morning, and found the men festively attired, and the small chapel decorated. They even had their own melodious choir.

Li-Yang tried to adapt his words to the understanding of these simple people, and he succeeded. They begged him urgently to come again. As for him, his heart throbbed with great joy over this beginning of his work.

On his return to the Palace, a message came from the Emperor summoning him. How would he find Hou-Chou?

The Ruler had grown more manly and free in his movements and speech. He received Li-Yang with great reverence, yet like an intimate friend.

"You finished even more quickly than I had anticipated," he said, "but not a moment too soon. I need your advice and instruction. You will have to accustom yourself to the thought of making this your primary place of residence.

"In order to justify your sojourn to everyone, I would like to entrust you with the classification and arranging of the extensive collection of manuscripts which I inherited from my predecessors. You are to complete it, and acquire whatever you consider desirable. Rooms and financial resources will be at your disposal without your having to ask for them.

"That is your task in the eyes of the world. But the kindness that you are to do me is to acquaint me with the belief in the One God. I want to lead the way for my people in this; with your help they are to follow me. Will you promise me that, my friend?"

Li-Yang consented joyfully. How could he better fulfil his task than by working at the Emperor's side for the welfare of the people?

Hou-Chou now told him that in the meantime he had married a charming Princess of noble descent. She had also borne him an heir to the throne, whose teacher Li-Yang must some day be.

"There will be a great reception tomorrow, Li-Yang, when I shall present you, the wise Lama, the new Curator of manuscripts, to the mandarins and all the people," the Emperor concluded.

And so it came to pass.

In the wise man who was incorporated into the court with special honours, no one recognised a son of their own people. But an immediate rift was apparent among the courtiers.

Some saw that he was still very young, and marvelled at his wisdom in having already attained the highest distinction! They also saw that he must be of the most noble descent; for his features were well-formed, his hands slender and graceful. He won their hearts. They expected nothing but good of him, and were prepared to do anything for him.

But the other, and unfortunately the larger faction, saw in him the foreigner intruding into the firm structure of their government. They were agreed in exerting their utmost to protect the Emperor from his influence, and doing everything possible to drive the intruder away.

Each mandarin however had numerous servants, who were completely in thrall to the master whose serfs they were. That explains why on this first day the division from the top downwards continued even among the courtiers and servants. These in turn spread their opinions among the people, where however they did not find such sympathetic ears. The people wanted to see and hear for themselves before taking sides.

With a fine intuitive sensing, Li-Yang realised what was happening around him, but it caused him little anxiety. When after the reception the Emperor, somewhat dejected, alluded to the rift that appeared to have come about, his Adviser exclaimed cheerfully:

133

"Did you expect anything else? They would not be human beings if they did not rebel against the stranger who suddenly received preference in everything. I am prepared for worse, but it cannot alarm me. God Himself has given me the task, He Himself will deliver me. Have I not sufficient help?"

This confidence also revived the Emperor, who knew better than Li-Yang just how much discord this rift could bring to the court. But perhaps it was just what was needed. He too would trust in the help that had brought Li-Yang to him.

He went with the Lama to his apartments, and sent for his small son. The little boy, just over a year old, stretched out his arms towards his father, and immediately afterwards towards the stranger, as though he sensed that he was a very special person.

"Just look at him, Han," said the Emperor in jest, "one day he will educate and instruct you, so that you may become a better ruler than your father."

During the next few days Hou-Chou arranged for work-rooms and the collection of manuscripts to be shown to the Lama, asking him to establish a definite time each day when he could be found at work.

This was done, and the Emperor appeared the very next morning to request instruction. It was decided that these lessons should always be the first thing on Hou-Chou's daily list.

He proved himself a very eager and thoughtful student, with many questions waiting to be asked. Nevertheless Li-Yang could only proceed very slowly with the actual tidings of the One God, for much of the old had first to be eliminated. Above all, the student was unable to recognise the demons as products of human thinking and feeling. He regarded them as animistic, and even endowed with reason.

In vain did Li-Yang tell him of his own experiences. Hou-Chou entrenched himself behind the objection that Li-Yang, being an entity from the Heavenly Gardens and not a real human being, was also given power over the demons and evil spirits.

"I shall not really be able to believe in this until I have experienced it myself," concluded the Emperor one day, after a lively discussion on the subject.

When the lesson was over, Hou-Chou liked Li-Yang to tell him what he had undertaken the previous day. The Lama travelled a great deal with Wai, to spread the seed of his teaching. Moreover the people now also began to visit him in the Palace under all kinds of pretexts. Some claimed to have need of spiritual help, others sought learned conversations.

Sometimes also sick people came wishing to be healed, but Li-Yang sent those away. In the Middle Kingdom there was a well-qualified medical profession which jealously guarded its rights. One day Hou-Chou learned of Li-Yang's refusal to visit one of the most distinguished mandarins and free him from a long-lasting ailment. The Ruler was of the opinion that with the great power bestowed on the Lama it should be easy for him to alleviate or put an end to people's physical sufferings.

Li-Yang tried to explain to the Emperor that it would only render his path unnecessarily hard if he tried to interfere with the duties of others.

"We have people who give alms to the poor," Hou-Chou persisted, "and yet you visit the huts of the poor to alleviate their misery."

"That I do in secret, so far as I am able," replied Li-Yang. "Nor does it cause any sensation, as healing would. If I give to a person in need, I do so to make his soul more receptive. If I heal an incurable patient, I thereby demonstrate that I am able to do more than the doctors. I am to be a helper of souls and not of bodies."

With that Li-Yang ended, as though he wished to say no more on the subject, but then immediately, half smiling, again took up the thread:

"Of course I must indeed do something for the bodies as well, O Emperor. We will have serious epidemics in the country unless we urge greater cleanliness upon the people. Here in your Palace, in a cultivated environment, you cannot imagine the filth that smothers your subjects. Something must be done about it."

"Do you think, Li-Yang, that I could go out with you one evening in servant's clothing to see for myself?" asked the Emperor, hastily adding: "Not because I disbelieve you, but because I really want to see all that you tell me about with my own eyes for once."

"That will be easy to arrange, Hou-Chou," Li-Yang agreed readily. "We can go this very evening, if it suits you. Only you must allow Wai to accompany us; for he knows ways and people, and can also serve to protect us."

135

"What kind of person actually is this Wai?" the Emperor wanted to know. "He is not a son of our Realm. To me he seems more like a Tibetan, and his conduct suggests that he is of noble lineage. Do you know anything about him?"

"I found him as a depraved beggar in a miserable hut, and took him into my care. Since then he has repaid this small kindness with unwavering loyalty. He is Tibetan, Lie-Tse told me that. More I do not know. I have never wanted to question him. But if you wish it, O Emperor, it shall be done."

The curiosity of the young Ruler had been aroused; he confessed that he would very much like to know who was concealed behind the person of the attendant. Then Li-Yang recalled Lie-Tse's promise that he would learn more about Wai later. Perhaps that time had now come.

Li-Yang sent for his servant, who easily concealed his surprise at being permitted to appear in the Emperor's presence, and greeted the illustrious ones with stately courtesy. When he learned why he had been summoned, he flushed scarlet. Perceiving this, Li-Yang felt sorry for Wai. He addressed him kindly:

"If you prefer to keep silent about your past, Wai, your wish shall be respected, even though the Emperor would like to know a little about you. Your loyalty is deserving of implicit trust."

"I hesitate, not because I have anything to hide, Master," said Wai candidly, "but because I fear that you will no longer wish to keep me in your service once I have spoken. But speak I must, since you have asked me to do so. Lie-Tse's command was: Keep silent until Li-Yang himself asks you. Then the time to speak will have come."

"In that case let me promise you, Wai, that whatever you reveal to me will in no way change our relationship."

Wai gave a little smile, then he began:

"I was still very young when as a student I entered the monastery which you, Master, also know."

Li-Yang had difficulty in suppressing an exclamation of surprise. He did not wish to interrupt the speaker, but was now most anxious to hear what he had to say.

"I had been studying for several years, when Lie-Tse informed us that in the Middle Kingdom had been born a little boy who came from the

136

Heavenly Gardens, and was destined to bring the Light from his Spiritual Home to his people. One day, when he entered upon his mission, he would be in need of many helpers. Lie-Tse described the mission in glorious words; we were all spellbound. But I was particularly moved, and called out: 'Oh, if only I could be one of these helpers!'

"Lie-Tse looked at me with his penetrating eyes, as if to read in my soul, then he said: 'Wuti, if you are in earnest about your wish, repeat what you have said. But consider well before you commit yourself.' Filled with great joy, I called once more: 'Let me be one of these helpers!'

"'Never forget that you have pledged yourself to serve the Truth-bringer, Wuti,' said Lie-Tse earnestly. Then for years nothing more was said about it. Our spiritual father was called away to a distant land on a secret Divine mission – we were told no more at the time. Nobody knew if we would ever be permitted to see him again. His deputy, Fu-Tse, was a good leader for us, but he could not replace Lie-Tse. Meanwhile I had advanced to a higher level of the Brotherhood, and attained to the rank of Seeking Brother. Then one day, when his deputy had been called away a few days previously, Lie-Tse was again in our midst. Our joy was indescribable."

Pausing for a deep breath, Wai was silent for a moment and looked at his master. The latter gave him a nod, and Wai continued:

"A few days after his return Lie-Tse sent for me, and asked if I was prepared to fulfil my vow. Blissfully I affirmed it. Then he told me that the time had now come for me to set out for the Middle Kingdom. He himself had prepared everything for me there, with the acquisition of a miserable hut in which I was to live as a beggar. Then he instructed me that I would have to appear as coarse and unrefined as possible, so that you, Li-Yang, would really believe me to be destitute and depraved. The beggars' priest had instructions to mention my name and my hut to you. Everything else would proceed as willed from above.

"Hardly had I arrived in Kiang-ning and moved into the hut than you already made your way to me, Master. You know the rest. I have often felt ashamed that, in the attempt to appear as bad as possible, I dealt with you in such an offensive way. Forgive me!" concluded Wai.

Li-Yang's head was almost swimming. So here too there was guidance, as indeed throughout his life! But why had Lie-Tse chosen this way of sending him a helper? He would have welcomed him joyfully, had he come on behalf of Lie-Tse. Why this disguise? While Li-Yang was still racking his brain in search of an answer to the question, the Emperor uttered it unconsciously:

"How wisely Lie-Tse acted," he said, reflectively. "He knew quite well that upon his word you would unquestioningly have taken any servant. But he wanted you to gain the helper for yourself. You did Wai a kindness because you thought he was in need of it. But instead it was you who needed the opportunity to demonstrate that you were sufficiently mature to find your own helpers."

"It is as you say, Sire," said Wai, who henceforth was called Wuti once more. "Lie-Tse told me when we met again in Tibet that your kindness towards me had removed the first veils from your task. But now keep your promise and let me continue as your servant."

"Not my servant, Wuti," replied Li-Yang, "but my helper, as you once promised to be. We are Brothers of the same Brotherhood; that unites us!"

Li-Yang spoke the words with joy.

Now they also discussed the evening's expedition, in which the Emperor was to take part unrecognised, and to which he was greatly looking forward. It was something completely new in the life of this conscientious Ruler, who was always thinking of what would be good for his people.

But at night he returned home sorrowful. He had not expected to see such depravity, such vice, such dirt and filth. It required all Li-Yang's persuasive powers to prove to him that it was in his imperial hands to change all this in the course of time.

"Without you, Li-Yang, I should have continued to live in ignorance," cried Hou-Chou bitterly. "You had first to open my eyes to my own people. But now I shall not delay in passing the necessary laws to improve our conditions."

"I fear that it will not be accomplished by laws alone," replied Li-Yang. "We shall have to produce well-thought-out plans for proceeding against all that was revealed to you this evening, my Emperor. Let us retire to rest, perhaps sleep will bring us the ideas we need."

And while the Emperor went to his bed-chamber, Li-Yang knelt before his altar, and besought God's help in finding the right counsel to give.

In the morning Hou-Chou did not appear at the usual time; instead Li-Yang was summoned to the Emperor, whom he found in the throne room, surrounded by counsellors. They all seemed to be in a state of great agitation, so far as the term could apply to men who were fully accustomed to hiding their feelings.

"Listen, Li-Yang," the Emperor called out to him as he entered. "Something terrible has happened! My chief physician informs me that a highly infectious epidemic has broken out in one of the outlying slums. There is no choice but to burn down this slum, lest the disease should spread."

"Burn it down?" stammered Li-Yang, totally uncomprehending. "With all the people living there?"

"No, Li-Yang," the Emperor replied, "the people will be asked to leave their dwellings within a few hours, and to move into a camp far outside the city. This is our practice," he explained. "The houses are then burned down, taking care that no more than necessary are destroyed."

"So you would send both the healthy and the sick to the camp?" Li-Yang asked.

"Well, after all they live together now in any case," the physician answered for the Emperor. "But then they will be harmless to the rest of us, whereas now they constitute the gravest danger to the whole city. Usually the matter is then dealt with as follows: the healthy people automatically move farther out than the sick. Once safely established, they set fire to the sick-camp, in which hardly any remain alive."

Li-Yang shuddered, but for the moment he could do nothing against these long-standing practices. The main thing now was to take precautions for the safety of the city. Truly this was the best opportunity to enact the laws against dirt and squalor.

Li-Yang soon perceived that the Emperor had the same thought. For the present the counsellors were dismissed to carry out the usual measures in the circumstances. Afterwards Hou-Chou and Li-Yang resolved to take drastic measures for cleansing the city, which in turn were to lead gradually to the cleaning of the whole country.

It occurred to Li-Yang that the previous evening the Emperor had been in one of the worst slums. What if he had caught the disease? He voiced the thought, but Hou-Chou shook his head:

139

"I was on a good errand, so nothing could happen to me," he said solemnly.

Ever anew Li-Yang recognised that the Emperor had far surpassed his people's level of thought. How much easier this made everything for himself! Just how difficult his path would have been if the Emperor had been ill-disposed towards him could hardly be contemplated. And yet! Despite Hou-Chou's willingness to do what was right, it seemed almost impossible to eradicate the ancient customs and replace them with something better. They could only proceed gradually, tackling one thing at a time.

Today the two men, who had the people's welfare so much at heart, drew up a law by which daily ablutions were decreed for the entire population. The Emperor informed his subjects that a violent epidemic had broken out, against which they could only protect themselves through the utmost cleanliness.

Both knew that this was not enough, but they left it at that for the time being, since the new law would certainly cause unrest enough in the city and the country.

What they foresaw came to pass. Emotions were roused to fever pitch among the people. Never before had the Emperor laid down regulations for the life of the individual! Whether to wash, or to continue in the squalor that kept them warm, was their own concern, and beyond the confines of law. There was imminent danger of an uncontrollable uprising.

The priests supported the agitated people. They themselves were hardly acquainted with the benefit of water, nor did they wish to learn of it on command.

The mandarins, realising the rightness of the Imperial decree, opposed it because it came from the foreign Lama. The unrest within the population grew daily and hourly. They went indeed to the river, but only to rave and shout.

Then one man fell ill here, another there, elsewhere a whole family was stricken. Now terror intensified the agitation. The masses raged wildly. Where the beggars' slum bordered the river there was a veritable surge of frantic people.

And suddenly – no one knew how – there on the roof of a dilapidated hut stood the Lama in his lilac silk robe, which gleamed far and wide.

He raised his arms heavenward, and called out the one word:

"God!"

Thereupon the masses fell silent, as though seized by a strange power. Then he spread his hands over the people below him, again calling out just one word:

"People!"

It gripped them as nothing had ever done before. In silence they looked up at him, awaiting what was to come. He began to speak, in a voice that carried afar:

"My people, hear me!"

A murmuring arose:

"What does he want? He says 'my people'. We are not his people. He is not our ruler! He is not of our race."

The murmuring swelled, and Li-Yang realised that he must continue to speak. Again he raised his hands; the crowd was silent.

"I am not your ruler, but I come from among you. I am a son of the Middle Kingdom despite the apparel that I am permitted to wear. Why should not also one of our people become a Lama? God Himself commanded me to become a sage for your sake, and to learn all that can benefit you."

Instantly the mood of the over-excited crowd changed. Hardly had they heard that he was one of their people than they hailed him. Never before had a son of the Middle Kingdom attained to the rank of Lama.

How intelligent he must be, and how good! And God Himself had commanded him? They did not even notice that he spoke of God, and not of the gods. They were carried away by their jubilation. They shouted to him to go on speaking; they wanted to hear more. He complied, for he still had much to say.

He spoke of the dreadful plague that threatened the whole country, of the inadequate measures that were taken in the past.

"If we always resort only to burning buildings to the ground, there will be nothing left in the end. Fully aware, we would all perish, not lifting a finger to save ourselves while there is still time!"

"Do you know how we can be saved, O Wise Man?" A voice rang out from the crowd, and a hundred others took up the cry.

The voice belonged to Lai, who, inconspicuously dressed, had mingled with the crowd.

Again Li-Yang raised his hand, and called out in a resonant voice:

"Indeed, I know how! God Himself has revealed it to me! I will tell you, but you must listen, and resolve to follow me."

A hundred voices answered:

"We will. Speak!"

When calm was restored, Li-Yang proclaimed:

"Diseases of the body arise where the body is badly cared for. You have all often experienced how ugly a wound becomes when dirt gets into it. Diseases are established in dirty conditions where they can spread. Do you understand that?"

Cries of assent were heard, one louder than the other, and the crowd's excitement was heightened now in a different way.

"Away with the filth!" they shouted. "Let us burn down the squalid huts!"

Already some were prepared to suit the action to the words, naturally intending to set fire only to the huts of others, when a shout from Li-Yang checked them.

"Let us act like sensible human beings, not like fools!" he urged them. "Let each go to his home, and clear out everything that is no longer of use. We will carry these things to the open space here by the river, and burn them. Whatever is still usable must be washed in the river. Then you must also clean your houses and huts, inside and outside, and finally you your-selves must go into the river, and afterwards put on clean clothing."

"We have none," cried a number of voices.

"Then go to the priest of the poor, he will help you," Li-Yang encouraged them.

Together they established the times when everything was to be done. He pointed out that they must light no fires without supervision, for wind could spring up all too easily, and carry the flames on to the thatched roofs. He, Li-Yang, would ask the Emperor to send out many soldiers at about midday to watch over the fires.

The crowd assented cheerfully, and hastened to collect what was to be burned.

142

Unchallenged, Li-Yang walked back to the Imperial Palace, to inform Hou-Chou and request his assistance. The Emperor was elated.

"Li-Yang," he said, "if you succeed in guiding the people in this one district, the others will soon follow."

"God my Lord, Who helped me today, will continue to give help," said Li-Yang confidently.

In high spirits, he returned to the river with the servants and soldiers assigned to him. He had taken these helpers with him, not so much because of the fire risk, but because of the excited crowd.

When he reached the open square, he found mountains of evil-smelling rubbish, foul rags and rotting waste already piled up. He told the servants to form a circle, which was to be breached only at his command, whenever new masses of rubbish were brought.

Then he had the three largest piles set alight. They burned with smouldering, smoky flames; green and yellowish-red tongues of flame shot up here and there. And suddenly there was a shout:

"Look at the demons above the flames!"

With anguished cries the people fell back; some who seemed to be completely bereft of their senses jumped into the deep part of the river, and refused to be saved. Li-Yang prayed to God. He found no words; but he repeated the Name of God countless times in ardent fervour. And heavenly peace descended upon him.

A pile of large stones had been collected, to be used later to extinguish what would remain of the fire. The Lama stood atop this mountain of stones, raised his hands as he had done in the morning, and called out:

"Why are you afraid, people? The demons will retreat before the pure flame that consumes all impurity. They can do you no harm. They are not allowed to harm you, for you act at the Command of God; God Himself protects you."

His words had an immediate effect. Nevertheless a harsh male voice called out:

"Then prove to us that the demons are harmless. Look behind you; a horrible monster is creeping towards you; prove that it cannot harm you."

Li-Yang looked round, and actually saw a terrible, dragon-like figure approaching him. He stretched forth his arm commandingly and cried:

143

"Stand still!"

The demon obeyed. Now he turned again to the people, who were gazing at him and the phantom as though spellbound.

"Dear people, this monster has sprung from your fear. It will cease to exist as soon as you are no longer afraid!"

But he perceived that they were far too excited to understand him. He had to reserve the explanations for another time; the situation called for action. Without a moment's hesitation he turned once more to the dreadful apparition, which seemed to waver slightly, and called out:

"In the Name of Almighty God I command you to perish! You were born of fear, have arisen from impure thoughts; now be gone, as fear and impurity shall be gone!"

Even as he spoke, the colours of the demon grew paler; like grey mist, it still stood in its place for a moment, then it disappeared in the smoke that billowed across from the burning piles.

The crowd stood in silence. With some the enormous tension was released in weeping; others began to pray. At first no one dared to utter a word. But Li-Yang called to them: "My brothers, you see that the evil demon dissolved when the fear that gave rise to it was overcome by fearlessness. Just as I have driven away the demon today, so can you all, as soon as you regard it courageously, and pray to God the Almighty."

Then at last the anticipated question rang out:

"Who is God? We know nothing of Him. Will you tell us about Him?"

And Li-Yang promised to come to the main temple of the district and speak to them about God, once the great clean-up was completed.

"But you must clean that temple too," he concluded, and they promised to do so.

Li-Yang's victory over the demon had been witnessed not only by the inhabitants of this quarter, but also by the Imperial servants and soldiers. Whereas the people bore away the great experience in silence, allowing it to act on them as they carried out the work of cleaning, the Imperial staff spread abroad what they had seen. The news that the foreign Lama could drive away demons swept through the whole of Kiang-ning.

When Li-Yang returned to the Palace in the evening, he was summoned to Hou-Chou, who was full of what he had heard.

"How I wish I had been there, Li-Yang," he exclaimed as the Lama entered. "You know how I long to persuade myself about the nature of the demons. But I must still wait."

When Li-Yang described how calmly the inhabitants of the quarter had set about the work of cleaning, Hou-Chou said:

"That is due to your influence, Li-Yang. Only you would have succeeded in this. The commander of the soldiers told me that more than half of his men had been hostile to you. But after today's experience they all support you. Truly, God granted me a high grace when He gave me you."

In the days that followed, the work in the outlying quarter continued to progress. Li-Yang, Wuti and Lai were present, assisting by word and deed.

But messengers came from other sections of the city, requesting Li-Yang to come there and help them, as he had helped the poor by the river. And Li-Yang entrusted the supervision of this part to Wuti and went with a small troop of armed soldiers to another district, where craftsmen and porters lived.

Here he had little trouble in persuading the people to agree to his plans, since fear of the epidemic which was springing up everywhere, and the precedent set by the slum, were his best allies. Here too there was much to be burned, though far less than in the first quarter. When all the arrangements were made, he left Lai behind to supervise and moved on. Just outside the city, by the river, was a settlement of fishermen and boatmen; among them several cases of the plague had been reported.

There he planned to continue with the great cleansing. However a message from the Emperor reached him, requesting him to return to the Palace. Li-Yang set off promptly. Imperial servants had brought his steed. But the people grumbled as he rode away.

Forgotten were the many days he had sacrificed on their behalf. They were afraid, they needed his help, and now he was leaving them! Their discontented thoughts clustered around him, almost taking his breath away. He became aware of them, turned, and saw that a crowd of people were running after him to call him back. He saw their thoughts fluttering about like evil demons.

Reining in his horse, he called to them:

"Do you see how wicked you are? Look what is emanating from you!"

145

He pointed with his finger at the shapes which danced up and down, grimacing. And it was given to them all to see what he indicated.

Piercing shrieks burst forth from the crowd, which fell back terrified. But he banished the demons as he had often done before. The people broke forth in jubilation and shouted: "Li-Yang is not a human being, he is a god! We no longer need any other gods. Li-Yang shall be our god."

The Lama became sad. How easy it was to sway the people! They had no constancy. But at least a way of reaching their hearts was now offered to him. He spoke to them kindly:

"Listen to me! I am no god!"

Murmurs of protest interrupted him, but he repeated still more loudly:

"I am not God, but God is my Lord; I am His servant. Worship *Him* Who has granted me power over the demons and unclean spirits. Make Him your Lord, and you will be blissful. But let me go for the present. The Emperor needs me. I shall come back to help you. You can be sure of that."

Then they let him ride away, but for a long time they stood together talking about the dispelling of the demons.

In the Palace, Li-Yang had been anxiously awaited. No one knew what the Emperor wanted of the Lama, whose presence he urgently desired.

The wise man proceeded without delay to the Imperial apartments, where he found the usually so composed Ruler in a state of great agitation. His little son had shown symptoms of the plague.

The physician declared that there was no hope. The child would have to be taken to a remote part of the Palace so that he could die there alone. Only thus would it be possible for their Imperial Majesties to be spared. Of course the servants must not learn of this, for if they did they would all take flight without further ado.

As the physician spoke, Li-Yang prayed to God, and became convinced that through this experience the faith of the Emperor was meant to grow firm and secure.

Calmly the Lama let himself be conducted to the sick child, who lay whimpering alone in a lofty chamber. No sunlight or fresh air entered; windows and doors were tightly closed. The attendants had apparently fled, while the Empress had been locked in her apartments by the physician, as Li-Yang was told later.

In fervent prayer, Li-Yang went to the bedside of the little boy, bent over him and listened to his breathing. The whimpering had stopped when he entered. Then he ordered the windows to be opened wide. But there was no one to carry out his instructions. Without hesitation, Hou-Chou himself set to work, and the moment fresh air from the gardens streamed into the room, the child opened his eyes.

Gently Li-Yang placed his slender hand on the child's forehead and prayed. Silently the Emperor stepped to the other side of the bed, and something inexpressible moved through his soul. What if God allowed him to keep the child? That would be beyond all human comprehension, but the Lama had told him that with God nothing was impossible.

Li-Yang turned to him with a smile, and said:

"Behold, O Emperor, your son is asleep. Already the blue discolourations on his skin are fading, his breathing is regular. He will live! See to it that a reliable attendant comes to his bedside, and command that the windows be kept open day and night."

He turned to leave, but Hou-Chou held him back.

"How am I to thank you, my friend?" he asked, deeply moved.

"You must not thank me; thank God, the Most High, by serving Him with all your strength. But let us go and see the Empress, lest fear and anxiety make her susceptible to the poison of the epidemic."

Li-Yang had never seen the Empress before, but he walked quite naturally with Hou-Chou to her apartments.

Li-Fu-Ti was a petite, charming person. Even more captivating than her beauty was the expression of her almond eyes. Their gaze revealed great depth. She had been unspeakably anxious about her child, and went herself to his rooms to tend him, unmindful of her own needs. Li-Yang felt that she was indeed healthy and unscathed. He was about to return to the fishermen's village, when the Emperor drew his attention to the fact that the mandarins were indignant because the Lama devoted all his energies to the poor and despised, instead of helping those of rank and nobility.

"Did you not tell them, O Emperor, that they are intelligent enough to make changes for themselves, and take precautions?"

The Emperor agreed that he had done so, but added that they were all so anxious that they needed help.

147

Suddenly Li-Yang thought of Hai-Tan. He sent for him, and put him in charge of the cleaning of the palaces. Hai-Tan was not very pleased at having to do such inferior work, but on hearing that the Lama was similarly occupied in the poorest districts, he set about his task without delay.

Days and weeks passed in strenuous labour. It became necessary to penetrate ever further into the country from Kiang-Ning, but eventually the epidemic was brought under control. Now the Imperial edicts were truly of benefit: the people experienced for themselves the blessing of cleanliness; everywhere they wished to enjoy its benefits.

Li-Yang was well aware that it was God's Power with him that had contributed most towards the arrest of the disease. Yet he did not emphasise this at the moment, lest the people be given an excuse for relapsing into the old uncleanliness.

For some days now he had devoted himself again to the manuscripts in the Imperial Palace, awaiting a Command from God. He saw quite clearly that now he had to go out into the vast country, but he would wait until God Himself pointed the way. Then the time would have come.

Hou-Chou entered. Everything about him breathed a previously unknown joy and vitality. Since the control of the epidemic, the Ruler had been seized by a boundless courage to spread enlightenment. He envied Li-Yang, who would be privileged to speak publicly about God. Much as he would have liked to keep the wise man near him, he could hardly wait for the Lama to set out on his long journey.

"Li-Yang, do you know," he asked as he entered, "that a veritable demon-plague has broken out in the east of our Empire, where the ocean laps its shores? Yesterday some travelling merchants brought the news that for miles around the inhabitants were so shaken with fear that many have died. What do you think should be done?"

"What does my Emperor think?" enquired Li-Yang, who was certain that this was the sign for which he had prayed to God.

"I think that God Himself is summoning you to go there and put an end to the false belief."

"Then I will set out this very day," Li-Yang cried joyously. But the Emperor disagreed.

"Let us not act precipitately," he warned. "You must not go to these frenzied people alone. Servants and soldiers must accompany you, as befits your dignity. The greater the honour accorded you, the more readily will people attend to your words. It would be a pity if you had to lose time unnecessarily before they realise who you are. You must present yourself as a Lama and the Imperial Adviser. I will invest you with full powers. Believe me, Li-Yang, I know our people."

"Let us ask Wuti, O Emperor," said Li-Yang. "He was assigned by God to prepare the way for me; I must comply with his advice."

Wuti was sent for and came. He too was filled with joy at the thought that now the actual work was to begin, that he would be permitted to accompany the Truth-bringer. He fully concurred with the Emperor's suggestions. Much as Li-Yang would have liked to set forth quietly to bring God to the souls, he had to ride out in the midst of an imposing retinue, in order that the way might first be prepared for him in a gross material sense.

A large number of soldiers were called up, with Hai-Tan as their leader. He was to be the protector of the Lama, and as such felt very important. Li-Yang would have been glad to forgo his company.

It pained him that Hai-Tan had still taken no step towards God, although he had often been given the opportunity to recognise Him. Of what use was such a person in the holy work? But the Luminous Messenger of God, to whom Li-Yang brought all these questions, determined that Hai-Tan should travel with him.

Wuti and Lai had reserved for themselves the tasks of attending to the physical well-being of the retinue and supervising the numerous servants. Hai-Tan was given a striking brightly-painted scroll written at the Emperor's behest, stating that everything Li-Yang commanded was decreed by the Emperor himself. A banner with a golden dragon on a green background was also to be carried with the retinue.

The exodus began a few days later with a solemn Hour of Worship in the Temple, attended not only by the court but by the whole departing troop.

It was the first time that those who as yet knew nothing about God were deemed worthy to pray to Him with the others. The Emperor had decreed this deliberately, hoping that seed would thereby be scattered, to bear rich fruit after Li-Yang's homecoming.

Each morning of the journey before they set out, Li-Yang said a heartfelt prayer amid his entire retinue. In that way the soldiers and servants grew accustomed to hearing of God.

AFTER SEVERAL DAYS' journey, Li-Yang's procession approached a major city, the first in the region visited by the plague of demons. The Lama expressed his intention of beginning his work here, and gave Wuti instructions to see to accommodation within the city. And while the main retinue moved on slowly, Wuti and Hai-Tan rode swiftly ahead with a number of soldiers and servants.

When they reached the town gate, Hai-Tan had the dragon-banner unfurled; at once a large crowd began to gather round it. When Hai-Tan was satisfied with the size of the crowd, he ordered the gongs to be struck, as was customary for proclamations.

Then he raised the Imperial scroll high up for all to see, and then read it out aloud in a resonant voice. Now everyone knew of the exalted sage who was about to enter their city. The crowd dispersed, eager to spread the news. But Hai-Tan rode to the house of the highest dignitary, where he read out the Imperial words once more.

Thereupon the mandarin with several of his officials set out to meet Li-Yang, so that he was received with due ceremony as he rode into the city.

This was not really to Li-Yang's liking, and he decided to proceed differently in future. This time he could do nothing about it. He let himself be escorted to the house obtained for him by Wuti, a house joyfully vacated by its occupants to make room for the Lama.

That did not please Li-Yang either. After all, he did not wish to drive anyone away! He felt sorry for the people whom he imagined to be out in the street without a home. But Wuti explained to him that these people were the envy of the others. It was a high honour and great good fortune for them to be permitted to serve a Lama, the Adviser of the Emperor himself.

The house was rather untidy, but within a short time the servants had put it in order most satisfactorily. It was evident that Wuti had brought with him everything that could contribute to Li-Yang's comfort.

As was customary, an altar was set up immediately in the largest room available, so that Li-Yang could now worship there. But he was reluctant to admit his band of attendants, who still believed in gods, to this very personal altar. Therefore he ordered a large tent to be pitched for the purpose in an open space nearby.

There he prayed every morning with his men and spoke to them of God, and in due course a few townspeople appeared, whom he did not turn away.

During the first few days, Li-Yang walked about the town with some of his companions, awaiting an opportunity to approach the people. But wherever he went, the crowd fell back in reverence. He had to confine himself to a superficial acquaintance with the city and its inhabitants.

He visited the various temples and pagodas, hoping in that way to establish contact with the priests. But they too were unapproachable owing to their veneration for him.

So he resorted to his old expedient: in servants' clothing he and Wuti participated in temple-festivals and devotions, and entered the huts of the poor. What he saw there distressed him. False belief and unbelief held sway everywhere. Squalor, corruption and depravity ruled the masses. In this respect things were certainly worse than in Kiang-ning.

The mandarin sought him out. He came surrounded by pomp and splendour, for he wanted to show that even in the provinces they knew what was fitting for a representative of the Emperor. Now Hai-Tan was in his element. In every way he strove to surpass the city official. The pomp displayed around Li-Yang, without his knowledge and against his will, was unequalled.

Although this was inwardly repugnant to the Lama, he accommodated himself to the setting around him. An indescribable dignity emanated from him, who met his visitors without any self-importance. He observed the customary ceremonies, but ensured that they were given no more importance than was absolutely necessary.

Then he began to question the mandarin about the fear of demons, which was ostensibly the reason for his coming. The dignitary was evasive, not wishing to engage in this conversation, but Li-Yang persisted. He put his questions calmly and firmly, and at last the dignitary had to admit that things were in a sorry state in his city.

The very poor seemed to be under the special protection of the gods: no demons approached them, no dragons appeared to them. But everyone else lived in fear and trembling. Only the previous evening a terrible figure had appeared to him, which had forced its way into his palace even with the gate closed.

"And how did you banish the demon?" asked Li-Yang kindly.

"I sent for the priest of the main temple. But when this was of no avail, when the esteemed man began to tremble with fear just as I did, then..."

The Lama completed the unfinished sentence:

"Then you both hid in the dark so that you need see no more. Was it not like that?"

The mandarin nodded. But Li-Yang began to explain to him that demons, in all their dreadfulness, were simply the forms of human thoughts.

"If that is your opinion, then you have never yet seen any," said the visitor nervously.

On this point too he was enlightened. Finally the Lama promised to come next day to the mandarin's palace, where such a monster manifested every evening at the same hour. Promptly at the appointed time Li-Yang arrived at the palace of the civic leader. Great confusion prevailed there, for the demon had appeared earlier than usual, thus dispelling the Lama's fears that just on this occasion it might fail to manifest.

To conduct the visitor to the master of the palace was hardly possible, for no one dared to enter the rooms where the demon was pursuing its activity. So Li-Yang made his own way, directed by the babble of frightened voices.

He found the mandarin on his knees, surrounded by several persons of rank; they had turned their faces, veiled with silk cloths, to the wall, while a huge, fierce demon billowed up and down in the centre of the room. When Li-Yang entered the people stopped whimpering, and the outlines of the form became less distinct.

"Hear me, Fu-yi," the sage addressed the master of the house, who seemed to straighten a little at the sound of the clear voice; "this demon is a product of your own fear. Trust in God, at Whose Command I stand here! Have the courage to turn round, and look the enemy straight in the eye. I promise you it will disappear."

The words had a compelling effect on the faint-hearted man. With a jerk he tore the veil from his face and turned to look fully at the demon.

"He has become smaller!" he shouted joyfully.

No sooner did the others hear this than they likewise turned to behold the miracle with their own eyes.

"Product of human fear, I command you to dissolve!" called Li-Yang.

He knew that the words were no longer necessary, but he uttered them for the sake of the disbelieving people. The form vanished. For a few moments there was a fine undulating haze, then no more was to be seen of it.

Now they all fell on their knees before Li-Yang, wanting to worship him. He rebuked them firmly for it, and asked them instead to gather round him. Then he told them about God the Almighty, Who is Lord over Heaven and Earth, over gods and men.

Joyfully they listened – all those who had just been so afraid. What they were permitted to hear was something completely new, that there was a Being Who was well-disposed towards them, and would give them strength and help.

Trustfully they received the tidings. And Li-Yang perceived how with each word his own strength grew. He spoke ever more convincingly. Then he explained the nature of demons to them, but they could not understand him. So he decided on an experiment.

He forbade them to say anything outside the room about the dispelling of the demon. Servants should be forced to enter the room. Their extreme fear would produce new demons. Then they could all be convinced of how their courage would cause the forms to disappear.

And it came to pass as he had determined. A number of little monster-shapes entered the room along with the trembling servants. But laughter broke out among those who had witnessed the dispelling. It seemed to them impossible to conceive that they could have trembled before such things. Amid their laughter, however, the demons vanished.

The mandarin's gratitude was boundless. He knew no better way of showing it than to vow instant allegiance to this Supreme God, in Whose Power Li-Yang had accomplished the great deed.

"If you are in earnest, Fu-yi," the Lama said, "then come tomorrow to the temple that has been built not far from my home. There you will learn more about God, and be able to pray to Him."

153

That evening, as he reflected upon the events of the day, it struck Li-Yang that everything had come about quite differently from the way he had planned it in Kiang-ning. Now he suddenly realised how good it was that he had made his entrance with such pomp, and thereby commanded respect from the outset. Moreover, how good it was that he had fought the first demon in the house of the mandarin. Had he done this work in the slum, the distinguished man might well have become his opponent, whereas now he had a well-disposed helper for his further work.

The more Li-Yang mused upon this, the smaller he became in his own eyes. Everything he did would have been wrong, had he not let himself be guided from above.

"Sublime, Almighty God," he implored, "I no longer wish to be anything myself. Make me into an ever better instrument of Thine, into Thy servant!" –

The next morning Fu-yi and his officials arrived at the temple, and listened devoutly to Li-Yang's address. Then they asked to be allowed to come every day; this was granted to them.

But the news of the previous evening's events had spread throughout the town. From every quarter the people flocked to see the Lama, to prostrate themselves before him, and to ask for his blessing. They assailed him with requests to banish their demons as well.

He tried to explain that it lay with them not to give rise to the demons in the first place. But they could not grasp that. In their great need they wanted to see help, to experience help from outside.

He referred them to Wuti, so that he might determine where Li-Yang should go first. Wuti knew how to deal with them. He spoke reverently of the Lama, but not in the exaggerated manner affected by Hai-Tan. Cheerful and confident, he promised those who besought help that they would receive it, but at the same time he also called attention to their inner state of mind.

He advised them to replace despair and sheer fright with courage and trust. For the Lama he was in every respect the helper who worked according to his wishes. And Li-Yang thanked God for placing this Brother at his side.

For about a month the Imperial Adviser banished demons in that city and its environs. The people recognised the Truth in the words of the Lama, and in this way a great many of the inhabitants found their way to God.

Now Li-Yang had a large, beautiful temple built, which was dedicated to God. He gave no name to God; it would have seemed to him a desecration. He used the designation once found for Him by his devout mother: the Supreme One.

Now he had to find a priest for this temple. Wuti could not be spared, and he himself could no longer remain in this one place.

In his predicament he turned imploringly to God. He was deeply anxious not to leave without help the people who had only just found the One God. They would relapse too easily into their former unbelief. And because his entreaty was so earnest it gained in strength, became overwhelming, and rose upwards to the very Steps of God's Throne.

Now Li-Yang heard again the clear voice of the Luminous Messenger:

"Do not despair, Li-Yang. The souls that you were allowed to deliver from the power of the Darkness belong to God. He provides for His own. Before you called, He answered and sent help."

Li-Yang was filled with great confidence. He resolved to stay in the town until help arrived. When he went to the temple the following morning, a simple man whose features seemed familiar stood before it.

The stranger bowed and entered the temple behind Li-Yang, devoutly participating. On leaving, the man again joined the Lama. Hai-Tan wanted to send him away, but he explained that he had a message which he must deliver personally to the sage. At that Hai-Tan left him alone.

It was a strange thing about Hai-Tan. At his request he had recently been permitted to take part in the Hours of Worship in the temple. The Power from above worked mightily on his soul, but he feared that it would become too great within him. He did not yet wish to belong to God, for he quite rightly sensed that he would then have to surrender himself. And Li-Yang let him be. Hai-Tan must himself come to realise the error of his present ways; until then he would not find the right path.

When they reached Li-Yang's home, the stranger approached the Lama, and handed him a slender scroll written by Lie-Tse. Now Li-Yang suddenly knew where he had seen the stranger.

"Were we not together in the monastery, my brother?" he asked kindly.

The man assented, and reported that some months ago Lie-Tse had asked him to go with Li-Yang as a helper. First he had been in Kiang-ning, then he had followed him on his way. He was happy to have met the Lama.

Lie-Tse wrote only a few words:

"My son, God the Sublime One is with you in all that you do. Together with you I thank Him. At His Command helpers will come to you at certain intervals. These are reliable Brothers, to whom you can entrust temple and community."

A few days sufficed to introduce the Tibetan to his office; thereafter Li-Yang journeyed on.

Wherever he went, events transpired in a similar way: he helped the frightened people, and through this help he led them to God. But his work did not go unnoticed. Word of his activity went far in advance of him, and while it gave hope to the fearful, it unleashed bitter enmity among the priests.

Whether the people believed in their gods or in others was basically all one to the priests, but their very existence was at stake. Were the people to become estranged from the gods and the temples, the sacrifices and offerings on which the priests lived would cease. Their priestly prestige would decline, and with it also the outward life of luxury which they had hitherto enjoyed.

Although now and then one of the Tibetans, who always arrived in time to take charge of the newly-built temples, tried to win over the local priests to God, it was of no avail. They clung tenaciously to their wrong belief, and inveighed against God and His followers.

Li-Yang had set out to bring peace, yet he left behind discord and unrest. At times his soldiers had to intervene in order to enable him to work.

Li-Yang became sad. He was meant to be a Truth-bringer, yet it appeared to him that he brought dissension. Was it not better for him to return to Kiang-ning, and leave the people here to themselves? Although they suffered from the demonic plague, they suffered together in unity. It was his activity that brought about the division.

If only he could have spoken with Hou-Chou! What would the Emperor think if reports of agitation, bitterness and fraternal strife came from the very part of his Realm where his Adviser sojourned.

156

And Li-Yang entreated God from a troubled soul:

"Lord, show me where I have failed, that these are the results of the work done at Thy Command. Show me whether I am to return home or whether I may continue to work in Thy Power."

Then a picture was shown to him in the night:

He saw men engaged in the building of a magnificent temple. Excellent beams had been prepared; the colours were exquisite. Wonderful silk lay in readiness to cover the ceilings and walls. But Li-Yang was horrified: they were erecting the building on top of a structure that lay partly in ruins, of which it was not possible to tell what purpose it had served.

"Stop!" shouted Li-Yang excitedly. "You can build nothing new so long as the old, with all its falseness, remains beneath it."

But the men hardly looked up, and went on working. One of them however said calmly:

"It will be right as we are doing it. It is the will of the Lama Li-Yang that God's temple be built within mankind, without the need to eradicate the old. Removing the old is noisy and difficult. But he wants everything to proceed gently and quietly. He is a Lama, he must be right!"

The picture disappeared, but Li-Yang had his answer. He felt ashamed. Out of the shame arose his resolve to act with greater determination in future to bring about the more rapid collapse of the old.

In this connection he thought of Hai-Tan. How much he had neglected him by letting him continue in his irresolute and cowardly way. After all, Hai-Tan had been entrusted to him. He must be precious to God, otherwise he would not have been placed by his side. And he would have calmly allowed this man to take the wrong road!

He must speak with him. If he ardently implored God's help in this, he would be victorious. He passed the night in gratitude and praise. Very early in the morning, completely contrary to custom, Hai-Tan entered his room. Some special urge must have impelled him, and this urge must be strong, for Hai-Tan began without the usual ceremonies:

"Li-Yang, are you still my friend?"

More emphatically than would have been possible the previous evening, the Lama affirmed that he was.

"Is it worthy of a friend to leave the other so completely to himself as you

157

do me?" Hai-Tan asked resolutely. "I resisted your God, whom I was prepared to acknowledge, though not as my God. I refused to let myself be overpowered by Him. And now He has become too powerful for me after all. Wuti came to my bedside last night and said earnestly:

"'Hai-Tan, how much longer will you seek to defy God the Almighty? You have long since recognised Him, but you love yourself too much. Beware, lest you sink into Darkness!'

"I could not answer him. But now I come to you, and demand that you help me to surrender myself and belong to God."

Then Li-Yang told his friend all his experiences of that night, and from the ruins of Hai-Tan's defiance and self-love their friendship blossomed more beautifully than ever, never again to wither.

WITH ALL THESE events, years had passed. Li-Yang had reached the place where the waves of the ocean washed against the shore, having turned off sometimes to the left, sometimes to the right on his journey, in order to traverse as much of the country as possible.

The ocean itself had made a deep impression on his receptive nature. It seemed to him to proclaim God's Omnipotence in a very special way. Demons and other forms could not withstand the salty tang borne on the wind from the sea. The people who lived here were used to braving all dangers. They had little thought of dread and fear.

On the other hand there was something else here: the people were too self-assured. They relied on their strength and their skill, on the keenness of their eyes and their presence of mind. They believed that they had no need of any help whatsoever from above.

Li-Yang, who felt very drawn to this quite special race of men, deplored their attitude and tried somehow to bring God closer to them. He spoke to the women repairing nets on the shore while they waited for the boats.

Hitherto he had avoided approaching the other sex. But the thought of his mother, which he carried within his heart like a sacred treasure, led him to the numerous mothers who did not hide here as they did elsewhere.

They too were accustomed to a rough life and hard work. When he first addressed them, a woman threw a coiled-up rope at him, which nearly

158

struck him. It was evident that they wished to drive him away. Only when they were told by Wuti that he was a priest did they condescend to listen to his words.

He asked if there were not often misfortune, and what they did then. Did they realise that their fate lay safely in the Hand of God? Their astonished looks told him that he might just as well be speaking Tibetan; the women had no idea what he wanted of them.

Again Wuti had to intervene and mediate. He asked one of the women for a fish. She gave it to him hesitantly, but when he offered kaolin coins in return, other women also brought him fish. He took them all happily, piling them up beside Li-Yang. Then he began a friendly conversation with those who had become more trusting. Jestingly he enquired about their sons, what age they were and whether they too aspired to become seafarers one day.

While this small talk, to which Li-Yang listened in surprise, was going on, an elderly woman broke away from the group; she walked slowly towards the Lama, and looked at him. He was not sure what to make of this look, and assumed that it was directed at his lilac robe. Then the woman began to speak slowly:

"Sir, are you from Tibet?"

Li-Yang said that although he was born in the Middle Kingdom, Tibet had become his second home.

At that the woman's features relaxed, and she said:

"My mother came from Tibet, and told me about the devout Brothers who grow up in monasteries. She also described to me people who wear robes like yours. She called them Lamas and said: 'My child, should you ever meet a Lama, beseech him to tell you about the Eternal God Whom they worship in Tibet.'"

Overjoyed, Li-Yang began to bear witness. He told of how vast areas of the Middle Kingdom had now also found their way to this Supreme One.

The woman called a few of her friends, and asked them to listen. Before long, Li-Yang was sitting in the midst of the crowd of women; as they repaired the nets he spoke about God. Gradually some of the veiled eyes grew brighter, and the weather-worn features seemed slowly to relax.

The sage remained with the simple fisher-women until evening. Then when the boats came in view, and brisk activity began at the shore, he set out for his lodging.

Filled with anticipation, he returned to the shore the following day, only to find it deserted. For hours he waited, but nobody came. Then Wuti suggested that they go to the fishermen's huts, from which smoke was rising, a sign that they were occupied. They did so, but none of the women would let them enter. None even dared to speak with them.

From hut to hut they went. Everywhere they were met with the same rebuff, which they dared not defy. Finally they found the old woman who had first addressed Li-Yang. But even she turned her back on them. Then the Lama implored her in memory of her mother to tell him what had caused this dreadful change.

"The men beat us," the woman said in a low voice. "We are not to speak with other men. They also said that what you told us is heresy and will incur the wrath of the gods. Go away, otherwise they will try to kill you."

Having obtained this information Li-Yang could do no more, and it made him very sad. In the night he asked God what he should do. The Luminous Messenger told him to leave these people to themselves for the present. Some of the seed-grains he had scattered would bear fruit after his departure. He should return to Kiang-ning, where he was needed.

So the following day they prepared for the homeward journey, and decided to visit all the towns where temples had been built. It was a ride with ever changing impressions. The unrest disseminated among the people through the proclamation about God had not yet subsided. They came to places where the former wrong belief had triumphed once again. The Tibetan priest barely made a living, if he was not altogether banished. The temple was demolished or burned down.

In other places there was an active spiritual life. Although the believers in God met with hostility, they cheerfully pursued their work and their faith. Not infrequently a second or even a third temple had been built in addition to the first. In such places Li-Yang was received with joy. He had to address the crowd in each of the temples, and experienced many a proof of deep faith and genuine change of heart. Demons no longer appeared anywhere.

The journey took many months, but one day the pagodas of Kiang-ning appeared in the distance, and now Li-Yang looked forward to the reunion with Hou-Chou.

Hai-Tan had sent messengers ahead in good time, and the Emperor himself rode to meet his Adviser. He had changed a great deal. The young face had become manly, lean, with sharply chiselled features. A very thin, well-groomed beard hung in two long points down to his chest.

But the eyes held the same warm expression as before, and once the friends were alone in the Imperial apartments, Li-Yang perceived that Hou-Chou's soul had become even more mature. Again he had the impression that the Emperor towered far above his people.

"You have returned at the right time, Li-Yang," Hou-Chou greeted him. "My son, Han, has reached the age when he needs your instruction. Also, a messenger came this morning from Tibet to seek you out. He is awaiting you in your rooms."

When the Lama went there a few hours later, he found a Serving Brother from the well-known monastery. The latter gave him a voluminous scroll, with the assurance that he was at his disposal to provide any particulars that Li-Yang might still need after studying the document. The latter spent all night reading. More than once he had to put the parchment aside to reflect on what he had learned.

Lie-Tse wrote that he had grown too old to continue as Head of all the Lamas. At God's Behest he had summoned them, and permitted them to decide on his successor.

As a result the choice fell on two Lamas. The one, who was henceforth to bear the name Miang-Tse, was named as head of his monastery. But the other Lama, who was chosen to be Head of all the Lamas wherever they might be, was given the name Lao-Tse, and was none other than Li-Yang. The choice of the Lamas was made in accord with the Divine Will.

Lie-Tse now asked him to set out for Tibet at once, so that he himself could introduce him to his duties. Thereafter he would be free to return to the Middle Kingdom, for his new position would never remove him from his tasks there. On the contrary, as Lao-Tse he would be even better able than before to fulfil his task among his people. But speed was essential, the High Lama should set out forthwith.

So the following morning, Li-Yang had to inform the startled Emperor that he must leave him for an indefinite period. But when Hou-Chou learned the reason he was deeply moved, and joyfully thanked God, Who granted his people such high grace.

"As Lao-Tse you will become an even greater blessing to us, my friend!" he exclaimed repeatedly. "How rich we are to be permitted to have you in our midst!"

The loyal followers also rejoiced and bowed low before him who was invested with the new office. That very day they started for Tibet by the shortest route. Since he rode in this direction for the first time Lao-Tse had experienced much. While his steed covered mile after mile, now hastening through a gorge at a swift trot, then sure-footedly climbing the rocks, the Lama had time to reflect on it all.

He became ever more aware of God's Grace, the guidance that had shaped his whole earth-life increased in clarity before his inner eye. It was wonderful how just what he most needed was always there before he asked.

Like the intricately constructed beams on the gates of his homeland, so had events followed one upon the other, yielding a complete whole. But no beam must warp, no human being must resist his guidance or indeed be deaf to it. His own experience was sufficient proof of this.

To point human beings toward this Divine Guidance must now be his main task. Men wanted to do far too much. By their over-eagerness they created unrest, and thereby misery for themselves. They needed to be still, to open themselves, listen within, then they would become happy and contented, then they would rediscover the path to those Heights from which they originated.

He would talk all this over with Lie-Tse. Lie-Tse! He thought of the old man with infinite gratitude. How would he find him, he wondered?

No sooner had he thought this than three Brothers from the monastery came riding towards him, bringing a welcome from his aged teacher. He was still alive, and longed to see and to bless the Truth-bringer. The messengers showed the travellers an even shorter route, which led in relative comfort up the mountain to the monastery gate.

There everything was just as Lao-Tse had left it many years before. Nothing seemed to have changed. The same figures strode through gardens and corridors. In joyful haste Lao-Tse followed the Brother who led him into the guest-rooms, where everything needed to remove the traces of the ride was provided.

A lilac robe, exquisitely embroidered, was laid out; beside it lay the Yellow Cap. Lao-Tse hardly dared to touch it. Now he knew what a Yellow Lama was! And he was to occupy this high office?

When he was ready, a Brother led him to Lie-Tse's apartment, where he found his teacher alone. And alone they remained, these two who had so much to say to each other. Lie-Tse had grown old, very old indeed, but his eyes shone with youthful ardour; it seemed to Lao-Tse that their radiance had become even deeper.

"My son!" the old man greeted his guest, "My son! I rejoice that my old eyes are permitted to see you once more, that they behold the Sign of God upon your forehead. You are the Truth-bringer sent by God for your people. Now help our people also, lest they forget God. Call the Lamas in all the monasteries to account for their activities, and encourage them to live in the Laws of God. A new spirit from evil regions seeks entry among us too; drive it away just as you scatter the demons. China is your mother, but Tibet is your father. Do not forget the one for the sake of the other."

Lao-Tse had listened, deeply moved, to the venerable man's words. Now he ventured to interpose: "My father, if I live in the Middle Kingdom, looking after my own people, how am I to know what takes place here? If out of love for Tibet, which imparted all my knowledge to me, I try to see that everything is in order here, how can I be certain that I am not deceived?"

"Do not forget that today you will become a Yellow Lama, Lao-Tse. As yet you have no idea what this implies. At the ceremony tonight, I will make it known to you. Until then have patience. But now promise what I have asked for. Do you think you would have been chosen by God if He did not provide the means for you to fulfil your vow? If you remain loyal to your vow He will not forsake you."

"How can I prepare myself for the Festival this evening?" Lao-Tse asked quietly.

Lie-Tse looked at him kindly:

"Your ride here was the best preparation, my son. During that time you learned a great deal. I rejoice over you!"

163

The two conversed at length, and Lao-Tse expressed his admiration for the Divine Guidance which had affected him deeply.

"Are all human beings so guided down to the last detail, my father?" he asked thoughtfully.

"Certainly, if only they would attend more closely to their guidance," replied Lie-Tse. "Each one could experience miracles, if he did not time and again spoil everything for himself."

A servant entered and announced Miang-Tse, who wished to greet the new Head of Lamas. An elderly, dignified man, in the same attire previously worn by Lie-Tse, approached Lao-Tse. He recognised in him the yellow-clad Lama who had once attached the Yellow Ribbon to his robe.

Joyfully the two, who were called to watch side by side over Tibet, recognised each other. But then Miang-Tse left teacher and pupil alone again; they shared a meal together, after which the aged man wanted to rest.

"Go into the garden, Lao-Tse," he suggested. "You will find many good thoughts awaiting you there."

Lao-Tse followed the advice, smiling a little to himself at Lie-Tse's choice of words. But this smile disappeared after he had been walking up and down among the flowers for a few minutes. It seemed to him as though, with the fragrance of the blossoms, thoughts which had never before entered his mind flowed to him unceasingly.

Majestic figures from a supra-earthly world arose before his spiritual eye, and as he absorbed them, marvelling, he became aware that he must have beheld them at some time in the past. A sense of being interwoven with other planes enfolded him.

What he perceived and experienced spiritually was glorious! Only with difficulty could he find his way back when servants came to escort him to the Temple. First he was conducted to a bath-cell, as once before.

The glorious male choir that was one of his most precious memories greeted him as he entered the Temple in which the dignity of Lama had been conferred upon him. As before, he found all the other Lamas assembled. They sat in a semicircle round two chairs, on one of which Lie-Tse was seated. The other was assigned to Lao-Tse. Miang-Tse stood in front by the Altar, which was adorned with flowers.

He was a worthy successor to Lie-Tse, and yet there was a vast difference in the way each performed the duties of his office. Lao-Tse became ever more conscious of this, asking himself involuntarily:

"Which of the two do you resemble?"

With all his heart he longed to become like his old teacher. Miang-Tse read a manuscript which explained the appointment, at God's Behest, of another Lama superior even to the High Lama.

He was to ensure that all Lamas complied fully with their duties, that they did not stray so much as one step from the right path. Dreadful to say, unbelief and atheism had penetrated even into Tibet. At least the monasteries had to be preserved.

Lao-Tse had not only the right but also the duty to admonish, to warn or to punish every negligent Lama immediately, in accordance with what would be demanded by God. Every Lama was to appear before Lao-Tse at his bidding, wherever he might be.

The Supreme Lama was dazed. How was he to call the Brothers to account when he was miles away from them! How was he to know what was taking place in Tibet?

Suddenly a wave of calm seemed to pass over to him from Lie-Tse. Could the venerable man know what preoccupied him? Could he read thoughts?

Again glorious choruses resounded; Miang-Tse uttered a prayer and returned to the ranks of the Lamas, who stood and knelt around the two chairs.

Lie-Tse rose to his feet. With a firm step he moved forward, enveloped in a silver-grey robe on which sparkled exquisite violet stones set in silver.

He directed his full attention to his former pupil, whom he had summoned, and who knelt humbly before him.

"My son," he began, "you are overwhelmed by the new responsibilities which you are to assume at God's Behest. Always remember: to him who is given a task by God, the requisite strength is also granted. He demands nothing that His servant is not capable of achieving.

"At this hour your inner faculties will be opened wider than before. You will be able to see things that are hidden from human eyes. Luminous messengers will accompany you as your servants. They will bring you tidings of all happenings that you need to know about.

"Whether you are staying in Tibet or in the Middle Kingdom: the actions and words of those entrusted to you will be known to you as though you were in their midst. To a lesser degree this ability and grace is bestowed on every High Lama; Miang-Tse too was endowed with it on the day of his consecration; but you, as the foremost Lama of all, have received even higher grace in the spiritual servants who will constantly surround you."

A stream of exultant Power and sublime happiness flowed through the kneeling one. Truly God had provided for him beyond all prayers!

Lie-Tse went on speaking. He reminded Lao-Tse that he had already found the secret of success for his activity. He was not to do battle, nor to provoke battle; but in calmness and harmony with God's Laws, he should teach human beings how they also were to seek peace by fulfilling the Divine Will.

"Two tasks were assigned to you, my son, even before you entered our world: you were to destroy the demons. That was the first task, and you have faithfully accomplished it. The second task was: you were to prepare the way for the good spirits. You have brought the tidings of God to men. That was self-evident, for you could have had no success in any other way. But in addition, it should be your concern to pave a way for the people to establish contact with the helping beings. Your people need helpers. Hitherto they beheld only demons, which spread fear and terror. Teach them to find the beings from whom they can learn how to serve God aright. You will find open hearts if you replace the Dark with the Light. I need tell you no more. You are guided."

In fervent prayer the aged man raised his hands over Lao-Tse's head, and let them rest upon him for a moment longer.

Then he took from the Altar a piece of jewellery the size of a hand. It was intricately fashioned of gold, and consisted of two intersecting equal arms, each bearing four precious stones. The stones were of different colours, and shone exquisitely. In the centre, where the arms crossed, glowed a huge crystal-clear stone. The splendid ornament was suspended on a heavy gold chain, which the aged hands now placed round the neck of the kneeling man.

"At God's Behest, bear the sign of your dignity and your duties. Never be without it. Where you do not wish to wear it openly, conceal it in the folds of your robe. Each stone brings you something different: Purity,

Truth, Love and Justice speak to you from them, but also knowledge of Divine things, wisdom in your dealings with men.

"May you discover for yourself the significance of the last three stones. Once you have absorbed that within you, you will have reached the boundary of what mortal spirits are able to grasp. Beyond that there is nothing. And now rise, speak from here to those entrusted to your care, and as the representative of the Most High, let them pledge to you the loyalty which they owe to Him."

Unprepared as he was, Lao-Tse found the right words to touch every heart. He found Lie-Tse's promise fulfilled in a wonderful way: he was able to see whose vow was spoken in earnest, but he also recognised him who only approached hesitantly, and him to whom any kind of supervision seemed unnecessary.

The Festival was over, and the Lamas were preparing to leave the chapel, when Lie-Tse begged:

"Tarry yet a moment, my son."

Lao-Tse willingly seated himself on the chair beside the aged man. Soft singing enveloped them. It did not come from male voices; the tones sounded wondrously soft, unearthly in their loveliness.

"Do you hear them?" Lie-Tse asked with transfigured countenance, which he turned upwards, "Do you hear them? They wish to conduct my soul home to the Eternal Garden, where henceforth I may continue to work as God's servant."

"My father!" stammered Lao-Tse in alarm.

But when he saw the radiance on the ancient man's features he was silent, and listened with him. It was as though the music came closer; thereupon a bright ray of light seemed to descend from above, completely enveloping the venerable Lama. Then the tones withdrew, taking the radiance with them. But with that Lie-Tse's soul had also departed.

For a long time Lao-Tse stood beside the lifeless cloak of him who had been his teacher and friend. His whole inner being was filled with gratitude. Gratitude towards the man who had guided him, gratitude towards God Who had taken away the precious soul so graciously.

Finally the Lama broke away, and went to call others. Though the grief of the whole monastery was great, it was observed in stately solemnity. It came to light that Lie-Tse had made detailed preparations in every respect for his departure. Like his predecessors, he wished to be interred in one of the tombs hewn into the rocks behind the gardens.

That very evening the Brothers opened the tomb designated by the deceased, which proved to be a completely empty grotto. It was decorated with flowers; bowls of incense were arranged, and oil lamps lit. In the centre of the grotto a platform was erected, on which they placed the anointed body.

Once more all were permitted to behold the cherished face; then Lao-Tse spread a silken cloth over it, while Miang-Tse draped the whole body with the robe. For three days everything remained unchanged. Several times during the day male choirs sang solemn melodies. The morning and evening devotions were held at the graveside rather than in the chapels.

Thereafter a specially solemn Divine Service conducted by Miang-Tse took place. Lao-Tse was also to speak. During these days he had immersed himself wholly in prayer, and often it seemed to him that his soul was wandering in other planes. When he stepped forward now to address the devout, he was a mere instrument for what another would proclaim through him.

"Hear me, Brothers!" he began, and his voice resounded far beyond the assemblage. "Lie-Tse has ascended to heights of which your spirit can form no picture. He has served the Supreme One faithfully, without wavering or self-will. Now he may also serve Him in the Eternal Gardens, where all volition becomes instant fulfilment. Now he beholds Him Who sent us to bring the Light of God to the world which is turning to the Darkness; he beholds and worships Him. We however should emulate him, so that like him we may one day be raised On High.

"Glorious are the Eternal Gardens in which blessed spirits walk and work blissfully in the service of God. Supreme joy fills them, for they desire nothing but to serve, to praise and to worship. Lie-Tse's spirit moves freely and easily among the others. He has been granted the reward for his loyalty.

"But terrible things await him who knows of God, and does not act according to His Commands; as also him who weakens and slackens in his work. Brothers, do not cease to serve God; the welfare of the whole people depends on your loyalty. God will one day demand of you the souls of these human beings. See to it that not one of them is lost through your fault!"

To the strains of sacred songs, the grave was sealed. Later a beautiful stone, of the kind already standing before several of the burial chambers, was to be placed at the entrance.

The following day, Lao-Tse set out on the return journey to the Imperial Court. His farewell from the Brothers was heartfelt; they would have liked to hold on to him for good, sensing as they did the great spirit that spoke out of him. But they understood that his duties lay with his own people, and knew that he could be reached at any time. With that they had to be content.

Much sooner than the Emperor had expected, his Adviser returned. But for Hou-Chou, who had missed him, it was not a day too soon. In the meantime the Ruler had contemplated great plans: he wanted to close some of the temples of the gods, and in their stead build others in which the Supreme One was to be worshipped. It was time to lead the people to the right faith! Hou-Chou could hardly wait to execute these plans.

During the very first hours of their reunion, he spoke to Lao-Tse about what he had most at heart. He had feared that the Lama would wish to dissuade him. How he now rejoiced that Lao-Tse was in complete agreement, and urged an immediate start of the building projects.

The friends were happy and eager to immerse themselves in the work that lay ahead for the coming months. At the same time, the lessons of the little Prince began. Han was a very bright child, open to instruction in everything, but most of all he loved the hours of the day when his teacher told him about God and His Commandments.

"Why do so many of our people still believe in false gods?" he often asked. "When one day I am Emperor, I shall have any subjects who do not pray to the Supreme One killed."

Only with difficulty could Lao-Tse persuade him of the error of that intention. Han thought, as had his forefathers:

"What is a human life? If it is in my way and thwarts my intents, it must be removed."

But Lao-Tse's untiring patience succeeded in eradicating this wrong attitude, and bringing to life the many good qualities that slumbered in Han's soul.

LIFE AROUND Lao-Tse had already begun to assume a quieter course, so that the sage wondered whether he was really fulfilling all his tasks, when he was rudely shaken.

The former rift proceeding from the court, which had split the nobles of the Realm into two camps, was only apparently bridged. At first they all bowed to the fact that the Lama had been invested with a previously unknown dignity, which made him appear unassailable even to his enemies.

But now that he lived so peacefully by the Emperor's side, intervening and supporting him with advice, hostility again reared its head. What hitherto had been unable to manifest openly became all the more active in secret. It only needed a strong hand to enable these dangerous sparks to blaze up into a disastrous conflagration. And this hand emerged.

Moru-Tan, one of the most distinguished mandarins among the Emperor's closest advisers, who thought himself entitled to the most in-fluential position, was deeply offended by the preferential treatment accorded to Lao-Tse.

After trying everything to advance his position with cunning, and after every one of his clandestine plans had failed, he found no further peace, either by day or by night. A search for like-minded persons began.

He proceeded with extreme caution. It was only difficult to find the first three or four; thereafter these brought him ever new supporters, so that he soon had a large following.

As yet no one knew the purpose and goal of this alliance. They all vaguely sensed that it was aimed at the overthrow of Lao-Tse, which was important to them all. Some were annoyed because he had withdrawn from them altogether, not associating with anyone; others grudged him the Emperor's confidence, and others again were indignant that he had divested the old gods of their rights.

All Kiang-ning seemed to be corrupted by this secret alliance, which even began to spread to other large towns. The time had come for Moru-Tan to consolidate it systematically.

To that end he convened a meeting of the available members on a specified evening. Far outside Kiang-ning he owned a large country-house, which had formerly been occupied. But a gruesome, unsolved mass murder, imputed to the demons by superstitious priests, had been committed there some decades ago. Ever since, the building had fallen into disrepair; everyone avoided it. To that place Moru-Tan summoned his supporters.

At the appointed hour he entered the hastily-prepared hall, and found it packed with men of every class and age. There was a tremendous number of people. The air was heavy with various odours, which took Moru-Tan's breath away as he entered. Demons produced by fear, seen by few but felt by all, fluttered round the heads of those present.

Moru-Tan had to summon all his courage, had to intensify within him all thoughts of hatred, in order to be able to step on to the slightly raised place meant for him. Then, as he addressed the people with growing eloquence, he seemed to be carried away by some strange, sinister force.

He described how much harm could arise for the people from the new faith, and demonstrated that the stranger was alien to their customs and practices. Innovations could not be brought about as desired by the decree of the Emperor and his Adviser. It must spring only from the will of the whole people.

His words roused the hearers to enthusiasm. As he concluded, they asked what he proposed to do. He replied that he would make this known at the next gathering; for the present they should go home and reflect on what they had heard. But that was not to their liking. Shouts were heard:

"Lao-Tse must return to Tibet!" – "The Emperor will not let him go!" – "Then the Emperor must abdicate the throne!"

Like a ball starting to roll, this last call passed from mouth to mouth. Moru-Tan's cries were all in vain. He could no longer check what he had unleashed.

But this had not been his intention! The Emperor should come to no harm, he was only to take him, Moru-Tan, as his adviser. He had only intended Lao-Tse's downfall or, better still, his death.

But to appease the crowd he acceded to their shouts. He promised to devise ways and means of overthrowing the Emperor. But they should undertake nothing lest the secret alliance be uncovered prematurely. This they had to promise. Afterwards they dispersed, glad to take leave of the eerie place.

Moru-Tan, however, climbed hastily into his carrying-chair, troubled and fear-driven. He knew only a handful of his followers. Could he rely on this excited crowd? But if the Emperor were to learn of the plans prematurely, he would be rewarded with the silken cord. He himself would have to put an end to his life in such a shameful way. While all this was taking place far outside Kiang-ning, Lao-Tse was in his room alone, engaged in deciphering some manuscripts which he had recently found. But while his intellect struggled to make sense of the intricate symbols, his soul was pursuing other pathways. It was led to a different place.

He saw himself sitting at the big table covered with manuscripts, saw how his head drooped, and his vacated body slumbered. He, however, floated out of Kiang-ning, and was led to the abandoned country-house. He saw all the visitors entering. He knew many of them; other faces impressed themselves on his mind. And then he witnessed what took place there.

Neither anxiety nor indignation stirred his soul. It simply absorbed what it had to know, in order to forestall disaster in the country. It felt safe under the Guidance of God; it knew that what it now experienced, indeed its being witness to this meeting, was willed by God. Hence Lao-Tse's soul would also learn what must be done after this.

The same tranquillity filled the Lama when his soul had returned to its body. He thanked God and asked for further enlightenment. But he decided to say nothing to the Emperor for the present.

The following day Moru-Tan visited him. This had never happened before, and Lao-Tse was eager to learn the motive for the mandarin's visit. It was at once apparent that it could only be some pretext.

The visitor spent himself in demonstrations of respect far exceeding the otherwise customary ceremonies, before he began:

"Exalted Father, I feel impelled not only to pay lip service to the new faith which you teach, but to absorb it with my soul. I have come to ask you to accept me and six like-minded friends as your pupils and to instruct us."

Lao-Tse's eyes rested thoughtfully on the petitioner. It was as though only his outer ear heard the words, while his inner ear perceived something altogether different. He knew that the mandarin sought this connection with him in order to lull him into a false sense of security, to be informed about all his movements, and finally, to gain the opportunity of eliminating him.

With a man of Moru-Tan's character, this was so natural that it was no surprise to the Lama. However, the necessity to respond not to this, but to the request he had heard outwardly, was difficult. A few moments were required before he was ready to answer; then he said:

"I am honoured by your request, Moru-Tan. It honours you, as well, if indeed it has sprung from the desire for knowledge of God. If it has, then I may grant it..."

The visitor sought to interrupt him with assurances, but Lao-Tse did not permit it:

"No, Moru-Tan, you must not give me a reply now. Commune with your soul, and if you are then convinced that the urge to seek me out comes from there, then return on the first day after the next full moon."

The day was deliberately chosen, for Lao-Tse knew that the next meeting of the secret alliance was to take place on the night of the full moon.

But Moru-Tan was not so readily satisfied. He begged Lao-Tse to be assured even now of his sincere intentions. He could not imagine what other motives might induce a human being to make such a request.

"Do you really not know?" asked Lao-Tse calmly.

This composure somehow provoked the mandarin. He tried once more to persuade the Lama, but the latter replied with the same impersonal courtesy, stating that he must abide by what had already been said.

His confidence shaken, the visitor left. That same day a pedlar who had beautiful articles of Tibetan workmanship for sale was announced to Lao-Tse. Wuti was told to look at them. He was delighted by the beauty of the bowls, vases and little boxes. Nevertheless Lao-Tse felt disinclined to see the wares for himself. Only when he heard that the pedlar was very poor could he be persuaded.

At once he recognised the man who now entered the room: it was one of the late-night conspirators. Lao-Tse knew that he must be on his guard.

He deliberately touched none of the proffered articles, however much the pedlar urged him to do so. Finally he bought several items, only to be rid of the man.

Then from under his garment the latter produced a phial, ornately painted in gold and containing a watery fluid.

"I wish to present this costly little phial to the benefactor of the poor," he

173

said glibly. "It contains a wonderful fragrance that will delight your senses. You must smell it at once to tell me whether this scent is pleasing to you, or whether I should exchange it for another."

With these words he loosened the stopper of the phial, and held it out to Lao-Tse. But the latter took a step back, and said:

"It will suffice if you smell it! I will then know immediately what the fluid is like!"

The pedlar awkwardly declined to do so, asserting that the fragrance was too precious for his nose. That struck Wuti and Lai, who were present, and Lai went up to the man.

"When the Lama gives a command there is no refusal," he said, grasping the man by the hand that held the phial, and raising it to his nose.

As he did so, the loosened stopper fell to the floor. A foul odour emerged, causing Lai to close the phial hastily. He grabbed it just in time before the pedlar fell to the ground, dead. Wuti and Lai were deeply shaken. It had been an attempt on the Lama's life!

Wuti in particular could not stop reproaching himself, for it was he who had admitted the pedlar, against the will of the sage. Lao-Tse himself remained as calm as before.

"Remove the body," he commanded; and with regard to where the man and his belongings should be taken, he responded without hesitation:

"Let him and all his wares be taken to Moru-Tan. He will know what has to be done next."

Although neither could understand why just this mandarin was singled out for the purpose, they were used to unconditional obedience, for they knew that whatever Lao-Tse commanded was right. This command too they obeyed, all the while expecting a highly-indignant Moru-Tan to enquire what the dead man had to do with him. However, no question was asked. That gave them food for thought.

The mandarin was greatly alarmed when the dead man was brought to him, and he recognised him as one of his friends. If not even his confidant was able to bide his time, what was he yet to experience with the others? Fear and anxiety were his constant companions.

Meantime the days seemed to pass quietly, as usual. Lao-Tse had made no changes in his customary way of life. Every morning he conducted the

Hour of Worship in the newly-built Temple; several times each week he visited the Tibetan place of worship in the slum. During one of these visits, a man jostled against him. The Lama saw through him, and said in a clearly audible voice:

"My friend, give the dagger that you carry to my servant. It is not yet time to assassinate me."

The man was so terrified that he actually drew his hand from his garment and surrendered the curved, sharp-edged weapon to Lai. The crowd would have fallen upon him, but Lao-Tse protected him:

"He was acting on behalf of another; let him go. But you, my friend, tell this other man that it is foolish to attempt to lay hands on Lao-Tse so long as God protects him."

The man quickly disappeared, but he delivered his message.

Now Moru-Tan's dark soul was gripped by even greater fear. He would so have liked to postpone the next meeting, but that was impossible. Too many, who could not be reached, knew about it. And if he were to stay away from the meeting? Without him they would certainly decide on some foolish course of action. And were it to be discovered, they would most definitely not spare him. He must continue with what he himself had begun.

His anxiety drove him to one of the few remaining temples of the gods. He would buy peace of mind for himself with rich offerings. But in the very temple he encountered a demon more hideous than any he had ever yet seen. He was terrified; but then it seemed to present a good opportunity to harm Lao-Tse.

The mandarin presented himself to the Emperor; he complained that despite Lao-Tse's presence in Kiang-ning, demons could still commit their dreadful mischief. The Emperor asked for a description of where and how Moru-Tan had seen such a creature. Then he asked:

"Why were you afraid, Moru-Tan?"

Moru-Tan, greatly alarmed, swallowed a few times as if he found it hard to speak; then he replied:

"Why should I have been afraid? There is nothing that could cause me to fear."

But the words sounded rather pitiful.

175

"And yet you must have been afraid, Moru-Tan," persisted Hou-Chou. "Only fear produces demons."

"Then someone else must have been afraid," Moru-Tan maintained. "In that case it was a demon produced by someone else. That is how it must have been, for the demon did nothing to me. I was free to leave the temple."

The Emperor sighed. Still this fear of demons! One day, when he himself fully understood the connection, he would also be better able to take a stand against it. But now he had to say something, in order to get rid of Moru-Tan. What was there left to say?

At that moment Lao-Tse entered. Without asking what was going on here, and without being summoned by the Emperor, he turned to Moru-Tan, and said pleasantly:

"Turn round and look."

Almost against his will the mandarin did as he was bid. Even the Emperor looked in the direction indicated by Lao-Tse's pointing finger. From the dark corner of the room a huge demon was taking shape. It looked shaggy, although it seemed to be dressed in rich mandarin attire. Slowly it swayed to and fro; then it began to grin in a sinister way, and moved towards Moru-Tan.

"Lao-Tse, worthy Father, save me!" pleaded the latter, beside himself with fear. Hou-Chou watched and listened intently.

"Who has produced this demon?" asked the Lama, who could not help smiling a little. "I have only just entered the room; and surely you would not accuse our supreme Ruler of cowardly fear. Who then remains, Moru-Tan?"

The form advanced on the mandarin, whose teeth were chattering with terror.

"Throw off this senseless fear," commanded Lao-Tse, "and the demon will vanish."

"I am no longer afraid," lied the trembling man.

Now something which Lao-Tse had never witnessed before took place. A second demon emerged from the corner, joining the first. It looked as though it would overpower the first demon; then suddenly it too turned on the mandarin.

Now even Lao-Tse watched intently, completely forgetting the quaking

176

man, who began to scream frightfully. No such thing had ever happened in the Emperor's presence. The man had now lost all self-control. He threw himself on the floor, and pulled one of the thick mats over his head.

The forms immediately placed themselves on top of the mat, as if to deprive him of air. At that Lao-Tse ordered them to release their victim. When Moru-Tan heard the commanding voice, he regained some courage, and the demons faded accordingly.

The Emperor witnessed how they slowly fell back, lost their colours, and then seemed to dissolve into mist. At the same time Moru-Tan struggled to his feet, and slunk out of the room humiliated and ashamed.

Lao-Tse stepped to the window and opened it. They must have fresh air from the gardens, but at this moment he was reluctant to send for a servant. He had to be alone with the Emperor, for he knew that now Hou-Chou was deeply affected.

The latter was sitting, still quite stunned by what he had just experienced. Then slowly he began to ask:

"So it was fear after all that gave rise to the demon? I only said so because I had heard it from you, my friend, but I did not believe in my own words."

"That is also why they were of no avail. We must experience inwardly everything we say, otherwise it is worthless, and better left unsaid."

"Why did you come to me just at the right moment?" Hou-Chou went on. "And how could you know what we had been saying?"

"I saw you from my desk, O Emperor," returned Lao-Tse, as naturally as if such seeing from another part of the Palace were an everyday occurrence.

The Emperor stared at him. Several times already he had experienced that the Lama possessed special powers, but this knowledge verged on the supernatural.

Pacing the room slowly, Lao-Tse began to explain to the Emperor that being a Lama was not only an outward dignity, but that Divine gifts of grace were associated with it as well. One of these was the ability to see important happenings which might be taking place quite far away.

It was some time before the Emperor had understood, but then his friendship for Lao-Tse changed to such lofty reverence that he thought it impossible ever to continue a harmless association with the highly-gifted sage.

"What is an Emperor in comparison with you, O Lama?" he asked humbly.

But then he desired to know for what reason Moru-Tan could have been afraid.

"He is pursuing evil paths," replied Lao-Tse. "His conscience haunts him day and night; he is afraid of himself. That explains the manifestation of the demon in the temple. Here, however, it was his wish to harm me, and when I entered your room at that very moment he began to tremble, and the form appeared."

"But it came out of the corner of the room," the Emperor objected. "If it had emanated from him, it would have had to hover above him. Yet it arose behind him, and moved towards him."

"Even that can be readily explained," said Lao-Tse. "Whenever a person is fearful, any darkness increases his fear. Hence the demon comes forth where the person's anxieties adhere. But once it is created, the originator begins to fear the demon, and then the form moves towards him."

"Be that as it may, I am certain of one thing now: the demons are products of men, and must disappear the moment a courageous person confronts them," said Hou-Chou. "I would love to try my strength against them one day."

"There will be an opportunity for that too," said Lao-Tse, ending the conversation.

The Emperor was a little disappointed. He had expected the Lama to bring about the opportunity for him at once. But the latter, sensing the Emperor's thoughts, said:

"It is not a good thing to produce such opportunities at will."

Then he left the room just as he had entered it.

There were still a few days till full moon. Lao-Tse had implored God to show him what to do. After that he gave no further thought to the conspiracy. His manuscripts claimed a great deal of his attention. They were the writings of an old sage who had lived about two hundred years earlier, and were well worth snatching from oblivion.

Lao-Tse intended to record them in a more up-to-date language, thereby making them available to others as well. He rejoiced over such profound sayings as:

"If you do not take death seriously,
　　life will plunge you into seriousness.
But if you live with death in mind,
　　life will not be able to harm you.
With death in mind and that which follows it,
　　you will stride through life as one who lives it,
　　and feels not its severity."

Filled with this work, the last days also slipped by, and the night of the full moon approached. This time Lao-Tse planned to join the assembly in full view of all those present. Wuti accompanied him. Both wore loose cloaks over their robes.

Many people were already assembled when they reached the doorway of the tumbledown building. They went inside, together with others likewise demanding entrance. Anyone who came was heedlessly admitted.

In the same spacious room where the crowd had gathered previously, Lao-Tse mounted a slight elevation directly opposite the one on which Moru-Tan had stood before. It was far more difficult for the Lama to discern anything in the semi-darkness with his physical eyes than it had been for the eyes of his soul on the first evening.

But no sooner had this thought crossed his mind than the eyes of his soul were opened once again, and now he saw distinctly all that went on in the hall and in the human souls. He saw hatred and jealousy, envy and scorn, but also curiosity and indifference, as well as the craving for wealth and fame anticipated by some.

It filled him with loathing. Countless demons again polluted the air in the room. But he saw something else besides. Behind Moru-Tan's place stood entities who supported the walls. Even the beams carrying the ceiling were held by huge animistic beings.

Lao-Tse had never seen the like before, but he knew at once that these were God's animistic servants about whom Lie-Tse had told him. He gazed and marvelled. Something horrible was brewing, and he must not prevent it. Nor would he do so.

Now one of the animistic beings approached him, indicating that he and Wuti were not to leave the stone on which they were standing. Countless beings crowded round him. He knew that they were waiting to rescue him.

179

The room had slowly filled; there were even more people present than last time. Now Moru-Tan came also, richly attired, but pallid with fear. Lao-Tse saw that he was only waiting to speak in order to gain courage by speaking. Now the time had come; Moru-Tan began:

"Men! You have assembled to bring about a change in our country. It does not befit us to cringe under the fist of a stranger in our land, who exploits his power over our weakling Emperor in order to rule over our people through him. He has brought us tidings of a god who is said to be more powerful than our gods whom even our ancestors worshipped. Who apart from him has ever heard of such a god? This god has sprung from his thoughts ..."

For a few seconds he was unable to continue. A sudden thunder-clap interrupted him, a dull rumbling came from the earth.

He regained his composure as quickly as possible.

"Do you hear," he called loudly, to make his voice sound firm, "our gods resist the product of an imagination that lusts for power! We must not tolerate this god to be worshipped in our country."

"And why not?" Lao-Tse's clear voice asked from the other end of the room.

He had thrown off his cloak, and stood there robed in the whole glorious splendour of the Supreme Lama. It was as though all the light was concentrated on the gold embroideries, such was the radiance that emanated from him.

All heads were turned in his direction. But Moru-Tan, who saw his influence endangered, shouted:

"Out, you traitor! What business have you here? Who asked you to come today?"

"The God Whom you deny, Moru-Tan," was Lao-Tse's calm reply. Then he turned to the assembly:

"I knew that you would sit in judgment on me today. This was of no importance to me. I knew also that you would dare to pass judgment on the Emperor. That will bring you harm, for he is the best Ruler this Empire has ever had. But you have the audacity to impugn the Supreme One in thought: at that I cannot keep silence! As His servant I stand here and call upon you to leave this room before judgment overtakes you!"

The resonant voice had penetrated to the farthest corner of the room. Lao-Tse stood motionless, Wuti beside him. It would seem that any stone that was hurled could strike the two; but none dared to take one in his hand. Terror had seized upon their souls.

Spellbound by the great personality, a few actually began to leave the hall. The others attempted to hold them back. Moru-Tan became senseless with fear. He shrieked and roared:

"Destroy him who dares to defy me. Destroy him lest his God destroy us!"

What kind of words were these? The listeners did not understand them. Did he now believe after all in the God Whom he had just described as so powerless?

Lao-Tse's calm voice rang out again in the midst of the confusion, and all the clamour ceased:

"Men! God is above you! He, the Supreme One, will not suffer His creatures to raise themselves above Him in thought. It is His Will to put an end to idolatry and heresy. Let me tell you about Him. I will do so every day in the Temple. Let yourselves be guided! But now leave the room before the judgment overtakes you."

This time he was cut short by reverberating thunder, and the earth rumbled and quaked perceptibly. Great fear seized them all. They shouted and raved. And once again Moru-Tan raised his voice above all the clamour, bellowing:

"I curse you and your invisible God!"

At that the earth rocked. The walls collapsed; lightning flashed, and the prolonged rumble of thunder drowned the death-cries of the people.

Lao-Tse and Wuti, however, escaped into the open unharmed, with the help of the animistic beings.

Deeply shaken, they walked back to the city. Wuti was as though in a daze, while Lao-Tse pondered the working of God's Omnipotence.

As they approached the houses, it was evident that even here the earthquake had left its traces. Many an imposing building lay in ruins. In the slum-district through which they had to pass, whole streets of houses had been reduced to rubble. There was devastation and misery everywhere; agitated people wandered about, and the wounded reached in vain for help.

When he came upon those who were maimed or injured, Lao-Tse went to them, and bandaged them as best he could. In the absence of other material he tore up his and Wuti's underclothing. He proceeded in a calm, matter-of-fact way, as though he had come for this express purpose, and not as if he had just witnessed the most ghastly of all spectacles.

He urged Wuti to help him, in order to rouse him from his stupor. Then Wuti realised the great danger from which Lao-Tse had just escaped, and how the collapse of the old building had put an end to an evil conspiracy.

It was already daylight by the time the most pressing work had been done, and Lao-Tse walked towards the Palace.

"In what state shall we find it?" lamented Wuti. "It is such a tall building that it is bound to have suffered the most damage of all."

"I think that not a single stone will have been moved," replied Lao-Tse confidently. "What we experienced last night was a punishment. But Hou-Chou had no need of that."

The sage proved to be right. The Palace and the Temple of God were intact, but many other palaces had suffered severe damage. The worst of them was Moru-Tan's estate. A pile of ruins was all that remained of the imposing building; only a few servants had been able to save themselves; ruefully they reported that their master must be buried beneath the ruins.

Lao-Tse walked slowly among the palaces, finding the confirmation of what he had expected: the homes of all those involved in the conspiracy, who now lay dead under the stones out there, were so devastated that no one could say who had perished in the collapse.

"So it is God's Will that the conspiracy should remain a secret," mused Lao-Tse. "How wondrously every trace has been eradicated. No one will search out there for the hundreds of missing men. Everyone will assume that they died in their homes. Then I will not speak of it either. It is better so for Hou-Chou."

He could rely upon Wuti, after explaining the need for silence.

In the morning he called on the Emperor in order to hear from him about the night of horror. Hou-Chou was so full of the many different impressions that his Adviser's failure to discuss it did not strike him. Numerous reports of missing mandarins had already come in; Lao-Tse also mentioned a few other names of those he had seen in the country-house. Later that day these too were reported missing.

Great devastation had also been wrought in the largest temple of the gods still open. It was the one in which Moru-Tan had last worshipped. The idols were overturned, shattered and destroyed, causing much damage as they fell, even killing the high priest.

"Let us take it as a sign to proceed even more eagerly with the building of the Temples of God," suggested Lao-Tse, who realised that more must be done to avert a similar conspiracy.

The Emperor agreed, although he was unaware of the Lama's motive. He availed himself of the opportunity to have it proclaimed in all the streets that the earthquake had been a punishment from God, which had claimed many innocent victims along with the guilty. He had not consulted Lao-Tse about the wording, which seemed to him splendid.

But the Lama was not satisfied. He explained to Hou-Chou that in this way he was presuming to judge God's action: "God is Justice; it is not possible for innocent people to perish in the raging of the elements unless God has ordained it for some reason."

"But I cannot imagine how people like Moru-Tan and his friends could have deserved God's punishment," the Emperor said thoughtfully.

The Lama would have liked to supply the right answer, but he had an inner warning that the time had not yet come to speak of the conspiracy, so he said nothing.

In the days that followed, reports about the natural phenomenon came in also from surrounding towns. Nowhere had it been been so severe as in Kiang-ning, yet all places from which people had come to the meeting had suffered considerable damage.

There was work enough to be done everywhere, clearing away rubble, digging out the dead, and rebuilding. The numerous bodies were removed to the river bank, and burned all together. The remains were so mutilated and disfigured that identification was impossible. Therefore none were laid in a grotto, as was customary with the nobility.

Lao-Tse had nothing to do with this work. He was sitting once more over the manuscripts, eagerly deciphering and translating, immersed in the ancient wisdom brought to light there.

ONE DAY HIS SOUL quite consciously set out on another long journey. He felt himself removed to a monastery which he did not know, but whose name was at once made known to him. It was one of those in the lowlands, about which Lie-Tse had already been concerned.

He found the Lamas of this monastery assembled in a great hall, but not for worship. They were debating a proposal laid before them by the High Lama. He was an intense, younger man who argued his point of view most emphatically.

Lao-Tse's soul shuddered when he learned what was under discussion. The High Lama, Wi-Fu-Yang by name, thought the time had come for the monasteries to free themselves from the supremacy of the Mountain-monastery. They should inform Miang-Tse that they regarded themselves as having an equal right to self-government, and to establishing rules of their own. They were no longer prepared to be so cut off from the world.

God could be best served if they associated with those of different beliefs, who could be converted to the true faith. Moreover this monastery wished to abolish the time- and energy-consuming school. It wished to devote itself to studies of its own and to all kinds of arts, in which it would assume a pioneering lead. Generally speaking, Tibet was still far too backward. The progress enjoyed by others must be adopted. Monks should be sent to the Middle Kingdom to learn there.

Not all the Brothers shared the view of their Head Lama. The older ones all opposed it, but they were shouted down. Yet also younger Brothers spoke out, declaring that it was not good to violate hallowed rules. Conflicting opinions raged back and forth. Suddenly Lao-Tse perceived that one of the older Brothers was able to see him; so he communicated with him. The Brother, Ra-Chou, trembled with joy at what he was permitted to experience. He was seeing the highest of all Lamas! He could hear him speak! And now Lao-Tse was even instructing him to tell the Brothers what he had heard!

Ra-Chou raised his voice in the midst of the uproar, and silence ensued. Everyone had to listen to him, as if a command had gone out from within to every single soul.

"Brothers, hear me," called Ra-Chou, "Lao-Tse is among us!"

There were exclamations of surprise, of doubt, countered by cries of the greatest delight. Again the old man made himself heard.

"You must allow me to speak, Brothers. Lao-Tse commands it!"

Now all was hushed. Some eyes searched for the manifestation, but in vain; only Ra-Chou was blessed to perceive it. He now continued:

"Brothers, I, Lao-Tse, am shocked by your thoughts. I cannot comprehend that Tibetan Brothers can stray so far from the right path. The organisation of the Brotherhoods was wisely ordered. The Will of God is clearly discernible in it. And just as the circles of Brothers are structured in each of the monasteries, so are the monasteries connected inwardly, one with the other, one supporting and furthering the other.

"That you do not recognise this, that you no longer know it, is very sad. Nevertheless you have no right to undo with clumsy, impatient hands that which God has joined together. Whoever removes himself from the firm structure, be it an individual, be it a whole monastery, thus removes himself from communion with God, and falls prey to the Darkness. Lie-Tse, your departed master, feared for you; that is why, in accordance with the Will of God, he appointed me to keep you together.

"If you go to the unbelievers, you will defile yourselves, and thus do injury to your souls. The hands of him who touches the soot of lanterns will be blackened. Beware of these black hands, Brothers!

"I, Lao-Tse, have been sent to you in the hour of danger. In this you see how God guides you! I am with you, and demand that you now vote on who will joyfully and willingly remain in the monastery in accordance with the old rules, and who would leave it, to live in freedom as he pleases. But do not think that you can deceive me. Just as my soul can see all your bodies, so it can see and understand what goes on in your souls. Now decide!"

The Brothers responsible for such tasks set to work counting the votes. The result was that out of two hundred and seventeen Brothers, only five were against remaining. They were separated from the others, and placed against a wall of the hall. Wi-Fu-Yang, as High Lama, had been allowed to abstain from voting. Once again Lao-Tse's soul instructed Ra-Chou to lend his voice, and the old man joyfully complied.

"Brothers," he called into the crowd of silent listeners, "Brothers, you

185

have chosen! I rejoice over all those who have retreated from the disastrous path, even at the last moment. Set about your previous tasks as before, with fresh enthusiasm and deep humility, and God's Blessing will be with you.

"Wi-Fu-Yang is to come to me in Kiang-ning. I shall expect him in three months from today. He is to set out tomorrow at sunrise. God Himself will send him guides to escort him in safety.

"But the five Brothers who have chosen freedom shall have it. Take their robes from them, and dress them in the things you have at hand for beggars and the poor. They are to leave the monastery, and henceforth not to show themselves to any of the Brothers!"

And Wi-Fu-Yang rose, and handed over the direction of the monastery for the duration of his absence to one of the other Lamas, who ensured that the five renegades were expelled that same night. Wi-Fu-Yang, however, set out at sunrise on his long journey to the capital of the Middle Kingdom.

Lao-Tse had now experienced how everything promised to him by Lie-Tse was literally fulfilled. He was able to participate in what was happening in Tibet without having to forsake his duties in the Imperial Palace. He became ever more deeply absorbed in worship of the Almighty, Eternal God.

SEVERAL DAYS LATER as Lao-Tse was strolling in the garden, he listened to the song of a little bird which seemed to be trying to tell him something. Over and over again the same notes fell upon his ears. They grew ever more urgent, but the Lama could not understand them.

"Little feathered messenger," he said warmly, "what tidings have you for me?" The same notes answered him, filled with such sweetness that it seemed the little songster's throat was about to burst.

"I do not understand you, little bird," said the Lama regretfully. "You are so beautiful, and have such a lovely voice. Are you trying to proclaim the Greatness of God to me through yourself?"

Abruptly the notes broke off, the bird flew away. Servants came running to summon Lao-Tse to the Emperor. Something extraordinary had happened. The servants would have liked to report precipitately what they knew, but Lao-Tse gave them no opportunity. What he was to learn he would hear from Hou-Chou himself. Kind-hearted as he was to all under him, he always drew a line to keep familiarities at bay.

The Emperor was in the so-called government-chamber, a huge hall in which the splendid throne was the sole adornment.

The hall was filled with an excited crowd, pressing forward in the direction of the throne, from which it was held back by a heavy red cord running across the width of the hall through two gilded dragons' mouths at the walls, where it was also held by servants.

Willingly the crowd made way for Lao-Tse as he entered. It was as though everyone sensed that calm would now prevail over the excitement, and clarity would replace confusion. The Lama, with his buoyant, not at all ceremonious step, went up to the red cord, which was lowered at a sign from the Emperor, to allow him to step over it. Hou-Chou motioned his friend to his side. One of the mandarins stepped forward and called for complete silence. The Emperor wished to speak; anyone who so much as uttered a single uninvited word would be removed from the hall.

The babel of voices ceased; the Ruler spoke. Although he addressed himself only to Lao-Tse, he spoke so clearly that all those present were able to hear him.

"A strange thing has happened, O Lama of all Lamas," Hou-Chou began. "Three men were found after the earthquake, and though still alive, they were so interlocked that they could not be separated from each other. It was assumed that they were overtaken by the event out-of-doors, and had become deranged. The strangest thing is that they are of three different classes: a mandarin, a priest and a beggar!"

The Emperor paused for a moment. But to Lao-Tse it was immediately clear that these three men must have escaped the collapse of the country-house. Had God allowed them to be saved in order to bear witness? Was that why he, Lao-Tse, had been obliged to keep silence about what had taken place? Now the Monarch continued:

"The unfortunates were cared for in the best possible way. Eventually a physician gave them a sleeping draught, and while they slept their cramped limbs relaxed. Last night they recovered their speech. But their story is so fantastic that it might be regarded as a delusion. I have decided to question the men myself. They are just being brought hither."

187

Again the crowd stirred restlessly, but everywhere the servants raised their curiously-shaped staffs as a sign that each individual was keenly watched. Thus silence was restored.

Servants entered from a side door with the three rescued men. They stood before the throne, by the red cord. Their faces were pale, all reflecting a seriousness which guaranteed that they would speak only the plain truth. Lao-Tse recognised all three. They were the ones who had tried to leave the hall after his first appeal.

The Emperor addressed them kindly.

"You must be weak, friends. Sit down on the mat; you can answer from there also."

This was what attracted Lao-Tse to Hou-Chou again and again: the humanity and goodness which no Emperor before him had displayed. The present Monarch never thought of himself, he was only concerned about his people ... and yet it had been possible for such an uprising to be plotted!

The mandarin and the priest sat down on their heels and looked up gratefully at the Emperor; the beggar remained standing, supporting himself only on the cord. That too gave food for thought to Lao-Tse, who always saw the underlying meaning in everything.

In response to the Emperor's command to relate how they were caught in the earthquake, they looked at each other as if trying to find the answer to a question that occupied them all. The mandarin and the priest looked away; but the beggar regarded the enquirer with wide-open eyes and said:

"Forgive me, O Emperor, that I, your most unworthy servant, dare to speak here. In the horror of the event I have found God, the Only True One, the Supreme One. He bids my soul tell you the truth. But you must have patience; for my story is long."

Hou-Chou turned to the other two.

"I approve that this one should speak, but is it not for you to report to me in his stead?"

They maintained an embarrassed silence. So he motioned the beggar to begin. He described how he had been prompted by others to attend a meeting in Moru-Tan's country-house. The listeners were unable to suppress a cry of surprise, but the servants raised their staffs, and there was silence.

Although the beggar's description of that first meeting was awkward, it was indeed vivid. He omitted nothing of importance, neither the proposed violent overthrow of Lao-Tse, nor the audacious, excited demand for the abdication of the Emperor.

A shadow passed over Hou-Chou's open countenance, but he did not interrupt the speaker, who began to tell of the second meeting. Now even the Emperor was as amazed as were all those present. Lao-Tse had attended the meeting? Lao-Tse had knowingly ventured into the midst of his opponents? The Lama had spoken?

"Thereupon the three of us and a few others made for the exit," the beggar concluded, "for the Lama of all Lamas had said that we should leave the hall before God's Judgment should come. But the people standing around us would not allow us to retreat. Only by clinging firmly to one another did we three, complete strangers to each other, manage to escape their clutches and get outside. We tumbled down a hill and remained there, senseless, until we were found the following morning. What happened in the hall I cannot tell."

The Emperor's eyes sought Lao-Tse, who stood beside him in his usual calm manner.

"Can you tell us more, my friend?" he addressed him, completely forgetting that he was using this familiar form in the hearing of all.

But before the Lama could speak, the Emperor sought confirmation of the truth of the beggar's statement. He turned with this question to the mandarin and the priest, who both nodded with downcast eyes. But after a moment's thought the mandarin said:

"I realise that I am certain of the silken cord, whether I keep silent or speak; for only with my life can I atone for taking part in the conspiracy. Then at least I shall not depart in a cowardly way; what the beggar has said is literally true! Everything happened just as he has described it."

The Emperor threw him a kindly glance. Then Lao-Tse recounted what else had taken place. When he told of Moru-Tan's curse, there were cries of horror everywhere in the hall. Those present listened with the greatest excitement to the end of the ghastly drama.

When the Lama had finished, the Emperor was silent for a long time. Then he began:

"So what I perceived intuitively about the earthquake being a judgment of God was right! But it was also God's protection for our country. Picture to yourselves the misery into which a war of the masses, one against the other, would have plunged the whole people.

"You had no need to resort to such violent measures to remove me. I will go as soon as you demand it. The Goodness of God has prevented war and rebellion in the heart of our country, in that the Almighty killed the insurgents with a single blow.

"You three, who have escaped in order to bear witness, shall be allowed to go your way, free and unhindered. The poor man will be given land and a dwelling, work and assistance as a reward for his honesty. You, a nobleman of my Realm, may live as before, but do not forget that above you is the Omniscience of God. You, the priest, are to give up your office, for you lack all that is needful to be a servant of God. The idolaters shall vanish from this land if I continue as its Ruler.

"I shall issue a proclamation to all the people. They must themselves decide whom they wish to have as their Ruler in future. And now go, all of you, and thank God with me for His helping Mercy!"

It took a long time for the hall to empty. The crowd was slow to leave the place where it had heard such astonishing things. With a few mandarins and Lao-Tse, the Emperor left through a side door for his apartments. Here he asked to be left alone with the Lama.

"My friend, why have you kept all this from me?" he asked urgently.

"God enjoined silence upon me. I did not understand why this had to be. Today the reason for it became clear: had I told you what had happened, it would not have made so deep an impression. Besides, the masses would have disputed the likelihood of such a conspiracy. In the way you learned of it today, representatives of all the classes also heard the account, and satisfied themselves that it was based on truth."

And now Lao-Tse related everything he had experienced at the first meeting, and what he saw and heard at the second. Hou-Chou found only words of praise and gratitude. It seemed inconceivable to the Ruler that he could have been mistaken in Moru-Tan right up to the last moment.

"Now I shall no longer trust anyone," he averred, and he was in earnest about it. But Lao-Tse rebuked him, and said:

"Just because a few in whom you trusted failed you, why would you reject them all? Consider, Hou-Chou, how the Supreme One deals with us human beings!"

"He is Omniscient, but how am I to know whom to trust?"

"Do you not have me by your side to warn you? And if I am forbidden to bring something to your attention in advance, then you are meant to learn from the experiences, and God's protection will be upon you."

Slowly calm returned to the Palace and the city, and not even the Emperor's announcement of a plebiscite on his possible abdication could excite the people. Those who had been discontented were dead, and the others never even considered whether a different kind of rule might possibly be advantageous.

The people decided unanimously in favour of Hou-Chou's continuing to rule. A few however seized the opportunity to laud the Emperor, and thank him for the leadership he had given them. But Hou-Chou had become so suspicious that Lao-Tse first had to confirm that these declarations flowed from grateful hearts, before Hou-Chou dared to rejoice over them.

IT HAD BEEN HOT and dry for some time. The rice and other grains dried on the stalk before they could come into ear. The cattle found but meagre food. The people were threatened with starvation at the time of harvest. And the carefree, happy-go-lucky inhabitants of the vast Realm were roused from their unconcern, and yielded to despair.

Hou-Chou himself had given it no attention, and his counsellors had been just as carefree as the people. For as long as they could remember, the harvests had always been adequate. It did not occur to them that things might one day be different.

Now the distress was great, and while many people succumbed to dull brooding, others were seized by a great fury, which increased from day to day.

The Emperor summoned his counsellors and asked for suggestions on how to alleviate the misery. What they suggested was useless; they spent themselves in lamentations and complaints. The only recommendation on which a final decision was to be made was that every fifth man should emi-

191

grate with his wife and children. But where to? That was left to himself, but he must leave the Middle Kingdom.

Although most of the counsellors agreed enthusiastically with this proposal, no one knew how it was to be implemented. How was it to be known in the interior whether those expelled from the country were actually leaving it, or settling down somewhere else? Then another counsellor suggested that a law be enacted by which the sick and infirm should be given no more food.

Angrily Hou-Chou interrupted him. In thunderous words he charged the last speaker with inhumanity, censured the incompetence of his counsellors and dismissed them all in total displeasure. Left alone with Lao-Tse, he turned to him, still greatly agitated:

"And you, my friend, why do you say nothing? You see my plight, which is that of the entire people, and yet you can remain silent? Are you struck dumb with the impossibility of any help?"

"I am silent, O Emperor, because the Supreme One has commanded it. He will not have His Counsel mixed with the foolish deliberations of men. Long ago God showed me how to remedy the affliction; but I had to keep silence so that the people could recognise that without the help of the Supreme One they are as nothing."

Hardly had Lao-Tse begun to speak than the Emperor's agitation subsided. The calm and tranquillity which had become so familiar to him re-entered his heart. He listened attentively. Lao-Tse told how, at the Behest of the Most High, he had arranged for grain, tea and fruit to be purchased in large quantities in the plains of Tibet, where there was a particularly good harvest that year. The provisions had been placed in store.

The people must be divided into groups in accordance with the provinces which already divided the land.

In each province there should be twenty-four groups, with leaders to supervise each. These leaders must ascertain without delay the number of people in their group and the quantity of food available. Any deficiency would then be made up from the supplies in stock which Hai-Tan was even now administering with great skill.

The Emperor was filled with joy as he listened, but he had certain misgivings.

"Many sections of our population are poor. How will they be able to afford the food? And I have no means of compelling the rich to pay for the poor."

"Do you think, Hou-Chou, that when the Supreme One deigns to reveal a plan to human beings, it would be flawed or inconsistent? Should He, Who surveys everything, not have thought of this as well?"

"It is as you say," Hou-Chou conceded, shamefaced. "Tell me what the Supreme One demands of us, so that here too we may find a way."

"The way is very simple. The food will not have to be paid for with money, but in kind from our white earth, kaolin. Wherever I bought provisions, I promised articles made of kaolin in return: bowls, vases, utensils for food and drink, as well as ornamental objects. Everything that must now be produced has been listed. Places where these things will be made must be established in every province.

"He who is too poor to buy food must work for it. This will also check idleness, which unfortunately is a widespread evil among our people. After these times of want we shall have human beings who are more cheerful and happy."

Now purest joy entered the Ruler's heart. He thanked the Supreme One fervently from deep within, and repeated:

"Truly it is easy to be Emperor when God is one's Helper!"

Once Hou-Chou knew what he had to do, it was always easy for him to initiate action. He was especially gifted in large-scale planning, and was not without help from above. Thus within a short time the groups were formed, the leaders chosen and appointed to their posts; and workshops for the processing of kaolin were set up all over the country.

On Lao-Tse's advice each workshop undertook a different kind of manufacture. One produced only shallow dishes, another tall vessels, yet another made the much-sought-after dragon-figures, and other things besides. Whoever wanted work found it.

But then came reports from almost everywhere that countless women had no male breadwinner. So Lao-Tse decreed that the manufactured articles should be entrusted to the women for painting. They were more nimble-fingered for doing brushwork.

Up to now the articles had been painted with only a few colourful strokes, but now they were covered with quaint little figures, flowers, tendrils, pictures of animals or landscapes, according to the skill of the artist. Each woman was allowed to paint only what she undertook in the first place. This brought about a more highly developed skill and a rich flow of ideas, so that the standard of performance constantly improved.

Already everyone seemed to be well provided for, when reports came from the south-western part of the Empire that no more kaolin earth was to be found. Their earth did not contain it, and the other provinces were unwilling to part with any. At that Lao-Tse urged the people to make use of the vast supplies of silk which they had in reserve. They should try to decorate the plain fabrics with the brush, then send their handiwork to him; he would see that a market was found for it.

And find it he did. With the assistance of the Brothers in the Tibetan monasteries, he sent the silk fabrics far and wide into the great neighbouring country.

Amid all the brisk activity, the dreaded famine passed unnoticed by many. Certainly some who would not work had to pay for their folly with their lives, but every such death merely spurred the others on to renewed efforts.

When seed-time came, many toiling hands were absent from the workshops, since there was much to be done in the fields, but the others worked all the more keenly. This they did because on the one hand, until the harvest was in, they still had to earn their food, and on the other, because they had found joy and happiness in the work.

The silk-growers also set about their activities with increased diligence. The entire population of the Middle Kingdom had received an impetus; they had become active, and thereby more contented.

AT THAT TIME Lao-Tse's soul resumed its wanderings. Now it visited the monasteries in Tibet, now swung itself to distant regions, where it absorbed wondrous things. It was granted the gift of seeing and speaking with the animistic beings once worshipped by the people as gods, until they had made caricatures of them.

From these beings his soul learned a great deal; its comprehension of the

Divine, but also of the human, grew steadily. The animistic beings who had once guided the people knew the good which slumbered within them, but was overgrown with Darkness; and they showed Lao-Tse how he could set free this light within the souls, how he could gain access for the Light from above.

When Lao-Tse set out on such soul-wanderings in the quiet hours of the night, he usually remained by himself in the daytime. But if he had to go among men, everyone intuitively perceived the purity that emanated from the Lama. His clear features reflected a childlike serenity, his words breathed peace and harmony, and his counsel was helpful and kind.

The Emperor's son, Han, matured under his wise guidance into an intelligent, strong human being, who promised to become just as good a ruler as his father one day. He learned with ease, and was interested in everything.

Lao-Tse made use of this to see that he learned even such things as he would not need to carry out when he was Emperor, but would nevertheless have to judge. Once he let him work for some months in a nearby kaolin workshop, and great was the rejoicing when the works of the young Prince were specially highly commended.

Through this activity Han came into close contact with all levels of the population. The artist who produced the designs for manufacturing the wares was no more of a stranger to him than the foreman who received the painted articles from the women, or the potter who turned the dishes and bowls.

At first there was no lack of noblemen who considered it their duty to draw the Emperor's attention to these activities. They regarded it as quite unworthy of an Emperor's son to mingle in this way with working people. But Hou-Chou advised them to occupy their thoughts with other things. Han was being educated according to the Will of God, which no one understood better than the Lama of all Lamas.

He told Lao-Tse nothing of these conversations, but the sage knew of them in any case, and was grateful to the Emperor for making things easier for him here too.

As soon as Han was old enough to be able to judge what he saw and experienced, Lao-Tse took him to the slum. At first the childlike pleasure in being disguised and remaining unrecognised took precedence with the

195

Prince, but then his soul was affected, and his spirit preoccupied with ways and means of providing relief.

How was such wretched poverty possible, side by side with the enormous wealth that prevailed in the palaces all round the Imperial Palace! In everything that Han wished to undertake for giving real assistance to the poor, he was supported by his teacher and his father. But they never interfered, he always had to devise his own plans, and to find the means of executing them. If he went to them later for advice, they were ready to help him.

Three younger brothers grew up beside Han at the Imperial Court. They were carefully educated by good teachers, and Lao-Tse supervised their instruction. He had no time for more.

Again and again his soul was called to Tibet, where first one thing, then another, had to be attended to. Once he even had to ride there personally to look after matters. That was when Miang-Tse, although he was still young, was called away to enter the Eternal Gardens.

The tidings of this received by Lao-Tse's soul came in such good time that he arrived at the Mountain-monastery on the day before the death of the High Lama. His coming forestalled great complications, for contrary to usual practices, the dying High Lama had not appointed his successor.

Voices were heard saying that now, for once, another monastery was entitled to the leadership. The Brotherhood on the Mountain would not relinquish its privilege. Delegates came from other monasteries to advance their views. All this was cut short by the arrival of Lao-Tse.

With unequalled dignity he took the reins of government firmly in hand. No one would have dared to dispute his right to do so. Cordially but firmly, he sent the visiting Brothers home, after telling the assembled group in one of the halls why it was the Will of God that just this monastery should remain the leading one.

"Not without good reason is it situated on the Mountain, higher up than all other monasteries. As it towers above you physically, so also spiritually. Customs and practices have remained purest here, but still more important is the connection with the Supreme One which is stronger here than elsewhere. Moreover I also have emerged from this monastery. So long as I live, there shall be no High Lama from another Brotherhood."

They had no choice but to go home. The Lama of all Lamas however had made such a deep impression on them that they did not even think of complaining.

Then Lao-Tse went to the bedside of Miang-Tse, who had awaited him with longing. He greeted Miang-Tse kindly and said:

"Brother, I had first to set things to rights about you, before I could help your soul to sever its earthly ties."

And Miang-Tse, who had not uttered a word for weeks, so that all the Brothers believed him to be bereft of speech, opened his mouth, and said clearly and audibly:

"What you say is true, High Sage, that you must release my soul. Heavy are the ties in which it has become entangled. I cannot enter into the Eternal Gardens unless you help me."

Even before his departure from Kiang-ning, Lao-Tse had seen what oppressed the High Lama, but he wished to hear it from his own lips, so as not to deprive him of the blessing of unburdening himself.

And Miang-Tse confessed that he had been proud of his office, that he had often carried out his duties without seeking God's Counsel or Command. In the awareness of his superiority over others he had often arbitrarily oppressed Brothers, and troubled their souls.

Lao-Tse listened in silence. He felt sorry for the Brother, who had fallen prey to human conceit. And he had not been allowed to warn him. God Himself had warned Miang-Tse through a number of occurrences, which however the deluded one did not heed.

So he now had to live through his deeds to the bitter end, had to see with how many fetters he had shackled himself, and now had to recognise his own inability to sever even one. But Lao-Tse's soul knew that once the very last thing had been said and confessed he was permitted to bring comfort and help. Therefore he now also encouraged the dying man to continue speaking: "Do you know why you are called away from your post and your work so soon, Miang-Tse?"

"My wrong actions were not pleasing to God, that is why He calls me away."

"But what was the immediate cause of your illness? Do you know, Brother?"

To make this last confession was hard for the High Lama. Had he suspected that Lao-Tse was well aware of this too, it would have been easier for him to speak. But that very knowledge was not to be his. To stoop so low in the face of his conceit was part of his redemption.

At last he was able to break the silence that had seemed to embrace him ever more firmly.

"I will confess, O Lama of all Lamas," he groaned. "But the confession will cost me my life."

Again silence, heavy, oppressive silence. Lao-Tse did not say a word, but he removed the chain with the emblem of the Lama from his neck, and laid it on the breast of the heavily breathing man.

"Brother," the latter cried out enraptured, "this you do for me! Nothing will be difficult for me now."

And without faltering he confessed that he had wanted to discover how far his power as High Lama extended. He succeeded in all kinds of experiments. He was able to heal the sick by the laying on of hands. The fact that they later succumbed to even worse illnesses he blamed on their sinfulness, instead of seeking the fault in himself. He was able to decipher writings which until then had been accessible to none.

All that had induced him to make ever wilder experiments. One day strangers, erudite men from the country in the west, came to him. He secretly admitted them to the monastery in order to learn from them. It did not occur to him to ask God for permission. He thought that if he learned many new things it would benefit the monastery and the whole of Tibet.

The men had showed him many things, but above all they instructed him in the art of meditation. They taught him to send his soul consciously out of the body. And so he had appeared in the cells of the Brothers, spying upon what they did and thought, and becoming more and more arrogant.

A few months ago the strangers had returned to their homeland, laden with valuable gifts. Then, without their help, he had conducted ever more daring experiments. One night he was about to send his soul to the Eternal Gardens, to look for Lie-Tse, and to show him that he was capable of more than the former High Lama. And then Lie-Tse had actually appeared to him. Not as an admirer, but as a severe judge, he had stepped before him, and said:

"You fool, who use the powers given to you by God for trifling and to gratify your conceit, know that you could have attained to far greater heights in prayer than you have now done in your recklessness. You are still at the outermost boundary of the second Creation. You will never reach the first unless you change your whole life from the ground up. The Supreme One will call you away, that you may be purified; after that you may make a fresh attempt to ascend, but it will not again be made so easy for you."

Exhausted, the speaker fell back silent, the tears coursing down his emaciated face.

Lao-Tse was deeply moved. Although he had more or less known everything, it gripped him to hear it from the lips of the one who had gone astray.

"Miang-Tse, your path is marked out for you. What Lie-Tse has told you about it is the Will of God, the Supreme One. You are permitted to begin once more the ascent to the Eternal Gardens, and your present experience will be branded in your soul, warning you against every wrong step. You may confidently pass over to where purification awaits you, whence you will be allowed to set out on your new pilgrimage."

"I cannot go," Miang-Tse wept, "for I have angered God too deeply. Consider, Lao-Tse: to us Lamas Divine Power is granted to a far greater extent than to other human beings. And this gift of grace I have disregarded and abused!"

The words died away in agonised weeping. But Lao-Tse bent over the fallen Brother, grasped his burning hand and said gently: "What were you once permitted to tell the sinner who repented with all his heart? Miang-Tse, what were the holy words decreed by God Himself?"

The Lama of all Lamas straightened himself, and held his right hand over the dying man:

"Brother, you have sinned. Brother, you repent. As deep as is your repentance, so lofty is the Grace of God. In His Name I sever your bonds. May the core of your being rise upwards in purity, and atone for all that encumbers it. Thereafter begin your course anew in the Power of the Supreme One, Who does not close the gate to betterment on any who repent. Go in peace!"

"Lord God, Thou Supreme One, I thank Thee," were the words wrung from the lips of Miang-Tse; then his soul departed.

It was the second death experienced by Lao-Tse in this monastery. How different was the passing of these two! What would his own departure be like one day?

He stood in prayer by the bedside for a long time; then he called the Brothers. They did not need to know about the transgressions of their leader.

But he himself retired to the guest-rooms prepared for him, to seek God's Will in prayer. Who should be the successor?

And it was given to him to reach Lie-Tse in one of the Luminous Gardens; this filled him with great happiness. His old teacher said:

"You would like to know whom you should appoint as High Lama. Make the choice yourself!"

And it was as though a ray penetrated downwards, its brilliance seeming to cleave through the Universe, but its trail remaining like a path of light. Following the ray, Lao-Tse looked down.

There he saw the Lamas assembled in the monastery, praying for the departed one; above each one stood the picture of his spirit. In the main they were beautiful pictures, pure and clear. Only a few were clouded. But one picture outshone all the others. Spontaneously Lao-Tse said:

"I wish to choose this one here, my father."

"That is Fu-Yang, who was your teacher for a short time. You have made the right choice."

The ray faded. The picture vanished, but Lao-Tse's spirit still tarried consciously in the Garden beside Lie-Tse, who said to his former pupil:

"When you have settled everything in the monastery, ride back swiftly to Kiang-ning, where the second part of your task awaits you. You are to direct your people to good, helpful spirits; they cannot be without them. In their childlikeness they will find support in the animistic servants of God the Lord."

"Father, it seems to me that I have not yet rightly fulfilled the first task," lamented Lao-Tse's soul. "True, I have been able to reduce fear and dread; true, I have destroyed the worship of demons by proving them to be the products of evil human thinking, but this has not disposed of them!"

"You have done enough. By fulfilling the second task, the first will also benefit. Direct the human thoughts to the good, then the bad will have no place!"

The next day Lao-Tse revealed to the assembled Lamas, and thereafter to all the Brothers, that in accordance with the Eternal Will of God, Fu-Yang, from that day Fu-Tse, was chosen to be the High Lama.

All rejoiced, for the aged man was popular with students and Brothers. Yet he himself could not understand that it was really he who was appointed to this high office; he asked Lao-Tse to consider whether he had understood the name aright. Fu-Hi-Yang was far better qualified than he.

But when Lao-Tse assured him that no error was possible, he assumed the duties of his office with devout earnestness, and was allowed to discharge them for many years.

After the remains of Miang-Tse had been buried with dignity, though with neither the splendour nor the love that once accompanied Lie-Tse to the grave, the Lama of all Lamas set out for the Middle Kingdom.

Again he had had deeply moving experiences. In the course of the ride he let the memories pass through his soul. But then he was filled with the thought of his second task. How was he to set about telling his people of the animistic servants of God?

He implored the Supreme One to show him the way, and full of good cheer rode into Kiang-ning.

During his absence, all kinds of things had happened here to cause trouble for Hou-Chou. He missed Lao-Tse's advice sorely, although he was aware that this meant a time of testing for him personally. He must learn by himself to seek connection with God. Hitherto he had always only worshipped the Supreme One. He had always done what God required of him through the mouth of the Lama; now he must endeavour to discover the Will of God for himself.

Lao-Tse's ride to Tibet was not kept secret. With all the honours due to him, the Lama had ridden away accompanied by a great retinue. No one knew when he would return. In any case he would be away for months; this time had to be made good use of. And the priests of the few remaining temples of gods in and around Kiang-ning met with former priests and secret enemies of the Lama, to deliberate on how to attain power and esteem in the Realm once more.

Some called attention to Moru-Tan's horrible fate, but they were shouted down. Moru-Tan had cursed the new God; they would not do that, they simply wanted to help the old gods to regain their rightful places, and thereby put themselves in the lead.

One suggestion led to another. Some were carried out, bringing unrest among the population. Two workshop foremen were won over. One day these two declared that henceforth they would only employ workers who before the day's work began would pray to the idols set up in the ante-room.

At first those who were in earnest about their faith refused to do this. But after only a few weeks they felt acutely the lack of their earnings; and to avoid starvation together with their wives and children, they submitted.

Although the enemies appeared to have met with success in this way, they realised that it was not permanent. They had not won back the hearts of the renegades, and rumours of what they had done spread abroad and aroused indignation everywhere. They made no further attempts to win over other foremen.

With promises of great gifts, they tried to induce the poor who still remained faithful to the gods to win back people of their own kind to the old belief. They offered a reward for every penitent soul. But only a few made any effort to gain the reward, and these few were opposed by those whom they attempted to persuade.

So strong was the opposition that it made the others think. They sought to discover what bound the faithful so firmly to God. In this way they heard – perhaps for the first time – of the blessing wrought by that faith. And instead of leading souls back to the gods, they themselves renounced the old belief.

Suddenly one of the priests thought of a unique scheme. They would win over Prince Han. Once they had the future Emperor under their control, they could impose their conditions.

At first they believed that he could be enticed with the help of a very beautiful girl whom they set in his way. However the Prince, who was mature beyond his years, had no taste for any of the inducements offered him. On the contrary, he simply sent away the servants who offered to bring him in contact with the girl.

He wanted to tell his father about the incident, but met him at an awkward moment. Hou-Chou had just received news of what the workshop supervisors had attempted, and was very disturbed. Han had no wish to burden his father still further, and so kept quiet.

But the opponents were all the more determined. If the Prince could not be won over by such means, they must resort to force. Accompanied by just one servant, Han often strolled through the gardens on clear nights to observe the movement of the stars.

One day his loyal servant unaccountably fell ill, and had to be replaced by another. This one however was in the service of the priests, and disclosed his master's every move to them. Hence it was possible for the garden gate to be left open one night, and for a troop of armed men to fall upon the Prince and drag him away. To avert suspicion, the servant was also taken.

This took place on the very night when Lao-Tse arrived in Kiang-ning. No one knew of his return. Just as he was about to ride through the great gate with his retinue, he saw a picture before him: Prince Han, apparently lifeless, being carried towards the river. Whatever could have happened? A fervent prayer to God filled him with calm.

He turned his horse round, calling to his companions to follow him, but to let the pack-animals and their attendants wait outside the gate; then at a gallop he took the shortest route to the river. In spirit he saw the place that he had to reach if he was to forestall the evildoers. There in the moonlight lay a great vessel, the kind used by traders to transport heavy cargo.

"Some of you must take possession of the ship as silently as possible," he commanded in a whisper.

Lai and a number of servants leapt from their horses, and rushed on to the ship. The scoundrels had been so confident that they had left only two oarsmen on guard. These were quickly overpowered, gagged and bound, and Lao-Tse's servants hid behind crates and hawsers.

Meanwhile the Lama had told some of his companions what he feared, and it was decided that half of them should ride back towards the city by a roundabout route, to intercept the villains from the rear.

But no sooner had they left than the troop approached the river-bank, carrying their precious booty. They had not dared to ride for fear of attracting attention. But their journey on foot was arduous, and their load by no means light. So they approached the ship at last in a state of exhaustion.

Lao-Tse rode towards them, at first alone.

When they recognised him the men were frightened, and recklessly dropped their cumbersome load. As a result Prince Han regained consciousness, and his astonished gaze followed what now took place.

Unarmed, the Lama of all Lamas stood erect before the evildoers, who grasped their weapons with lightning speed.

With a movement of his hand the Lama repulsed them.

"What are you doing, you misguided men?" he addressed them, but his voice did not have the usual gentle tone; it spat forth anger. "Do not dare to touch me! The God Whose servant I am would turn every weapon against yourselves."

They stood before him dumbfounded, letting their arms and weapons fall. Only one crept quietly behind the Lama, and tried to attack him from behind. But when Lao-Tse uttered the words that every weapon would turn against its bearer, the man stumbled and fell upon his curved dagger.

He lay dead on the ground, and Lao-Tse stepped aside so that the others could see.

"Behold how he condemned himself! Any one of you who dares to touch me will fare likewise."

They were all paralysed with horror, let themselves be bound, and were taken back to the city by the servants and held in custody at the Imperial Palace. The Lama, however, turned to the Prince, who still hardly dared to believe in his rescue.

Even before his disappearance was noticed in the Palace, Prince Han was back in his apartments, trying to recall how the capture and the rescue had come about.

Now Lao-Tse knew why Lie-Tse had insisted so urgently on his speedy return.

The following morning rumours about the events of the night coursed throughout the city. Hou-Chou was aghast when he heard of his opponents' infamous scheme, which had been thwarted by Lao-Tse's timely appearance. He could not understand how the Lama had obtained knowledge of the outrage. Lao-Tse had great trouble in making the Emperor understand that it was only the connection with the Light-world that made such things possible.

The Emperor then wished the inhabitants of the city to know what had been planned, and how it was thwarted. He summoned his dignitaries and had it all recounted to them. Then he arranged for a great reception to be held in the Palace. Anyone who was decently dressed was allowed to attend these events. Always a great multitude thronged to them, as it was customary for the Ruler to address his people on such occasions.

This time, however, there were too many for all to find a place in the throne-room. The officials responsible for supervising the ceremonies stood perplexed before the crowd. Finally they decided to inform the Emperor, for they dared not simply send away half of the throng. When they came before Hou-Chou to make their report, he called out to them:

"Lose no time in idle talk. Have the walls of the next room removed, and place the throne in the centre – that will suffice."

Indeed it did suffice to accommodate the masses, but the officials were anxious about the Emperor's safety on the throne; there was no way of knowing what the opponents were scheming. But Hou-Chou dismissed these misgivings.

"At receptions I am as safe as if surrounded by bodyguards. The barrier of the red cord is enough, as it was for all my predecessors."

The officials withdrew hastily to have everything made ready. To them this Emperor, who issued instructions without their having to ask, was uncanny.

A few hours later Hou-Chou, in magnificent golden attire, was seated upon the throne. Around and behind him stood his counsellors, foremost among them Lao-Tse.

Now the offenders were brought in, bound but not gagged. A row of soldiers separated them from those in attendance. Then Prince Han entered the hall and took his place near the Emperor. Everything proceeded slowly, with utter solemnity. The servants suppressed any disturbance with their strange curved staves, which enabled them to seize by the neck from a distance anyone who displeased them, and pull him out.

A mandarin went up to the red cord and announced that the Emperor wished to address his people. Then Hou-Chou began. He described how the opponents of the new faith had made use of Lao-Tse's absence to thrust themselves to the forefront again. To that end no means was too infamous for them, indeed they even attacked the person of the Successor to the Imperial Throne. The plot would have been successful if the Supreme One Himself had not intervened. Then the mandarin called upon one of the prisoners to relate how they had succeeded in seizing the Prince.

Hoping to save his life through a frank confession, the man spoke freely. So it even came to light that the royal servant had been poisoned to enable them to slip one of their henchmen into his place. The unrest among the people mounted. Repeatedly the speaker had to stop for some minutes, until silence was restored.

"We considered everything in detail, and the whole plot seemed a success when chance led the Lama to come upon us," the speaker concluded.

"It was not chance, my friend," said Lao-Tse. "The Supreme One wished to prevent Prince Han from falling victim to such an evil conspiracy. Your plan would have harmed the whole people, who love their Prince just as they revere their Emperor."

There were shouts of approval, and smiling, the Lama waited for the excitement to subside. Then he told them of the picture which he had been allowed to behold, and of all the help he was granted.

"Who among you, hearing all this, does not yet recognise that the Supreme One is higher and mightier than all the gods? Your people are of value to Him, otherwise He would not time and again show forth His Power; instead He would leave you to perish in Darkness and sin. Thank Him through the deed!"

Now it remained to pass judgment on the criminals, which the Emperor himself had to pronounce. He began by saying that these men, all but one, had only acted on the instructions of others. The ringleaders had been apprehended; the death of all enemies of the people awaited them. But the others should vow to improve themselves, and go free.

Although their fetters were immediately removed, the men could not believe their good fortune. Surely such clemency and mercy could not be! They looked up enquiringly at the Emperor, who said:

"If I were still a servant of the gods, my judgment would have been different. Go home and thank God."

A FEW DAYS AFTER this Lao-Tse, dressed in plain clothing, was again walking through one of the poorer quarters. He had heard that women and children there gathered regularly around a man who told them stories. No further information was available. Now he wanted to hear and see for himself.

It was about the time when the workshops closed, and the men were returning home. They all seemed to be heading in the same direction, and Lao-Tse, together with Wuti, joined them.

A fire had recently destroyed many houses, and the debris was not yet cleared away. Women and children sat on top of it in groups. As they arrived, the men placed themselves behind them. It all proceeded so naturally, as though it were a long-standing arrangement.

In the midst of the women, on a slightly elevated place formed by a pile of lumber, sat a simply-dressed man. His features distinguished him as a native of the west country. His black hair fell down to his shoulders, as did that of the Tibetans, but they smoothed their hair back from their foreheads, whereas the inhabitants of the west country parted it in the middle and pushed it behind their ears. Lao-Tse placed himself so that he was able to hear well, but could not be seen by the man.

When the men had stopped coming, the storyteller began. He accompanied his words, which were spoken in a musical voice, with slow movements of his long slender hands, and these gestures seemed to create pictures of everything he described. All that he recounted was brought to life clearly before the mind's eye.

He told fairytales adapted to the childlike perception of the hearers. They were about amazing events at sea and on land; rescues from distress; misadventures befalling bad people as just punishment.

In each of the stories it was little beings, visible to only a few human beings, who brought help or punishment. The crowd listened spellbound. When the man finished, many listeners brought him gifts. He and a companion, who suddenly appeared beside him, collected gratefully what they received; then both men disappeared all at once.

Now Lao-Tse and Wuti really mingled with the crowd, in order to find out who the man was and where he lived. No one could say. One day he had simply appeared, and begun to tell his stories. Every day he had new narratives, which were good to hear. But probably he would soon move on. The dwellers in other suburbs also wished him to visit them. This was all that could be ascertained.

Thoughtfully Lao-Tse went home. That which the man related was closely associated with the second part of the task assigned to him, Lao-Tse. This was a way to bring the animistic servants of God close to men!

Evening after evening Lao-Tse sought out the storyteller and listened to his fairytales. The man said not a word which the Lama could have condemned. And so Lao-Tse was certain that this man from the west country had been led his way as an instrument. In the night he called for God's Luminous Messenger, who showed him the man. No longer dressed in simple clothing but in a robe similar to that worn by Tibetan priests, the storyteller knelt before an altar of the Supreme One in a hut outside the city. And Lao-Tse heard the words of his prayer:

"O Supreme One, grant that I may soon find him whom I am to serve here on earth! I am ready to devote my life to this service, for Thou Thyself hast commanded me to do so. But I have been seeking for three years now, and cannot find Thy Blessed One."

And Lao-Tse's soul approached the praying man, and spoke with him. That brought him comfort and joy, and he promised to come to the Imperial Palace the following day. Lao-Tse, however, blissfully perceived God's guidance, and gave thanks from the bottom of his heart. While he had been anxiously pondering on how to bring to the people what he was commanded to bring them, God had already prepared an instrument and help for him!

The next morning Wuti announced that the storyteller from the suburbs had arrived, and wished to speak with the Lama of all Lamas. How surprised he was when Lao-Tse received the man like a close friend.

Sindhar was the name of the west countryman; his ancestors had already known of the One God. He had been a scribe, but his soul had been imbued with only one wish: to be permitted to serve God through his life. This wish became a daily prayer, penetrating right to the Throne of God. And he had heard a voice:

"Go to the Imperial City in the Middle Kingdom, and tell the women and children in the suburbs the fairytales which you tell your friends and acquaintances here in the evenings. In so doing you will find him whose helper you are to become. He is the Truth-bringer of God, who needs you. If you serve him aright, you will serve God."

The very next day Sindhar had left everything behind, and embarked on the long, long journey. His way led over tall mountains and through deep valleys with rushing waters; although nobody could tell him the name of the Imperial City or where to find it, he had not doubted even for a moment. After arduous months, his way brought him safely to Kiang-ning.

"Why did you not ask for me, Sindhar?" asked Lao-Tse. "Someone might perhaps have directed you to me if you had uttered the name 'Truth-bringer'!"

"Master, you probably do not remember that God's Command was: Tell your fairytales; in so doing, you will find him. I was not allowed to ask for you, but in all simplicity was to tell stories. And in that way I did indeed find you."

Now Lao-Tse decided to attend the story-telling that evening in the robe of the Lama. At first he would wear the dark mantle over it; then everything else would come about of itself.

So it did. That evening the tall figure of the Lama, enveloped in the dark mantle, unrecognised by any, stood beside the storyteller. All eyes hung on Sindhar. When he had finished another story, in which the little beings in the forest warded off a dangerous animal from a sleeping boy, thereby saving the child from certain death, Lao-Tse began to speak:

"Sindhar's stories are good to hear, are they not, brothers?"

Loud shouts from the crowd assured him of their agreement.

"But they are not merely pleasant to listen to, they are also instructive, for they are the pure truth!"

As he uttered these words Lao-Tse laid aside the mantle, and stood before them in the lilac robe so familiar to all. He continued to speak, pointing out that not only did God have His servants among human beings, but the whole Universe was filled with them. They lived and worked in every form.

"At one time, when men were not so evil, and still complied with God's Will, all human beings could see them. Then these small and great beings were friends and helpers to them, indeed even teachers. That was a life brimming with joy, for it is glorious to feel oneself surrounded everywhere by help and love. But human beings forgot about God, and in His stead set gods, whom they worshipped. Indeed, finally they so abased themselves that they made gods of the demons begotten of their own fear."

Loud shouts interrupted the speaker:

"We were like that!" – "We did that!"

When the commotion subsided, an old man asked in a loud voice:

"O great Lama, can we not then become good again? Can we not regain the connection with God's little servants?"

"You can if you so will, in earnest striving," was Lao-Tse's reply. "I will now come every evening with Sindhar, and tell you about God's servants. But you must strive to become truly servants of God. Then you will regain the connection with the other servants."

And as Lie-Tse had once predicted, so it came to pass: Eagerly the people absorbed the tidings of the animistic servants of the Supreme One. Like a wave of joy, it surged out of the suburbs into the city itself. Each spoke about what made him happy: the benevolent beings, great and small, who were helpful to human beings.

Thus it came about that people thronged to Lao-Tse, telling him that they had actually experienced help; indeed some even reported that they had seen the beings. Here also, however, it was granted to him to distinguish between truth and falsehood.

In a calm voice he responded to these accounts, repudiating exaggerations and exposing untruths. Thereby he prevented an unhealthy frenzy from taking hold of the masses. Only those to whom such things had become a reality dared to speak of them; and just these usually remained silent.

It became an inner certainty to the Lama that he must now accompany Sindhar for a time on his journey through the country, so that the tidings might be spread in the right way in other places as well. But he meant to travel with a retinue which included the west countryman.

When Hou-Chou had agreed to everything, Lao-Tse asked that Prince Han might accompany him. The Emperor instantly saw the great advantage to be gained for the successor to the throne from this journey. If he travelled through the country under Lao-Tse's guidance, everything he saw would be doubly beneficial; it would at once be explained in the right way. His son could learn unspeakably much.

Han himself was delighted to undertake the journey; for the older he grew, the more he was oppressed by the semi-idleness imposed upon him at his father's court. Although he learned and worked with the lowliest of his people, yet when he saw how unremittingly active his father was in his concern for their welfare, a great longing to be allowed to do likewise welled up in him.

The Lama always succeeded in overcoming these moods of the Prince; but even Lao-Tse acknowledged that valuable potential energies were going to waste in the young man. Now the journey, which would last for many months, could remedy the situation.

Having heard so much about the storyteller without ever seeing him, the Emperor had become curious. Sindhar was requested to take up residence in the Palace before the departure, and to tell his stories whenever the Emperor desired it. Sindhar was happy to do so, and recalled his most beautiful tales. On the first occasion, Hou-Chou invited no one else to listen, apart from his sons and Lao-Tse. He felt wondrously moved by the content of the narrative, and still more by the way in which Sindhar spoke.

"Are all your people like yourself?" he asked the storyteller when he had finished.

"Master, not all believe in God. Only a very few of us have been permitted to recognise Him. But these may very well be just like me. I do not know."

"How did you hear of God, the Supreme One?" Hou-Chou enquired further.

"Even my forefathers knew of Him. In our family the knowledge has been preserved to this day. It is said that in olden times a Truth-bringer journeyed through our country at the Command of God."

"I wonder if God the Lord gives every people the opportunity at some time to hear of Him?" mused the Emperor. Prince Han answered promptly:

"It must be so. God is Justice; hence He cannot allow peoples to exist who may not hear of Him at all. One people will hear of Him sooner, another later, but one day all will learn of that which can purify their souls."

211

"Why do not all hear of Him at the same time?" one of the younger Princes enquired, but immediately answered his own question: "It probably depends on the maturity attained by a people. To those who cannot yet understand, God allows nothing to be revealed."

It was now decided that Sindhar should tell his stories every evening in the presence of the Emperor, until the time came for the carefully-prepared journey. The nobles were invited to listen, and every day more hearers came. On each occasion Lao-Tse also spoke, paving the way in the souls for an understanding of the interaction between all the Divine forces.

"You are going, my friend," said Hou-Chou to the Lama as he stood before him on the last evening to bid him farewell. "Again you leave me alone, and I feel apprehensive. I still have not learned sufficiently to let myself be guided by the Voice of God."

"You will learn it in these months, my Emperor," was Lao-Tse's confident reply.

Whenever the Lama expressed himself with the calm certainty characteristic of him, confidence and peace also returned to the other soul. Agitation and faint-heartedness could never last long in his presence.

ON THE FOLLOWING DAY a stately procession set forth from the main gate of Kiang-ning. All the participants were happy and full of hope. New things were to be seen and experienced! There were probably none who would not have wished to change places with them.

Prince Han rode by the side of Lao-Tse, and marvelled at his teacher's horsemanship. He gazed at the Lama with such admiration that the latter finally said with a smile:

"You probably thought I could not ride, Han?"

"I knew that you could ride, otherwise you would have preferred the chair to the saddle. But I had not imagined you to be master of this art as well."

"He who constantly strives to do his best in all things will also be able to master that which otherwise lies far from his usual work."

According to the prearranged plan, they rode from village to village, from town to town. Everywhere Sindhar's art of storytelling created the receptive soil for Lao-Tse's teachings. But the allotted time was by no means adequate. Nowhere would the people let the heralds go; everywhere they were begged to stay longer. And often the reasons were so convincing that Lao-Tse had to consent.

This he did willingly, so long as his soul's nightly inspection of Kiang-ning revealed no cause for a speedy return home. Hou-Chou held the reins of government with a firm hand. He had become more strict in the absence of his gentle Adviser. This was good: no one would dare, as previously, to plot against him.

At intervals Lao-Tse sent a messenger to the Imperial Palace with news. At the same time he often wrote of events that took place during his absence, so that the Emperor was reassured in the knowledge that the connection between him and the Lama was unbroken.

The "fairytale journey", as the Prince called it, had now lasted more than two years. It did not seem too long to any of those taking part in it. They had now reached the eastern part of the country, and thus the sea-coast, the regions where Lao-Tse had once dispelled the demon-fear.

Here they found eager activity. Workshops had sprung up in nearly all the larger villages, where delightful articles were made from kaolin. Never had the travellers seen such beautiful things anywhere. The bowls were egg-shell thin, the painting, which for long had been done in the workshops by the men themselves, was delicate.

Demons and dragons were captured with the brush, but always in a manner which indicated that the painters neither worshipped nor feared them. It was much more like an expression of the relieved laughter of children at fears overcome.

Lao-Tse and Han liked to walk through these workshops, inspecting everything. It became apparent that among the workers were a number of an alien race. They were smaller, nimbler and slighter than the sons of the Middle Kingdom. Their eyes, more slanted and like mere slits in the face, gazed at the world with an inquisitive, greedy and cunning look.

Surprised, Lao-Tse enquired about the strangers, and learned that they had come in ships, at first only to buy goods. Initially they had paid more than the Tibetan traders, but later less and less, until the foremen refused to sell to them. Then all of a sudden they appeared as workers. No one was happy about it, for the strangers would hear nothing about God, and made fun of the customs and practices. Yet no one knew how to control them.

"But do you not realise, people," cried Lao-Tse, "that these strangers are cunningly learning your art by watching you, in order to pursue it eventually in their own country?"

"Will that harm us?" the men wanted to know.

"Of course it will harm our people, to whom the little servants of God have shown this wonderful art so that they may have a source of income for all time.

"Numerous as the grains of sand here at my feet are our people. We should all have to starve to death if we could not exchange food for our products. But if we teach other peoples our art, they will no longer exchange anything with us, and the starvation which the animistic beings sought to avert would conquer our land.

"God directed me here in good time, to avert further disaster. In the name of the Emperor I order all foreigners to leave the workshops. Henceforth only sons of our people and worshippers of the true God may be employed here."

The foremen of the nearest workshops, who had been summoned, were instructed to dismiss the strangers the following morning, in compliance with this order.

It was unnecessary: nobody came. The undesirable eastlanders had vanished without a trace, together with their ships. Now Lao-Tse gave orders that henceforth no town was to admit such people within its gates. Sale of the products could take place as usual through the Tibetan traders, who were well known to all.

The Lama feared that once inside the country the crafty aliens might acquire the knowledge of the art in some other way. They must be prevented from doing so. Wherever he went, Lao-Tse spoke to that effect with the foremen of the workshops, and found them all receptive.

Meanwhile Prince Han was working at a place which produced the paper-thin vessels. Yet however hard he tried, he did not succeed in fashioning such delicate kaolin. Then an old worker told him that a little man who was once with them had shown them how to mix another kind of earth

214

with the kaolin. It was since then that the work they produced was so exceptionally delicate.

Han advised the people that no doubt this was one of the animistic servants of God. It was a great pity that his instruction had now passed into the hands of foreigners. That strengthened the men's determination to tolerate strangers no longer.

"Could you learn nothing from the strangers?" Han enquired.

The men declared that they could not. While the eastlanders deemed themselves much better and wiser, they were lax in their morals, and above all their glib words could never be trusted.

"Sire, they are liars!" the man concluded with conviction.

THE THIRD YEAR was nearing its end when one day the long procession of travellers rode back through Kiang-ning's main gate, joyfully welcomed by the crowd. They had seen and experienced a great deal, there was much to tell, to recount and to ask. For days the whole of Kiang-ning was like a stirred-up ant-hill, and there was joy everywhere.

Only Prince Han had a thorn in his soul, which caused him many a sad, or at least a thoughtful hour. He felt that he had sufficient control of his thoughts for them to remain unnoticed, but he had not reckoned with Lao-Tse. The latter endeavoured to strengthen the dispirited Prince, and to show him discreetly how he could attain to inner contentment.

One morning Han entered Lao-Tse's room before the hour of their usual discussion. He seemed to be completely preoccupied with one thought, and the Lama knew that now his quiet sowing had germinated.

There was a marked difference between Hou-Chou and his son. When the Emperor had something on his mind, he voiced it directly. Within the very first minutes of their meeting, Lao-Tse would know why the Ruler had come to him.

But Han always began by speaking of something altogether different, and much precious time would be lost before the main issue could finally be brought forth. The Lama often drew the Prince's attention to this, but in vain. And if pressed to come to the point, Han's courage to address the subject of his concern would fail him.

215

The same happened this time. Han asked about the manuscripts that lay on the Lama's desk, and told how his brothers could not hear enough about the long journey. Lao-Tse waited patiently. Finally the Prince took a deep breath, and said:

"Do you not also think that I am too old to lead such an inactive life as I did before our journey?"

When the Lama was silent, Han continued:

"I have thought about how I could change this. And somehow I have been helped during recent nights. At last I have found a way which appears to be the right one. Fu-Kung, who has hitherto held office as treasurer, has become very old. I have heard that he intends to ask the Emperor to allow him to retire from his post. Lao-Tse, do you think that I might ask my father to let me assume this position?"

The young Prince spoke urgently, his eyes lending emphasis to his words. Lao-Tse was happy: this very post would give the future Emperor essential insights that would later benefit him. Han was old enough to assume such a responsibility, and he was extremely conscientious. Nevertheless the Lama wanted to make his former pupil aware of the far-reaching nature of his wish.

"Have you considered, Han," he asked, "that this office is one of the most responsible and most difficult? You will have little time left for studies, excursions on horseback and the like. For not only will you have to administer the treasures belonging to the Realm, thus to the people, but you will have to receive all monies, make all disbursements and be accountable for everything.

"No one else can deputise for you in any one of these duties. You may have officials, but you yourself must supervise their work, and know exactly how much money passes through your hands each day."

"That is precisely how I imagined it," Han replied happily.

The Lama did not give him a blank refusal; this kindled his hope of winning over the Emperor's Adviser as his ally if his father were to raise objections.

And now his hope was confirmed. Lao-Tse looked kindly upon the youth who was prepared to surrender his life of luxury and pleasure in order to become a useful part of the whole, and said:

"Let us go to your father, Han, before he hears news of Fu-Yung's intentions. Otherwise he might promise the post to someone else and be obliged to keep his word."

Together they went to Hou-Chou. There, the Lama left it to the Prince to speak. Han himself must ask his father, who was not a little surprised by his son's decision. He let him finish speaking, then asked almost the same questions as the Lama, and finally said:

"When I was your age I was already Emperor, but in name only. You know my life story, and you know how shamefully I was exploited by Wen. What I felt then helps me to understand your wish. Therefore I grant your request.

"But understand rightly: You cannot become Treasurer today, and then resign when the work or the responsibility becomes too much for you. Only my death or yours can release you from the bonds which you impose upon yourself. For any suggestion that my son might perform his duties badly, and therefore have to be recalled prematurely, is an assumption that lies beyond the realm of possibility."

Overjoyed, Han thanked his father, and it was agreed that immediately after Fu-Yung's resignation he should be introduced to the counsellors as his successor. Until then they would say nothing about the matter.

The Prince asked if he might first familiarise himself with his new post under Fu-Yung's supervision. Hou-Chou reflected, and then granted the request, but first he would wait for Fu-Yung's resignation, in order not to drive the deserving old man from his office.

But a few days later the venerable man placed the seal and documents back in the hands of his Emperor, from whom he had received them. He gladly undertook the task of acquainting the Prince with all the duties, only asking that Han might settle into his work as quickly as possible. The very next day the Prince assumed his new post, which caused him much work and trouble, but gave him deep satisfaction.

MESSENGERS CAME FROM the east of the country, bringing complaints from towns and villages. The eastlanders, who had been successfully denied entrance to the towns, were landing anywhere along the coasts, and trying to approach the workshops dressed in the costume of the country. Where they had been unable to do so, they had even abducted men on several occasions, probably in order to take them to their own country, and learn the method of production from them for payment or by force.

Lord Treasurer Han was with the Emperor just as such reports came again. Much perturbed, Hou-Chou cried:

"What can we do about this pack of thieves?"

Han replied thoughtfully:

"We must build a high wall along the coast to prevent the marauders from invading us."

"That is a very good idea," said Lao-Tse. "The grounds of the Tibetan monasteries are surrounded by high walls for the same purpose. Some nights ago I saw in spirit just such a wall, which armed men were charging in vain. Even if the eastlanders were to come with armed forces, the walls would thwart their intention."

They deliberated at length; then the Emperor promised the messengers speedy redress, and sent master-builders who were to erect the walls.

"The wall must extend as far as our land is washed by the sea," he commanded.

"That is not enough," interposed Lao-Tse. "The men are as cunning as foxes. They would simply land by night to the north of the Realm, and invade our country from there. An extension must be built some distance inland from the sea-wall. A solid watch-tower must be placed at the corner, so that the land in front of the wall can be surveyed in either direction. A similar tower must be built wherever a gate is made in the wall; for we cannot cut off our country completely from the sea."

"What are we to do at the point where our river empties into the sea?" asked Han. "We can hardly obstruct it."

"Perhaps such a short stretch can be guarded even without a wall," was the Emperor's opinion. "Surely it would be difficult for the eastlanders to travel upstream."

Provided with the requisite funds, the master-builders and craftsmen left Kiang-ning a short time later, to travel by ship downstream to the sea. They would recruit workers from the local population; they also hoped to find the necessary large stones there.

Han would gladly have gone with them; he was strongly tempted to take over control of the building of the wall, which was his idea; but his office withheld him. It was the first time that he had found it rather a burden. But he valiantly overcame the impulse.

On Lao-Tse's advice, the building of the wall was begun at ten different places, so that practically the entire coast was alive, and therefore guarded. When the people realised that the structure was being raised for the protection of their workshops and themselves, everyone who could be spared lent a helping hand. It made them happy to thwart the plans of the crafty aliens.

They laughed and joked like children as they worked, and the higher the wall rose the happier the builders became. But it was a long time before reports could be sent to Kiang-ning that any progress on the ten structures was to be seen. Stones had to be broken and cut into shape. They were not to be found directly by the sea. It was necessary to travel far inland, and the hauling of the masses of stone took time and strength.

But perseverance in the face of necessary tasks was one of the main virtues of the sons of the Middle Kingdom. Nothing demanded of them by the master-builders was ever too much. Even when the kaolin workshops had to be closed periodically because all the men were needed for the building, there were no complaints. Perhaps it was quite a good thing that any foreigners sneaking into the country no longer found anything to learn from and copy!

Long ago Lao-Tse had been told by the Luminous Messenger of God that the building of the wall was in accord with the Will of the Most High. Moreover, during the night he was often shown improvements to be implemented; sometimes he even learned completely new things.

Thus one night the command came that the walls should be made wide enough for two coaches to be able to pass each other. Hou-Chou immediately saw the practical side of this instruction, and passed it on to the master-builders.

The command aroused dismay, for they had started to build long stretches of the wall which were only one-third of the desired width. What was to be done? Surely they could not demolish everything!

A particularly clever master-builder had the idea of building *alongside* the completed portion. That was done. To the height of the wall was added the required width, and then the building continued on both foundations. It was for this reason that future generations marvelled at the incomprehensible – that in some places the base of the sea-wall appeared to consist of two different structures.

Meanwhile Prince Han was considering whether it was expedient to surround the whole country with such a wall. His father laughed at him. The country was sufficiently protected by the tall mountains that surrounded it over long distances. It had not yet occurred to any of the neighbours to invade the country.

But Han, who had read many old manuscripts, proved to the Emperor that this had in fact occurred several times. And what had happened in the past could happen again.

"Then you build the wall one day when you are Emperor," conceded Hou-Chou in high spirits. "I have other building projects in mind."

Surprised, Han and Lao-Tse stared at the speaker, who delighted in their astonishment. Then he began:

"Before I retire from office, I would like to demonstrate my gratitude to the Supreme One, Whose Power has guided us all so graciously; and at the same time give my people a symbol to remind them never to forget God. I therefore wish to build here in Kiang-ning a great Temple, such as is nowhere to be found in our entire Realm.

"I have pondered much over this, and have chosen the place where it is to stand, and the stones of which its walls are to be built. I want to see whether one of my master-builders is able to draw a picture resembling the one that I see before me in my mind's eye."

And Hou-Chou sent for the most talented builders, telling them of his intention and requesting them to prepare drawings. But nothing they produced could satisfy him. Then he had it proclaimed throughout the country that he who could submit the right picture of the future Temple would be richly rewarded.

Drawings, in black-and-white and in colour, came from all sides. They represented a pagoda in modified form, so that the structure had no further claim to beauty; or else they based the design on the form of dwelling-houses, elaborately painted and ornamented. But this did not please the Ruler either.

He was not able to describe what he saw in his mind's eye. As soon as he began to speak of it, the picture became blurred, and the listener could not grasp how what Hou-Chou described could be carried out.

Then one day a man bearing a letter from Fu-Tse was announced to Lao-Tse. The High Lama wrote that the bearer was a very learned man, who had come to the Mountain-monastery from afar. They would have liked him to remain, for much could be learned from him. But he would press on, and would not be detained. He did not say, however, where he wanted to go; it seemed as if he did not know. Therefore Fu-Tse referred him to the Lama of all Lamas, as he might be of help to him.

Lao-Tse looked closely at the man. He was tall, upright, with supple limbs. His hair, which he wore in the Tibetan way, framed a noble face of light complexion.

His apparel was clean and of good material, but completely different from the clothes worn in the Middle Kingdom or in Tibet. He was dressed in long, tight trousers reaching to the ankles, and up under the arms. Over this the man wore a short jacket of the same material. This too was close-fitting. Over these hung a very long cloak with many folds. His head was bare.

"What is your name?" Lao-Tse asked the guest.

"Call me Hai-Wi-Nan, that will do," the man replied in strange guttural tones.

"Where do you come from?" Lao-Tse enquired further.

"That I will tell you when you have answered a question on which a great deal depends."

The Lama sensed at once that there was something special about the man. He nodded his consent.

"Tell me, in what country did your ancestors originate?"

"My father called the country Tarim, but I do not know whether he rendered the name correctly, nor do I know where the country is situated."

At that, the stranger fell on his knees, and grasped the hem of Lao-Tse's robe.

"So at last I am at my destination!" he exclaimed joyfully. "I too am from Tarim, which is separated from Tibet by high mountains. I was to seek the one whose forebears had emigrated from our country in order that a Truth-

221

bringer could arise for the Middle Kingdom. Thanks be to the Supreme One that my eyes may behold you."

"And why were you to seek me, Hai-Wi-Nan?" enquired the Lama, whose soul foresaw that here again an instrument sent by God stood before him.

"I am to build a Temple to God the Almighty here in this country, a Temple as it once stood in our country. It is to be glorious and magnificent. Behold this picture!" With these words the man from Tarim pulled a scroll from his garment and opened it out. An exclamation of the most joyful surprise escaped Lao-Tse. What he saw in outline was the Temple which he was often allowed to behold from afar in the night, high up in the Eternal Gardens. It must be a very faithful replica of the lofty Edifice.

"Does it please you?" asked the man, delighted. "May I build it?"

"We must go at once to the Emperor. I am certain that he will welcome you with all his heart."

They went to Hou-Chou, who could hardly believe his eyes when he now saw on parchment the picture that he had always envisioned. Lao-Tse told him where the man came from, and how he had come hither.

"You must start the building at once, Hai-Wi-Nan," said the happy Ruler. "Find helpers and workmen, ask for whatever sums you need for your work, and do not stint anywhere; but above all establish your own income as well."

"What is built here will be done at the Behest of the Supreme One. To be allowed to serve Him is reward enough for me. Give me a dwelling and my upkeep. For that I will be grateful to you; more I will not take."

Hou-Chou would not press the stranger now, for fear that the man should leave. Later on he would surely listen to reason with regard to well-deserved payment. He arranged for rooms to be allocated to Hai-Wi-Nan in the Palace, so that he would always be available when the Emperor wished to speak to him. Then the Emperor himself took him to the site which he had chosen for the Temple. But the master-builder shook his head.

"The Temple of God must stand apart; it must not be surrounded by houses, and everyday hustle and bustle," he said quite firmly. "Let me show you a place which drew my attention yesterday on my way to the Palace."

And he led Hou-Chou and Lao-Tse out of the city into a palm-forest. It did not even occur to him that thereby he was compelling the Emperor to go on foot – he whose preference was to be carried in a chair.

At first Lao-Tse had thought of sending for the horses, but when Hou-Chou in his enthusiasm went quite naturally on foot with the stranger, he dropped his concern and was happy.

Now they reached the place designated by Hai-Wi-Nan. It was a large, almost circular open space in the forest. Tall palms dipped their crowns, a small stream rippled past not far away. It was striking that the wide space was enclosed by solid, tall stones. They stood there, upright and defiant, as though embedded in the earth.

"Do you like this site, Emperor?" asked Hai-Wi-Nan.

Hou-Chou assented. He was as though spellbound. All that he had seen in spirit seemed about to become reality. He had not realised that there was a place so near his Palace which corresponded so perfectly to the spiritual prototype. But Lao-Tse knew the place. He had often come here when his soul longed for peace and quiet.

All the essential matters were now speedily dealt with, and soon lively activity began in the glade. With the assistance of animistic helpers, splendid stones from remote quarries were carried to the spot and set in place.

From their animistic helpers the people learned how the work had to be done. Soon they had lost all their shyness of them, and worked in joyful partnership.

Everywhere in the country artists were tirelessly active, attending to the necessary adornment of the Temple in accordance with Hai-Wi-Nan's instructions. Once more the whole great Realm was alive with eager activity. Everyone wanted to contribute something worthy of the work; everyone wanted to take part in it. The activity brought about joy and cheerfulness. There was no time for petty quarrels, peace reigned in the years when the Temple was coming into being.

It was Hou-Chou's favourite recreation to visit the Temple-site after his consultations. Usually he went on foot, as he had done the first time. When Lao-Tse once asked him why he chose not to ride, he said, almost embarrassed:

"To approach the place where the Sanctuary of God is to stand other than on foot seems to me presumptuous."

Naturally those who accompanied him had likewise to forgo horses or carrying-chairs.

Every seventh day Hai-Wi-Nan suspended the work. This was something completely new in the Middle Kingdom: not even in Tibet had Lao-Tse experienced it. He asked the master-builder why he did this. The latter explained to him that his people were commanded by God to do so. On every seventh day all work should cease, so that the souls of men could draw strength from above. Therefore the Hours of Devotion on that day were particularly solemn and prolonged.

This pleased the Lama, who spoke to the Emperor, and asked whether they might introduce this day of rest in the Middle Kingdom as well. Hou-Chou was immediately prepared to do so. A beginning had been made in any case, since everyone engaged in the Temple-building was already permitted a day of rest.

The people were happy with this innovation, which gave even the poorest among them a day to spend as he liked. Although they understood that the day was meant to be devoted above all to God, they regarded it mainly as a day of rest for themselves. It was not quite as Lao-Tse had pictured it, but he knew that nothing could be achieved by coercion in the matter. The people must be brought slowly to a better understanding.

But the nobles were resentful. Now the wretched populace could stroll in the gardens and parks every seventh day!

Actually, the nobles were not always in agreement with everything that was now taking place in the great Realm. In the past, under the other Emperors, they had decided everything, everything revolved round them. Their forefathers had been the powerful ones; no one troubled about the common people.

It was Lao-Tse who had wrought a change in this, with his speeches declaring that before God neither position nor title mattered, but rather the state of the soul. Hou-Chou had adopted this precept only too willingly. He had always seen himself as Emperor of the people, not as Emperor of rank. Now all his laws were aimed at making the people contented, happy and civilised.

Among themselves the mandarins said quite openly that it would be far better if the people remained ignorant and licentious. Then the necessary distance would be better preserved.

That a Sindhar – of whom nothing was known, except that he told fairytales in the streets and market-places for money and gifts – could come and go freely at the Sovereign's residence, that he had travelled like a close friend with the Lama of all Lamas, this was the beginning of the end. Where respect for those in authority ceased, the decline of a people set in.

The nobility of Kiang-ning often met secretly. It was not their intent to plot an overthrow, but expressing their views to like-minded people relieved them. Occasionally they were joined by mandarins from other places, whose duties brought them to the Imperial Court. From them the mandarins living in Kiang-ning hoped to hear that things were better in the provinces, that the new ideas were not yet carried into effect there.

But Lao-Tse's presence in the whole country, and the quiet influence constantly exerted by him, even when he was not present, had allowed the new to arise triumphantly everywhere.

Then one day a mandarin from the south of the realm brought the welcome news that a very great sage had now arisen there as well. He called himself Con-Fu-Tse. He was still young, but people felt that his knowledge was important. At the same time, he was averse to anything new, and proclaimed the old in a compelling way. People flocked to him in droves, and took his advice.

"Does he believe in the new God?" the eagerly listening mandarins wanted to know.

"We do not know. If one asks, as I have done, he says that belief is man's personal concern. Each must believe what he pleases. What people believe is irrelevant, so long as that belief bears fruit."

"What does he mean by fruit?" was the next question.

"He demands that people should cultivate certain virtues, such as self-discipline and willingness to make sacrifices; but understand me aright: not a willingness to make sacrifices for the poor or for individual human beings, but rather for some great idea, for some common project. For the sake of such an idea, says Con-Fu-Tse, man must also be prepared to lie and steal, so long as the desired aim is achieved."

225

"It seems to me," began an elderly mandarin, "that the new sage endeavours to advance what we all lament as a loss: the licentiousness of the masses. Although I am little pleased by what you report of him, it seems that he intends to support our wishes."

There was much discussion. In the end they were all inspired by the urge to know the sage.

"He must also be a High Lama, since he appends the 'Tse' to his name. Do you know where he studied?"

"Nobody knows. The sage keeps silent about his life. He says it is nobody's business."

The following day several mandarins told the Emperor what they had heard. But they said nothing about the teachings of the new High Lama, for they knew that Hou-Chou would then be ill-disposed towards him from the outset. The Ruler, whose thoughts were occupied with the Temple-building in every spare moment, had no desire to make the acquaintance of the strange sage. When the mandarins became more insistent, he dismissed them with the words:

"If he has received his knowledge from God he will come here of his own accord. I can wait."

But a few days later Lao-Tse began to speak about the sage.

"Have the mandarins told you about him?" Hou-Chou asked, with a smile.

"They have not," said the Lama.

"I saw him last night. I tell you, O Emperor, the sooner we let him come the better it will be."

"Is he so important?" asked Hou-Chou in surprise, but was alarmed when Lao-Tse replied:

"He is important, but he derives his knowledge and strength from the opposite pole."

"What do you mean by that? What is the opposite pole?" the Ruler, whose interest was now suddenly aroused, wanted to know.

"God the Supreme One is the Light. Opposite Him stands one whom I am unable to name; he is the Darkness. Just as God determines my guidance, this Lord of the Darkness has the new sage so guided that he will reopen wide the door to sin."

226

"Then let us forbid him to teach!" Hou-Chou said hastily, contrary to his wont. "If he does not comply, we will exile him. Perhaps we can find a reason to kill him!"

"The Lord of the Darkness, whose servant he is, will not be fought in that way. We must send for this man, hear him personally, and brand his teaching as erroneous before the world," was Lao-Tse's advice.

It was decided that not the Emperor, but the Lama of all Lamas, to whom of course even this strange Lama must be subordinate, should send for Con-Fu-Tse. The matter could then be taken from there.

Even if he set out immediately after receiving the message, it would be some considerable time before the sage arrived. The Emperor almost forgot what was impending here.

All the more did Lao-Tse think about it. He knew that Con-Fu-Tse had not come from any of the Tibetan monasteries. He probably bore his title wrongfully. There would be a hard struggle with the Lord of Darkness, but God was bound to triumph. Of that Lao-Tse was certain!

The messenger had now been back nearly a month. He had reported that he had to ride through several villages in pursuit of the sage before meeting him. But Con-Fu-Tse expressed his willingness to set out for Kiang-ning as soon as he was able to do so.

ONE DAY an imposing retinue approached the main gate of the city. In front walked footmen dressed in colourful silk, clearing the way with brightly decked rods for their master. The latter reclined in a semi-curtained chair carried by four strong men. It was followed by pedestrians, and riders whose horses adapted reluctantly to the slow pace. At the rear came a long train of pack-animals and armed men.

The Emperor was informed that a foreign ruler was approaching. But when the procession requested admittance, it was Con-Fu-Tse with his attendants.

The sage demanded accommodation at once in the Imperial Palace, since he had come as a guest of the Emperor. Lao-Tse, who had anticipated this request, had arranged for a few rooms to be prepared for him in one of the other palaces.

Hai-Tan, whose duty it was to receive and attend to foreign guests, also went to meet this Lama, and greeted him with courtesy. Then he informed him that such a numerous retinue had not been expected. But it should not be difficult to accommodate them all in the course of the day.

The guest replied arrogantly:

"I am not accustomed to living apart from my students and followers. See to it that I do not find things here other than what is essential to my comfort."

The derisive smile playing around Hai-Tan's mouth escaped the other man's notice. He replied calmly:

"I shall immediately arrange for you to be accommodated with your people. But provisions will have to be made for it. Until these are completed, I shall have some tents pitched outside the gate, so that you weary travellers may rest."

The group had no choice but to wait outside the city for two days. Although the tents were comfortable, the visitors had to provide their own meals, as though they were still on their journey.

Finally on the third day Hai-Tan himself came to conduct Con-Fu-Tse to the city, where an unoccupied house beyond the ring of palaces had been adapted to his requirements.

There was accommodation for man and beast, and two spacious rooms were furnished for Con-Fu-Tse.

This was not as he had imagined it, but he perceived that he was no match for Hai-Tan's intelligence; moreover he had no wish to incur the Emperor's displeasure at the outset. He settled in, and then asked to be taken to the Ruler.

"When you are sufficiently refreshed to be able to pay a visit," said Hai-Tan courteously, "you will first have to call on the Lama of all Lamas, who summoned you here."

Con-Fu-Tse winced. He had not expected this, and he was not prepared to accept it.

"I am anxious to pay my respects to the Emperor first," he said haughtily. "I do not yet know whether I will call on Lao-Tse at all."

Outwardly calm, Hai-Tan rejoined:

"Whether you can be admitted to the Emperor's presence will depend on

Lao-Tse, stranger. You seem to be ignorant of the customs of our Realm, although you are a son of our people, unless I am altogether mistaken. Be that as it may: since you are a Lama, you will know that you are subject to the supremacy of the Lama of all Lamas. You have lost much time already in paying him your respects. Let us set out at once, so that we may meet him in the Palace; later he will be away."

And Con-Fu-Tse, wily as a serpent, complied.

Hai-Tan himself escorted the man to Lao-Tse, who received the new arrival with gracious dignity. Just as he beheld him now, just so had he seen him in the night when he received tidings of his activity.

He was a medium-sized, lean man, with awkward limbs and podgy hands, which bespoke his low birth. Black hair trimmed in the style of the Middle Kingdom surrounded the sharp features, from which gleamed cunning, restless eyes.

But Lao-Tse perceived even more than could be seen with physical eyes. He perceived the man's inner strife, the desire for admiration at any price, the avarice and the hunger for power. And Lao-Tse shuddered.

"O Supreme One," he implored inwardly, "give me the strength to tear the mask from his face and render his teaching ineffective!"

Meanwhile the prescribed obeisances were over. The two Lamas and Hai-Tan had seated themselves in the circle of several mandarins. Then Lao-Tse asked:

"You are a Lama. In which school did you acquire this title?"

The man hesitated for a moment, then he replied:

"God has commanded me to keep silent about it."

Lao-Tse rose slowly to his feet.

"In that case you will understand that I may not permit you to teach in our country."

"But you have heard that it is God's Will," cried Con-Fu-Tse impatiently.

With impressive dignity Lao-Tse replied:

"In this country the Will of the Supreme One is proclaimed to me alone. I am His servant. Had you been sent by Him, I should have known."

Furious, Con-Fu-Tse leapt to his feet.

"Prove that you hear God's Will!"

"You yourself demand it. Otherwise I should have remained silent," said Lao-Tse very slowly and with dignity. "Let me ask you: where were you before you presented yourself in this country as a Lama, which you are not? Is it enough for you that I know, or shall I utter it, Master Kung?"

In his agitation the stranger apparently failed to observe that Lao-Tse had disputed his title of Lama. Almost roaring, he demanded that Lao-Tse retract the suspicion he had voiced. He had not been in prison, he had never stolen!

"Do you hear him?" Lao-Tse turned to the mandarins, who were listening with rapt attention. "He accuses himself. I said nothing about it, but I know it to be the truth."

Not wasting another word, the Lama of all Lamas left the room with dignity.

Those who remained behind were overcome with great excitement. Con-Fu-Tse stood in their midst, full of anxiety and trembling. Only now did he realise that he had given himself away. His presence of mind failed him; his tongue, usually so glib, could not offer a single subterfuge.

The mandarins were all the more indignant when they saw themselves deceived in their hope of finding support against Lao-Tse from the new sage.

They were about to vent their disappointment and rage on the stranger, but Hai-Tan restrained them. The close association with Lao-Tse had gradually influenced the formerly so worldly Tan; even his nature now breathed a little of his master's quiet dignity.

"He is the guest of the Supreme Lama," said Hai-Tan. "Let him return to his quarters unhindered. None but Lao-Tse may decide what is to be done with him next."

As if only just remembering that he had to quit the scene, the impostor turned and scuttled out unceremoniously. But Hai-Tan considered it imperative to give orders at the city-gates that the stranger was not to be allowed to leave without the express permission of the Supreme Lama.

He reported this to Lao-Tse, who asked in surprise:

"Why did you do that?"

"I fear that he will make haste to leave the city before you can forbid him to continue spreading his teaching in our Realm."

"He will not leave the city, Hai-Tan, without making one or several attempts to vindicate himself. I am sure of that. As soon as he is alone his master, the Dark One, will indicate to him what to say, so that people will believe him again. I fear there will yet be a hard struggle," Lao-Tse added with a sigh. Conflict was alien to his whole nature. How happy he would have been to find a helper in the new sage!

Despite Lao-Tse's assurance, Hai-Tan secretly watched every move of the disagreeable guest; his followers were also kept under surveillance. But nothing happened to arouse suspicion. The stranger went only for short walks in the vicinity of his quarters; no one visited him. He made no arrangements whatever to leave Kiang-ning.

After a few days he sent a servant with a letter to Lao-Tse. Hai-Tan, who happened to be present, strongly urged him to return the scroll unread, but the Lama refused.

"It is exactly because I know," he said, "that here it is not one human being against another, not one opinion against another, but the Darkness opposing the Light, that I must not do or leave undone anything which could give the other a hold over me, or could be interpreted as an admission of weakness. Believe me, Hai-Tan, wherever the Lord of Darkness appears, adherents gather round him like vultures round carrion. Among the mandarins who were so indignant at Master Kung's deception, there are some who nevertheless would like to see him in favour."

Then he unrolled the parchment and began to read:

"If the Lama of all Lamas is really a servant of the Supreme One, he will know that He forgives the fallen sinner as soon as he mends his ways.

"If the Lama of all Lamas knows this he will see from it that I strive with all my might to serve God, that my deed has been wiped out by my remorse.

"If the Lama of all Lamas knows this, why does he condemn me?

"And if he does not condemn me, why does he not permit me to come into his presence, so that I may explain my teaching, and if necessary defend it?

"I await his summons."

"Cleverly put," cried Hai-Tan, who in spite of himself was impressed with the style of the letter.

But Lao-Tse waved his hand.

"Let him come. At this time tomorrow he shall reveal his teaching before a select gathering. Until then we shall have no peace."

The Lama carefully chose from among the mandarins those whom he regarded as his opponents. Asked by Hai-Tan why he decided to invite these particular mandarins, he replied:

"If they did not come, they would maintain that there was something not right about it."

Then Hai-Tan requested that at least as many well-disposed mandarins be invited, and Lao-Tse smilingly assented. When he informed the Emperor about the forthcoming meeting, Hou-Chou asked to be present. But then he realised that it would be doing too much honour to the stranger, yet he felt strongly urged to be there. So it was decided that the Sovereign should attend in the dress of a mandarin. The noblemen and servants were sworn to the strictest secrecy.

On the following morning, when all who had been invited were assembled, Master Kung was conducted into the hall. He feigned humility, but his very first words bespoke his true character.

"At last it has pleased the Supreme Lama to send for me, whom he does not consider to be a Lama. In that case it would have been unnecessary for me to obey his call, for if I am no Lama, I am not subject to his command either. Nevertheless I have come, because I am humble, and forgive the harsh words which the Lama uttered about me a few days ago."

"It is not our custom for the incomer to speak first," Hai-Tan cut him short. "You should have waited for the Lama's greeting. Your behaviour shows that you are not of noble descent, and not accustomed to polite society."

"Polite or not," shouted Kung, lost to all caution, "that is not important now. I am a prince of the spirit, with whom none has yet been able to compare.

"Lama of all Lamas, I challenge you to hear my teaching, and to refute it if you can; then I will do the same with yours."

Impassively Lao-Tse motioned the speaker to come forward. It was but a slight movement of the hand, yet it demanded obedience.

"I accept your challenge, Master Kung!"

The one thus addressed flinched, but dared not protest. Lao-Tse continued:

"I would like us to put the questions turn about, and thus compare the two teachings."

Kung made a gesture of indifference.

"As you wish. You may have the first question."

"Who is God?" asked Lao-Tse, in deadly earnest, and in a resonant voice that filled the spacious hall.

"Do you mean yours or mine?" Kung promptly asked.

"So you acknowledge that we serve different gods," Lao-Tse declared.

"I cannot tell, until I know the nature of your God," was the evasive answer.

The Lama was well aware that if he were now to describe God, Kung would then say: my god is exactly like that; we have the same one. Therefore he said calmly:

"All those present know God; thus it is unnecessary to speak of the Supreme One here. Tell us who your god is."

Kung realised that he faced a dangerous opponent. Inwardly he called for his helper, and felt him near at hand. That strengthened him, so that he readily began:

"My god is the supreme one. He has all the power on earth, because he cares for every one of his creatures. He strengthens our intellect so that we may be more clever and cunning than others; he gives us good thoughts so that we may triumph over our enemies. He loves battle and strife; he rewards our loyalty with goods of all kinds. He can also help us to honours among men, if that is what we desire."

After these words, Kung looked defiantly at the Lama, who spoke again in the unearthly, re-echoing voice:

"He whom you describe is indeed a lord over many, but he is the Lord of the Darkness."

"Call him what you will; you cannot deny that he is the lord!" cried Kung, who was like one blinded at that moment. "Go on with your questions!"

"What is the purpose of human life?" was Lao-Tse's question.

Kung was silent. He knew not what to reply. Had he never thought about it then? Desperately, he tried to listen to the voices that whispered and murmured within him; there was a ringing and buzzing in his ears; he could understand nothing. Yet he felt that he must reply. Finally a thought came to him:

"To work one's way up from the depths," he said in a tone of firm conviction.

When Lao-Tse was silent in answer to this, he thought he had struck the right note, and continued more eagerly:

"How a man is born, be it as a beggar or a mandarin, is immaterial. He must simply strive to train his intellect so that it becomes brilliant. He can then achieve anything, for he will be superior to a thousand blockheads."

"And where does this life lead after death?"

This time the answer came promptly:

"To the Eternal Gardens!"

"How do you picture these Gardens?" was the next question.

This Lao-Tse was becoming troublesome! What was the purpose of his question? Now, however, Kung heard the whispering voice, and said confidently: "That we shall know only after death, when we have entered them. Ruminating over it beforehand is pointless. You know as little how my house in Peining looks as we know what the Eternal Gardens are like. Foolish question!" he added scornfully.

"What must man do to be able to enter the Eternal Gardens?" the Lama wished to know.

"He must live as honourable a life as possible."

Hou-Chou could no longer contain himself.

"Allow me to ask a question, O Lama of all Lamas," he requested.

Delighted, Kung looked in the new direction. Perhaps this mandarin would be less disagreeable than the sage. When Lao-Tse nodded his assent with a smile, the Emperor said:

"What do you consider the greatest of all virtues?"

"At last a sensible question, worth answering," said Kung condescendingly. "The highest of all virtues is cunning. And why do I award it the prize? Because it is what helps us on in life. It alone enables us to achieve what we aspire to; it helps us out of trouble and unpleasantness. I am certain that even after death it will show us the way to the Eternal Gardens."

"It will never do that," Lao-Tse said emphatically. "It originates from the Darkness; the Eternal Gardens, however, are in the Light."

"What is your opinion of Truth?" Hou-Chou went on. Though shuddering, he wished somehow to relieve a little of the loathsomeness for Lao-Tse.

"That man has yet to be found who always speaks the truth," laughed Kung, who now felt quite at ease. "I do not hold with those who preach what they do not practise. Surely it is much more appropriate to tell people: always pretend to speak the truth, that is better than ..."

He could not continue. All those in attendance, notwithstanding the presence of the Sovereign, broke into tumultuous shouts. Lao-Tse could hardly restore calm. Then he said:

"I believe, dear friends, that we have heard enough to identify the teachings of Master Kung as harmful heresies, misleading the people. And for that reason ..."

Before he could continue, Kung interrupted with a storm of rage and abuse. Behind him, clearly visible to Lao-Tse, stood a tall, dark figure that seemed to incite him.

Thereupon Lao-Tse was seized by a mighty wrath. Taking a few steps forward, he stood suddenly in the centre of the hall – a solitary figure. He seemed to have grown as he now stretched out his arm and called in a ringing voice:

"Begone Satan, Lord of the Darkness! We have nothing to do with you!"

A bolt of lightning flashed across the hall, followed by the dull rumbling of thunder. Unwavering, Lao-Tse called out again:

"Out! In the Name of the Supreme One, I command you to depart!"

For several minutes pale light filled the space where the two opponents, Lao-Tse and the Dark One, stood face to face, visible to all. Those present had leapt up, but remained motionless at their places.

For the third time Lao-Tse raised his voice, with a sound never before heard in human speech. It resounded like the surging of the sea, and vibrated like the pealing of bells.

"You spawn and ruler of the Darkness, who through your deluded servant forced your way in here, in the Name of God, the Lord, I command you: Begone!"

235

It was as if the earth quaked. But the dark figure had vanished. Kung lay face down on the floor as though lifeless.

So deeply shaken were they all by the experience that nobody uttered a word. Finally Lao-Tse sank to his knees where he stood, and prayed.

Fervently he thanked God for His help. Friends and foes knelt with him; there was no one who did not join in giving thanks. The horrible Darkness had been too close to them. They had been able to see it with their own eyes. This they would never forget.

Thereupon all of them departed, leaving the man who lay on the floor to the care of the servants.

NEWS of what had happened in the Imperial Palace spread like wildfire far beyond Kiang-ning. No one spoke of anything else.

But as always in such cases the rumours took on vast proportions. Some would have it that the Lord of the Darkness immediately took his servant with him. Others told of dreadful imprecations hurled by him against Lao-Tse who was now no longer safe anywhere from his pursuit.

The rumours and gossip even found their way back to the Imperial Palace, where they reached the ear of Hou-Chou, who was annoyed by them. Must men drag down everything to the level of the commonplace? By inventing all kinds of fantastic things they thought to enhance the miraculous. Nothing could be more wonderful than the overwhelming event that so many had been allowed to experience.

The Emperor convened the noblemen and officials, asking them to put an end to this foolish talk.

"Who knows anything about Master Kung?" he then asked.

Very few had bothered about him; but Hai-Tan, who was keeping a watch on his dwelling-place, could say that he had resumed his walks and was still making no arrangements for his departure.

"Then we must banish him from the country," the Ruler said thoughtfully. "But who is to guarantee that he will not cross the borders again, spreading fresh heresies? Has any one of you a suggestion?"

Everyone, even those who were previously partial to him, realised that Master Kung must go, but they were unable to say how to accomplish it. It was decided that each should endeavour to solve the problem. They would meet again in three days' time to see whether a feasible solution had been found.

Meantime, however, Kung had not been idle. On the advice of his master he had bided his time only to consider his next moves all the more keenly. On receiving word of the decision in the Imperial Palace, he realised that he must make haste.

In the dead of night he had all the preparations made for departure, distributing his people and pack-animals over the various urban districts near the gates. When these were opened in the morning, solitary travellers, traders or armed men walked out through every gate, likewise horses and pack-animals laden with goods were led away. This aroused no suspicion.

The following day this individual flight was repeated, and despite all the vigilance it was not discovered either. Now only Master Kung and his most trusted servant were left. In the evening, shortly before the gates were closed, this servant appeared at the main gate, disguised as a priest, and spoke with the sentry. He managed to find out that even during the night a small door could be opened just wide enough for a single person to slip through. He would need to produce a seal from one of the mandarins.

On further questioning, the sentry said that every night several persons came, requesting entry or exit; it was not unusual. The priest exhorted the man to be very much on his guard, then moved off slowly as if merely out for a stroll.

But he simply went to another gate and waited. Finally a man came along who was apparently about to leave the city; he pulled a seal from under his robe. The disguised servant was promptly at his side, asking whether he was in a great hurry, or whether he would like to earn a small fortune first. One word led to another, and in the end the traveller turned back; the servant, however, had acquired the seal.

At another gate he undertook the same risk; here too he succeeded, so that even before daybreak he was able to return to Master Kung with two of the required seals.

They left the city separately through two different gates, and met with the escorts and baggage train far off in the forest. In utmost haste they rode north-west in order to hide in the mountains for the time being. Then

Master Kung sent almost his entire following back to the south, while he himself, with a few servants, proceeded north.

When the dignitaries gathered again with the Emperor at the appointed hour to continue their discussion, the object of their deliberations was already far away. But they examined the suggestions, none of which met with unanimous approval.

At that point Lao-Tse entered. No one except Hou-Chou had seen him since the eventful day. He had been too deeply shaken to return lightly to everyday life. But today he came to make an important announcement.

He informed the Emperor that in spite of the careful surveillance, the stranger and all his escorts had left the city. His spiritual helpers had shown him, the sage, that Master Kung had turned north.

"Then let us set out, to catch up with him and bring him back," shouted several hearers in their zeal.

Even Hou-Chou was of the opinion that it was a duty to bring the heretic into safe custody. Yet Lao-Tse told them that God, the Supreme One, had reserved to Himself the punishment of the evildoer.

"Do you know how it is to be done?" the Emperor asked, but the Lama said "no".

"It is not fitting for us to ponder it," he said. "God will reveal it to us when the time comes."

Now weeks passed, and there was no more talk of Master Kung.

Meanwhile the building of the Temple progressed vigorously. It was a spacious circular hall, around which were spread several smaller ones, differently decorated. While the large hall displayed beautifully-cut stones of varying colours: white, grey, black, yellowish and reddish, polished to a gleaming finish, the small ones exhibited different materials.

One was constructed of costly woods, another was sheathed in silk, elaborately embroidered; a third had walls covered in kaolin tiles, with figures of the same material gracing them. A fourth was hung with tapestries, the fifth was richly inlaid with silver, while the last gleamed with gold. Everywhere precious stones were mounted in lavish profusion.

Broad steps led up to the entrance-gate. Passing through it, one came to a kind of forecourt which encircled all the halls. The entire plan was completely new in the Middle Kingdom.

But in Lao-Tse it awakened memories of far-off times, when he had seen something similar, only much, much more beautiful! And as he thought about it, a longing, such as he had never known before, welled up in him. His soul yearned for those Eternal Gardens which were its home. Memories upon memories arose in him.

One night he reflected on the guidance which had led his life on safe paths. Suddenly before his mind's eye stood the picture which he had been allowed to behold on the day of his consecration as Lama: the wondrous Countenance that inclined graciously over him! It was familiar to him and yet so sublime. If only he might be permitted to behold It once more!

This wish became unconsciously a yearning, longing petition.

"Have patience for yet a short while, Servant of the Supreme One," the voice resounded within him, "then you will be permitted to behold Him for Whom your soul is longing."

Now great joy filled the Lama's heart, and this inner exaltation communicated itself to all his activities. It was all the more necessary, since fresh difficulties were arising.

From the north of the Realm came reports that a great sage, who called himself "The Mysterious One", had emerged; he proclaimed God and performed miracles. Immediately thereafter Lao-Tse learned that this man was none other than Master Kung.

What should be done now? God had reserved punishment of the heretic to Himself, therefore one must wait. But this waiting was difficult. From all quarters the Emperor was urged to put an end to the activities of the false Lama. The people could not understand why neither the Emperor nor the High Lama would proceed against the Mysterious One.

But the gladness filling Lao-Tse's soul allowed him to look on quite calmly, and even to reassure the others. What harm could come to the people when God's Commands were acted upon?

The reports about the activities of the Mysterious One multiplied. Apparently Kung felt safe because until now nothing had been done to ward him off. He ventured ever further south-east. Nothing impeded his preaching or his advance.

Then one day he stood again in the great square in Kiang-ning.

A loose robe of extreme simplicity covered his body, which had become stouter. Down his back hung a long, black queue, a hair-style which no one had seen before, and which was admired by old and young alike.

On his head he wore the round black silk cap of mandarins, with a huge red button in the middle. The people thought that he must be of very noble birth. A thin flowing moustache like that of the Emperor, but not as long, adorned his upper lip. No one was able to recognise Master Kung in this "Mysterious One", and those who had expected to see him had to admit that their expectation had deluded them.

Lao-Tse had received tidings of his arrival and, dressed like a servant, he was among the crowd of listeners. With great ceremony a student of the Mysterious One set up a wooden block, covered it with a carpet, and then helped the speaker to mount it. At once he began to speak:

"Men of Kiang-ning. The Supreme One sends me to you! He wants you to learn the Truth at last, which has been withheld from you for so long."

Grumbling, resentful scolding among the audience interrupted him, but he disregarded it, and continued in a louder voice:

"I know, birds can fly, they are shot down with arrows. I know, fish can swim, they are caught in nets. I know, four-footed creatures can run, they are caught in traps.

"But no one knows how to catch the dragon which, borne by clouds and wind, rises up belching forth destruction, and swoops down upon men. Do you know?"

Loud shouts answered him.

"There are no such dragons. They are products of our fear."

"Who has taught you that?" the speaker asked warily.

"Lao-Tse! Lao-Tse!" sounded from all sides, and it was evident from the shouts that they contained certainty about the truth of what Lao-Tse told them.

"You poor deluded ones," shouted the man on the wooden block. "Naturally your Lama wants to lull you into a false sense of security. By denying the existence of dragons he can carry on his mischief all the better. He himself is a dragon! I know him. He rules over your whole vast Realm. He rules over the great Tibet. He will increase his dominion over still further expanses of land and bring all of them to ruin. Seize him before it is too late."

240

A murmur of protest arose like the rushing of enormous waters. But something held the people spellbound so that they did not fall upon the slanderer.

He raised his voice louder still:

"I have been sent by the Supreme One to put an end to these ungodly pursuits ...."

Had he moved too abruptly, did the animistic servants of God have a hand in it? Before the Mysterious One could complete his sentence, the wooden block tipped over. The speaker plunged down, directly on to the short, curved sword of the armed man standing in front of him, who had raised it as though in defence.

His life-blood gushed forth. The Mysterious One was dead. As he fell, the small cap slipped from his head, revealing that the queue which had evoked such admiration was fastened to it.

The bystanders drew back, leaving a wide space around him.

No one would have anything to do with the man whom God had condemned before their very eyes. And again, just as months ago at the Imperial Palace, he was left where he had fallen until his servants removed him.

Nobody cared about where the dead body was taken. Everyone breathed a sigh of relief that the Mysterious One would no longer be able to speak.

Together with the other listeners Lao-Tse left the square and went to the Emperor, bearing news of the terrible, yet liberating event. He was firmly convinced that the dead man was Master Kung, and Hou-Chou shared his opinion. He informed the nobles of his Council accordingly. The matter was then no longer discussed. The reports about some popular teacher came to an abrupt end.

But the fact that such a heretic could find credence indicated to Lao-Tse that he himself should again appear in public more often. Actually, Hou-Chou and Han no longer required his advice; the people, however, needed someone to speak to them regularly.

When he informed the Emperor of his resolve to travel about the country, the Ruler tried to withhold him at all costs. He considered the Lama too old for such exertions, and besides he felt his own strength declining.

If the Supreme One called him away soon, it would be reassuring to know that Lao-Tse was by the side of his son. He spoke plainly to the Lama about these misgivings, but found little sympathy. Once he had recognised something as a duty, nobody and nothing could change Lao-Tse's mind.

Quietly he prepared everything for his departure, and then one morning he stood before Hou-Chou to bid him farewell.

"My Emperor," said he calmly, "throughout your life, you have always asked only for what could benefit your people. Would you have it any different at the end of your life?"

"I feel that I will see you no more," was the Ruler's reply. But Lao-Tse comforted him:

"I will always know how you fare, and will be able to return in good time to bid you the last farewell."

On that note they parted.

Prince Han, who was detained by his duties as Lord Treasurer, would have loved to ride with the Lama.

"Once I am Emperor, I will be doubly bound," he sighed, but the Lama did not share his view.

"As Sovereign it will be your duty to ride through your country, and to show yourself to your people, my Prince. But now you are more needed here. Farewell."

LAO-TSE BESTRODE HIS HORSE like a youth. He did not feel the strain of riding, for as usual his spirit was occupied with other things. He had entrusted his entire journey to higher guidance, and now allowed himself to be led.

Wherever he went, his presence seemed to be particularly needed just then. In some districts he had to stay for weeks in order to clear up errors, to remedy grievances, or to make new arrangements.

These did not always concern matters of faith. Very often he had to enforce governmental measures, to enable the people to live in outward harmony, and to find time for their souls. His teaching was gradually perfected during this journey, and could perhaps be summarised briefly as follows:

We human beings are creatures of the Supreme One, Whom nobody has ever seen, nor ever will see. He is supreme over us, yet He has a part in our destiny. He knows whether we conduct ourselves in a way that is worthy of Him. If we do, He grants us all the help we need.

The spirit-spark which He sank into us strives upwards again to Him. Therefore our ascent into the Eternal Gardens is assured after rightly completing our course on earth. But no man lives just once on earth. He returns there until he has laid aside everything earthly in the earthly. Being of the earth we must free ourselves from the earthly.

The spirit-spark teaches man what he must and must not do, in order to live according to the Will of the Supreme One. He who listens to his inner voice acts in harmony with the Laws of God.

The better man grasps this, the more he learns "action through inaction"; that is action which accords with everything that proceeds from the Supreme One. The intellectual activities of men, "action in action", interfere with the effects of the Divine Radiations. As long as man considers himself to be wise, he will not learn "action through inaction", and yet it is the greatest bliss.

But let no one suppose that this is to advocate indolence. Only he who unremittingly attends to his work, whatever it may be, only he can pass before the penetrating Eye of the Supreme One.

We must live from within outwards, not from without inwards.

The more abundantly God reveals Himself to us, the less we become. –

Proclaiming these teachings, admonishing and reforming, Lao-Tse had reached the sea-coast. The thunderous waves made the same deep impression on his soul as they had in his youth. It was there that the Majesty of God and His Omnipotence still stood most powerfully before him. That is why he always felt particularly drawn to this region. But he visited it only when the Luminous Messenger of God advised him that the time had come to do so.

He found peace and harmony. The wall that had been raised had fulfilled its task so far, and consistently rebuffed the spying strangers. But it had begun to crumble in some places. It would not be able to withstand the severe battering of the ocean gales much longer.

Considering the problem, Lao-Tse and the people of the region decided that it would suffice to fortify the observation- and watch-towers. With the establishment of a regular coastguard, the wall could safely fall into ruin, for the country would be protected.

"Now that we, our children and grandchildren know what is at stake, nobody will be indifferent about the watch," said an aged workman. "Woe betide the stranger who dares to set foot in our land!"

Nowhere in the country but here was such exquisitely fine kaolin to be found. The bowls were extremely thin, and recently the men had learned from their little friends to add the colours directly to the clay, so that delicately tinted articles were created.

It was clear to Lao-Tse that this art flowed from peace-filled souls. Such works could only come into being where harmony prevailed.

Reluctantly the Lama left this district, to turn to the south-west of the country. On the eve of his departure a man in plain clothing came to him, and asked to be permitted to become his student. Lao-Tse had never yet gathered students around him as did other sages.

It went against the grain even now. His teachings were intended for all, his words sought entrance into the souls of all his hearers. And yet there was something about this very young man that attracted him. He arranged for the supplicant to come on the morrow, and brought his concern before God's Luminous Messenger in the night.

"Have you never yet considered training a successor?" was the surprising reply.

The Lama said that he had not.

"I thought it was unnecessary, and that at the right moment the Supreme One would send a Lama who could occupy my post."

"Through me the Supreme One bids you to take this man Chuang with you, and to implant your teaching in his already-prepared soul. It will bear fruit."

Chuang's joy was great when he received Lao-Tse's permission to accompany him in the future. But greater still was the Lama's astonishment when he observed how every word he spoke was received with understanding.

In the course of time the student became a close friend whom he could trust completely. Chuang's relationship with Wuti proved equally gratifying.

The closer Lao-Tse and his retinue approached the south-west, the more traces they found of Master Kung's pernicious influence. His teachings had even encroached upon the priests of the Supreme One, so that they preached "virtue" more than God.

But what they meant by virtue were mainly those human qualities capable of gaining recognition and influence for men. To train and develop these qualities, above all the intellect, was their foremost task.

Wherever he went, Lao-Tse had to combat these erroneous views; he had to involve himself in controversies and make forceful speeches – he who would so have liked to keep the peace! But there was no alternative. The situation could not be remedied by mere reasoning. He must seek to convince at least a few, before having recourse to prohibitions.

Already Chuang proved very helpful. He was at pains to relieve his master of all unpleasantness, provoking quarrels with the priests in order to be able at least to express his opinion and combat their wrong views. Only after the way for improvement had thus been paved did Lao-Tse himself need to appear and to censure, proclaim and teach.

But despite all that it was nerve-racking work. Lao-Tse as well as Wuti and Chuang felt that the real instigators of the heresies so readily disseminated by the priests were in hiding. The sages could not get hold of them. In vain Lao-Tse implored God to show him a way to proceed against these stealthy adversaries. It was not in God's Will that drastic measures should now be taken here, and Lao-Tse acquiesced.

The Lama had now been living for over two years in this fertile and beautiful region which until then he had hardly known. Nor did it seem possible for him to continue the journey, for only little, very little, had been achieved.

Then one night the call came to his soul:

"Go back to Kiang-ning. Hou-Chou is preparing for his return home. Leave Wuti and Chuang behind here. Let them continue your work. As for you, ride back to the capital by the shortest possible route."

And Lao-Tse did as he was bidden. His heart would grow heavy when he thought of Hou-Chou's departure. Prince Han was indeed a worthy successor to his father. He would surpass him with regard to the outward splendour of his Realm, in the show of force and also the lust for power; yet he lacked the fine sensitivity to the Laws of God and to the inner needs of the people.

DID PEOPLE ALREADY know of the country's impending loss? Accompanied only by Lai, Lao-Tse rode into Kiang-ning one evening, and went immediately to his rooms in the Palace. He was welcomed joyfully by the servants, and even Hai-Tan rushed to the scene on hearing of his arrival.

"How is the Emperor?" the Lama wished to know. Hai-Tan assured him that he was in excellent health.

"He has merely become more solemn than usual," he added. "That may well be attributed to his age."

But when Lao-Tse stood before his Ruler the following day, he clearly perceived the looseness of the cord holding the soul in the body; the very first words of Hou-Chou showed him that the Emperor himself was aware of it.

"So you have indeed come in good time, my friend," cried the Sovereign in welcome, "to help release my weary soul from the earth! How happy this makes me. There is still so much that I would like to discuss and enjoin upon you."

Losing no time, the friends became engrossed in the thoughts that occupied the Emperor. He was not anxious lest his son govern the Realm differently. But he too realised that Han would make use of every opportunity to extend the borders, even at the sacrifice of peace.

"I believe that after all these years of outward calm he literally longs for military exploits and conflict," the Emperor said regretfully.

It was a matter of great concern to Hou-Chou that the Temple of God, now nearing completion, should not be neglected.

"I fear that Han does not derive the same joy as I do from the work begun by me. Nevertheless it is his most sacred duty to have the building completed. I have entrusted it to him as a legacy, but I am telling you also, so that you may remind him."

There followed a whole list of requests for the welfare of the people, but which so far anticipated the future that Lao-Tse smiled.

"Do you think, Hou-Chou, that I will long outlive you? We are almost the same age. My years here below are also numbered, and I too long for home."

Then the Emperor realised that he had not at all considered the demise of the Lama. He had hoped that the wise man would be at Han's side for a long time to come.

"I will stay on for as long as the Supreme One still requires my services here below, my Emperor," the Lama comforted him, and the Emperor allowed himself to be consoled like a child.

After a few days everything that the Ruler had at heart was discussed. No sooner had it been said than it lost all importance for him. All earthly ties fell away. His soul freed itself for the flight upwards.

Lao-Tse asked him whether he wished to hold one more great reception. Amazed, Hou-Chou stared at the questioner.

"Do you think I should take solemn leave of everyone?" he asked. "They will remember me better if I do not confront them as a dying man. But you, my friend, promise me that you will stay with me during the short span of time that I shall yet tarry down here."

The Lama readily gave his promise. Infinite peace surrounded the aged Ruler. Blessed spirits, figures from other realms, approached the departing soul in greeting; light and radiance flowed around it. The friends mostly sat together in silence, listening to tidings brought by Messengers of the Supreme One.

It was about the hour of sunset. Lao-Tse had opened the window to make it easier for the Emperor to breathe. The two were so seated that they could see the section of the sky above the tree-tops, which was gilded by the light of the setting sun.

All at once it seemed to them that heavenly song floated with the gentle breeze into the room. Louder and louder it grew, like mighty choirs. Lao-Tse was reminded of the glorious singing in the Mountain-monastery.

Suddenly the gold deepened, seeming to break forth from within in sheaves of rays, marking out an avenue from above downwards. The two gazed enraptured, hardly daring to breathe.

"O Supreme One, am I allowed to behold Thy Glory?" whispered Hou-Chou, raising his arms towards all the heavenly radiance.

But Lao-Tse called in a loud voice:

"The Countenance Which appeared to me at every crowning point of my life! I see It again! Thanks be to Thee, O Supreme One, that I am allowed to behold Thee in Thy Holy Son! Now I know Who called me."

The Light-Radiance in the sky faded, night fell.

When the servants entered the apartment to light the small lanterns, they found Emperor and Lama in the great armchairs by the window. Together their souls had passed over to Luminous Realms.

APPENDIX

"AS ALWAYS ON EARTH,

IN CHINA TOO HUMANITY DID NOT HOLD

FAST TO THE RAY OF THE LIGHT

THAT WAS OFFERED."

SEVERAL MONTHS had passed since the Lama of all Lamas and his Emperor had left the earthly covering. Both were buried with great ceremony in accordance with wishes expressed earlier.

The remains of the Emperor were interred beneath the uncompleted Temple of God, in one of the small chambers constructed for the purpose. Precious embroideries, and artefacts made of silver, gold and kaolin were placed there.

In the centre stood the gilded couch on which lay the embalmed body of Hou-Chou, covered by a dragon-banner.

Afterwards the chamber was walled up; no human being was to set foot there again. A large wooden panel, lacquered in red, on which the Imperial Dragon was painted in gold, was placed before the walled entrance. Beneath it was the Emperor's name, the period of his reign and the words which he himself had specified:

"Sovereign of the people, but servant of God."

In the endeavour to preserve the remains of the Lama of all Lamas they had likewise been treated with oils and ointments. On receiving the news of Lao-Tse's death, the numerous priests of Tibetan origin who officiated in the Temples of God all over the country had hastened to Kiang-ning to render all honour to their Supreme Lama, and to perform every act of love that was in their power.

Chuang and Wuti, whom Han had summoned, also arrived in good time, and under Wuti's direction, the earthly covering of Lao-Tse was taken to the Mountain-monastery in Tibet. Emperor Han escorted it all the way to the border of his Realm, at the same time setting out on the journey through his country.

Now Wuti and the remaining Tibetans had returned. All had resumed their duties; only for Wuti there was no more to do. Emperor Han was far from Kiang-ning, and the mandarins jealously guarded against the reassertion of Tibetan influence in their country. So Wuti disappeared from the Imperial Palace; no one knew where he had gone.

Chuang had remained in the Mountain-monastery. The High Lama had received instructions to train this pupil of Lao-Tse's, even as the Lama of all Lamas had once received his training there.

While Han, the Emperor, was absent, the work at the Temple of God came to a halt. Hai-Wi-Nan was not negligent, but he was alone now, whereas previously the Emperor had supported him, urging the workers on by encouraging or exhorting them.

The mandarins and the other nobles and officials worked against him. They declared publicly that it was wrong to spend on the construction of a single temple monies which could be used for the country. There was no one to whom Hai-Wi-Nan could turn for help and advice.

One day he appeared in the assembly of the nobles, which ruled the country in the absence of the Emperor, and declared that he would not proceed with the building of the Temple so long as the Emperor was absent. The mandarins laughed.

"Have you perceived at last that you are not needed?" they mocked. "If the building of your temple is to continue, we can find master-builders here in this country. We have no need of strangers."

"Let me tell you why I am suspending the work," said Hai-Wi-Nan very gravely. "The building of a Temple of the Supreme One is something so sacred that no conflict must creep in. Only willing hearts and hands may join in the work, only among a people of God's servants may such a Temple arise! Here envy, ill-will and greed lurk about the building: that is a disparagement of the Supreme One! I will not lend my skills to it!"

Now the nobles were a little frightened after all! For they too believed in the Supreme One, and certainly wished to render Him every honour. And this stranger declared so coldly that they were blaspheming! One of them leapt to his feet, and went after the departing man.

"Listen, Hai-Wi-Nan," he called urgently, "if you really are not willing to continue building, surely you will remain in the country, and wait until the Emperor decides on his return what is to be done."

"For the time being I will remain here. I do not know what God will bid me do eventually."

254

And Hai-Wi-Nan returned to the Palace; but after only a few days he had vanished from his rooms.

The Temple structure as such was completed, but the interior still remained to be decorated, and even for the exterior the Emperor had planned all kinds of adornment, which was still lacking.

Sorrowfully Hai-Tan had the great gates locked. At first he went every day to the glade in the forest where rose the Temple of God, and where lay the best of all Emperors; but then there were more and more excuses for not going. Finally the glade was completely deserted by men.

And the animistic helpers? What happened to them? They too disappeared, since they were no longer needed for building the House of God.

HAN HAD BEEN away from his capital for more than a year. With all sorts of excuses he sought to silence the voices within, warning him that what he was doing was not right. Had not Lao-Tse himself stated that when he became Emperor he must visit his Realm?

"Yes," said the voice, "so he did, but he did not expect you to set out immediately after your father's funeral, even before you had effectively taken hold of the reins of government. Have you given your successor in the Treasury any insight into the work? Have you satisfied yourself that all parts of the great mechanism of government continue to interrelate, and would function smoothly even without the Emperor in command?

"Prince, Emperor, it was made so easy for you to assume your high office! With your father, his Adviser also departed – he who would probably have become burdensome to you despite your reverence for him. You were allowed to establish your position unaided! You were allowed to act independently, and to exercise your sovereign authority at your discretion, without intervention from anyone whose advice you had to heed!

"When you now return home, you will find all the positions filled by the counsellors to replace their absent Emperor. There is no more room for you! Go back, Han! Abandon this wrong course! Be Emperor before it is too late!"

The warning voices were ever more insistent. Han's soul grew uneasy. Was it too late to be Emperor in the true sense? What was he to do? He had still traversed only half of his Realm. What had he accomplished by it? Little enough. Whenever Lao-Tse undertook such journeys, he bore witness to the Supreme One, remedying grievances and bringing about innovations at the same time, as commanded by God! God?

It shot through the Emperor like lightning: he had forgotten about God! Apart from entering the Temple in every place to attend to his devotions, he was not concerned with the Supreme One. That was where his guilt lay! He perceived it and his soul cried out for Lao-Tse! He would give anything to be with his old teacher for an hour. The Lama would help him to find God again.

"Does it require a mediator?" the voices whispered. "Han, consider: do you not know that anyone who strives earnestly can find God? Become small and humble, small in your own eyes. What did your father say? Sovereign of the people, but servant of God! Do you not wish to be that also? Seek God, He can be found!"

And in the stillness of the night, Han prostrated himself on the floor by his bed, confessed his guilt, which now appeared to him enormous and unforgivable, and implored God to forgive him. With that, peace entered his soul, and reinvigorated, suffused with joyful energy, he was able to give orders for the return home in the morning.

They took the shortest route to the capital, after the nobles who were allowed to accompany the Emperor had begged him in vain not to break off the journey too soon. They could no longer understand the new Ruler, who at first had been quite to their liking.

"He must have had a vision," one of them whispered when all were struck by the changed nature of Han.

Messengers were sent ahead to announce the Emperor's arrival to the city. There everything was adorned most beautifully; old and young were on the streets and at the gates to welcome the Emperor with the jubilation befitting him.

He delighted in the joy of his people, blind to the fact that as yet he had done nothing at all to deserve this joy. On entering the Palace, which he was now to occupy, the familiar apartments in which everything was as it had been before, he experienced the searing grief at the loss of his father as on the first day after his departure.

"You wanted to avoid this grief," the voices whispered, "now you feel it all the more!"

"Then I accept it as penance for all that I have done wrong in vain delusion," the Emperor vowed, and he was in earnest about it.

He had to take upon himself a great deal more! The whispering voices had not exaggerated: The mandarins who were left behind had ruled as they judged and thought best, raising themselves to high offices, and lining their pockets.

"Can I proceed against them with severity, when I myself am to blame for things coming to such a pass?" Han asked in despair during the night.

"Since you recognise that the guilt is yours, you will take yourself to task. That shall remain between your God and you. But you must deal rigorously with the presumptuous offenders, so that they feel the hand of their Emperor, and submit in good time. Every day that you let them have their way will make it harder, and eventually impossible, for you to govern the country as your father did."

The next day a relentless Sovereign confronted the Council. He commanded that everything be reinstated to its condition at his father's death, that all posts conferred in the meantime be revoked, all monies wrongfully disbursed be refunded. All measures taken contrary to Hou-Chou's former decisions were declared null and void.

The nobles put their heads together and complained that Emperor Han in no way measured up to their expectations. Above all they were afraid of what each new day might bring.

But Han had gone to the forest glade to visit the Temple of God. The motionless silence that surrounded it he did not perceive, for his soul was absorbed in prayer. All the greater therefore was his astonishment when he saw that the Temple was deserted, without of any sign of work. The gate was locked; he could not even worship there.

"Is this also my fault?" he asked himself.

Then Hai-Tan came. He had heard where the Emperor was, and now he wanted at least to bring the keys. He feared the Sovereign's wrath, which he had experienced in good measure that morning. But this time he was mistaken. Han was silent, only two tears rolled slowly down his lean, tanned face.

"My fault, my fault!" he sighed inwardly. "My God, Supreme One, canst Thou forgive me this too?"

"Where is the master-builder?" he then asked, while Hai-Tan struggled with the lock.

"We do not know, O Emperor; do not be angry; one day he was gone!"

A quiet hope arose in Han's soul:

"Might the cessation of the building perhaps be due to Hai-Wi-Nan's disappearance? Was he himself at least not to be blamed for that?"

But the very next words from Hai-Tan's lips dashed this hope. Hai-Tan recounted truthfully what had taken place, and ended by saying:

"Had you been here, O Emperor, the master-builder would surely not have left!"

Little did he realise how deeply he pressed the thorn into his master's soul with these words.

Alone, Han entered the Temple when it was at last opened, and humbled himself deeply before God. How much more would he find ruined through his fault?

O Emperor Han, your troubles are not yet over!

When he returned to the Palace, the Ruler had all the servants questioned with regard to Hai-Wi-Nan's disappearance. No one could say anything more than that one day he was simply gone. Then Lai, Lao-Tse's old servant, was announced to the Emperor.

"Master," he said, "when we find Wuti we shall also reach Hai-Wi-Nan."

"Has Wuti also disappeared?" asked the Emperor, horrified.

It seemed to him that all good souls had left the city.

"Yes, Wuti left because he had no work here," said Lai, rather indifferently. "But I think we can probably trace him through the Tibetan community."

"Do you think that he has returned to the monastery?"

"Not so, O Emperor, he certainly has not done that. He is awaiting your commands. Do you wish me to look for him?"

"Yes, Lai, seek him, and if you bring him back, you shall be amply rewarded."

Lai looked with amusement at the Emperor, who could speak of reward at that point.

"Lai needs neither money nor goods. Lai is rich, for he has the knowledge of the Supreme One."

Lai was indeed richer than he, the Emperor! Han perceived this clearly. If only Wuti were here! Wuti, who had always been close to Lao-Tse! He would be adviser and companion to him also!

Days passed, days that brought much unpleasantness to the new Emperor. Although he was determined to act with the utmost severity, so that his authority should be established from the beginning, the nobles and officials were no less determined to be at once unbending, so that the Emperor should not fail to know where he stood with them.

Outwardly they spent themselves in ceremonies, inwardly they offered silent resistance to everything that he decreed. It was enough to drive one to despair!

"All this you might have spared yourself, you fool," the voices whispered. "Had you remained in the capital and taken over everything from your father's hands in good order, the Realm would today be moving towards calm, peaceful times. But now civil war is imminent!"

Civil war! It was unthinkable! Was it to be again as it had been under previous rulers, when rebellion raged through the streets, when only death and destruction could induce the people to give heed?

And it seemed that Wuti was nowhere to be found! Hai-Wi-Nan was still missing! Emperor Han gave orders for the Temple to be opened; daily devotions were to take place there, even though its decoration was not yet completed. But to whom should he entrust these Hours of Worship? The priests in Kiang-ning were occupied with their own Houses of God. Then the Emperor prayed to God in fervent, urgent entreaty, and God's answer came the very next day.

From the Mountain-monastery in Tibet came a Lama called Fung-Yan, with a letter from the High Lama. Lao-Tse had commanded Fung-Yan to set out immediately in order to assume the priestly office in the new Temple of God.

"You are still in contact with Lao-Tse?" the Emperor asked, as though in a daze.

"Certainly, Master," the Lama assured him. "Fu-Tse, our High Lama, can still speak with him."

This first sign of God's forgiveness and help filled the Emperor with great joy. He would do nothing, absolutely nothing in future without asking God for His guidance. Only now had Han, who from his earliest years had been taught the belief in the Supreme One, truly experienced and found God.

The following day Wuti stepped over the threshold of the Imperial chamber. Han could not believe his eyes. The faithful one, whom he thought he had already lost, now stood before him so naturally.

"If you have work for me, my Emperor," said Wuti, "I shall be happy to be allowed to serve you; if not, I shall return to Tibet."

"I will never let you leave me again, Wuti, now that I have found you at last!" cried Han.

But it became apparent that Wuti had come at the behest of the Supreme One; Lai had not found him.

"Will you be my companion and adviser, Wuti?" asked Han. And Wuti assumed the new duties as a matter of course.

Now the Emperor enquired regarding the whereabouts of Hai-Wi-Nan.

"He returned to his distant homeland at God's Command," Wuti reported. "The Temple is to remain in its present state for the time being. The country will be overtaken by hard times, in which there will be neither leisure nor money for building. Perhaps you will be allowed to complete it later, my Emperor."

This was the harshest punishment which could be meted out to Emperor Han. Without complaint, he accepted it as well-deserved.

It became clear that Wuti had kept a watchful eye from afar on developments in Kiang-ning, and was able to draw the Emperor's attention to certain things which had hitherto escaped his notice. He did so in a quiet, unassuming manner. It was obvious that he had associated constantly with Lao-Tse, and learned much from him.

But there was increasing unrest among the nobles. Once more a Tibetan adviser had appeared after all! That he had already been in attendance at the Imperial Court under Lao-Tse did not help matters, for they could tell him no tales; he had witnessed the development of everything himself.

Although he was not a Lama, the priests at the Temples of God willingly bowed to his authority, and the Emperor treated him as an intimate friend.

Han had acted with iron severity to enforce his decrees. Outwardly, all was now as it had been in Hou-Chou's time, and the people lacked nothing.

However, the joyousness that had once prevailed among the officials and mandarins was absent. The counsellors came to meetings reluctantly. Often it happened that they had no suggestions whatever to make to the Emperor, who clearly perceived that this reflected their defiant attitude:

"He knows himself what he wants to do, why should we speak at all?"

The more intolerable this situation became for the Ruler, the more forcibly it impelled him to prayer. Han grew accustomed to bringing everything that preoccupied him before God. Only thus was he able to obtain clarity, and from clarity came strength. He could not account for this, but intuitively he perceived it with increasing awareness.

Now he also summoned up the courage to beseech God for help, and even though he often went about it in quite the wrong way, in desperate cases he always found the right way, and help never failed to come.

"How am I to turn the mandarins away from their obstinacy and discontent?" he asked one night, and out of the question arose the cry for Light.

And again he heard the whispering voices:

"Give them work! So long as they are idle, their thoughts will always revolve round the same point!"

"Where am I to find work for them all?"

"Build the wall that you planned years ago. Now is the time. It will give work to the nobles, and protection to your country from the neighbours who have long regarded your art and growing prosperity with envy."

Grateful for the advice, the harassed Emperor found peace. He told Wuti what he had heard, and was advised not simply to order the building of the wall, but to make it appear that the idea came from the circle of nobles. After lengthy deliberation, a way was found for the Emperor to accomplish this.

At the next meeting Han reported that he had received private information that the men from the west country were making secret preparations to invade the Middle Kingdom. This caused great alarm.

Simply for the sake of contradiction, several mandarins were about to question the truth of this statement, but before they were able to comment, those who could not bear the thought of others knowing anything before

261

they did made themselves heard. They announced loudly that they too had received similar tidings, in fact their words far exceeded the simple statement of the Emperor.

Then Han called upon his counsellors to think how this invasion could be prevented. He would be grateful for any good suggestion. Stimulated and eager, the counsellors left the meeting. They had not been so united for many a day. No one had time to complain about Wuti or the Emperor.

The next day one suggestion after another was offered. Actually none was of any use, but Han was clever: he offered no opposition; on the contrary, he promised to examine each proposal.

In conclusion he read out a document which he said had been sent to him anonymously. In it he was asked to build a wall for defence against the western realm, similar to the one raised long ago by the sea. Once the neighbours realised that the border had been made secure, they would not dare to risk such an invasion.

The Emperor made no comment on this suggestion either. But the others acclaimed it enthusiastically as the best. Since it had been received anonymously, each could claim it as his own idea. Hence nobody would compromise himself by supporting the suggestion. Even before the meeting broke up, it had been agreed that the wall should be built.

"What suggestion does Wuti have to make?" they asked. The Tibetan gave a little smile.

"I bow to your wisdom, counsellors," he said. "This suggestion is worthy to take precedence over all others."

On one of the following days, the Emperor asked which of his counsellors and officials were willing to take an active part in the building of the wall. The extremely long border must be divided into many sections, each of which would have to be supervised by a nobleman, to ensure that the work proceeded in the right way.

A sufficient number of nobles came forward. Preparations were speeded up, and after only a few weeks Kiang-ning was rid of the disaffected. And at the border they were far enough apart to prevent them from causing any mischief.

Thus the dangers of an uprising, and along with that of a sudden attack, seemed to have been averted, but it only seemed so. Emperor Han had been too preoccupied with his capital to be able to pay attention to what was taking place in the rest of the Realm.

Suddenly reports came from the south that the nobles there wanted to secede from the Middle Kingdom. It was said that two realms had existed even in former times – the cold and the torrid. To let them be governed by one and the same hand was absurd. He who knew what was good for the cold region would not on that account understand the torrid one.

Now the nobles of the torrid region had chosen from among them a special emperor, who claimed to be a true son of heaven. This man, a youthful hotspur by the name of Pei-Fong, challenged Emperor Han. He sent seven messengers with a letter in which he described himself quite matter-of-factly as the Emperor of the Southern Kingdom, demanding recognition from his neighbour, the Emperor of the Middle Kingdom.

To simplify matters, the great river should form the border between the two countries. If Han agreed to this, the two rulers and their peoples could live side by side in peace, otherwise Pei-Fong would use force of arms to gain his right.

Han, who had received the envoys in the presence of his counsellors, tore the document to pieces, hurling it at the feet of the messengers. But they laughed, declaring that Pei-Fong had expected nothing else, and was therefore already standing at the new border with an imposing army, unless in the meantime he had even crossed the river.

Everyone was filled with indignation, and the common danger welded Emperor and mandarins more firmly together. Those absent were hastily recalled; the building of the wall continued only to preserve a semblance of defence against the neighbours, and all the men had to hurl themselves upon the enemy.

Yet by the time all these preparations were made, Pei-Fong and his forces already stood on the plain between the rivers. They had ravaged the region which they had traversed. It was inconceivable that the invaders were sons of the same Realm, hitherto living together in profound peace.

Every evil instinct was roused: the men robbed, plundered and murdered, as though the tidings of the Holy God of Peace had never reached them.

What gave Han a distinct advantage despite the enemy's having a start of him in every respect, was the fact that Pei-Fong's men were merely armed hordes, whereas Han was able to send trained soldiers to the battlefield, and to make use of the armed masses to cover the rear.

The war, so infamously provoked, raged for months, and the country suffered indescribably. Rivers of blood flowed, making hardly any impression; for in the overpopulated country, people were unaccustomed to valuing a single life. But famine and epidemics sprang up in the wake of the conflict, which was conducted doggedly and with alternating fortunes.

Slowly Han succeeded in repelling the hordes from the south back across the river; slowly, almost step by step, he regained possession of the southern provinces. But each day could still bring a turn of events to his disadvantage. With God's Help, however, Han continued victorious. Pei-Fong was killed; the mandarins who had supported him fled in terror, and the people were thankful to be able to return home.

After almost two years of fierce fighting, Han was once more Emperor in the "torrid region", as his ancestors had been before him. Now he decided to choose a capital here too, and to live alternately in both cities.

No sooner had this intention been made known than emissaries from widely-scattered towns presented themselves to the Emperor, inviting him to take up residence among them.

Although he felt very much drawn to the sea-coast, he turned down all formal requests from that region, because he wished to dwell in the heart of the provinces. There he would be better able to oversee everything. Finally the Emperor chose the relatively small town of Chang-Chou. The defeated nobles had to meet the expenses of building an Imperial Palace. They did so without a murmur, happy to be able to live in peace again at last.

Only now did it become apparent what devastation the war had caused. Fields were trampled underfoot, herds of cattle were slaughtered, leaving no offspring. But above all, the workshops and silkworm nurseries, so abundant especially in the south, were completely destroyed. What had been ravaged so quickly must now be slowly re-created.

But all this provided work, and occupied the people of every class. The building of the wall was also resumed with greater zeal. Only the Temple of the Supreme One remained uncompleted. People had become used to worshipping in the half-finished building. The small halls had been stripped of their ornaments in order to complete the large one. Also Han could not imagine what purpose the six small temples were meant to serve. Now all kinds of equipment were stored in them.

YEARS PASSED uneventfully. Han's son Chong, and his slightly younger brother Chou, had grown to manhood. Both wanted a part in the government, and besought their father for it. Had Han altogether forgotten how he himself once aspired to be active? He was indignant with his sons, whom he accused of anticipating his death. Aggrieved, they turned away from him.

The atmosphere in the Imperial Palace and around the ageing Emperor had become cheerless. He saw his people slipping back imperceptibly into the old idol worship, as the Tibetan Priests died and were replaced by priests from the Middle Kingdom. An immense pressure seemed to have settled on everyone. Where were the times when a joyful people created works of art amid laughter and jesting? When a grateful people prayed to the Supreme One? Han implored God, but the only answer seemed to be Wuti's death. Did the faithful one have to die just then? Now the Emperor felt utterly forsaken. He prayed ceaselessly. If God did not help, who was to save the people from itself? And God did help.

From Tibet came a blue-robed Lama, in attire similar to that once worn by Lao-Tse. He was called Chuang-Tse, and was the only pupil Lao-Tse had ever had besides Prince Han. He offered himself as a helper to the Emperor, who received him with open arms.

"Be my brother," the Ruler begged. "We both once had the same spiritual father. Truly the Supreme One must have sent you to me in my great loneliness!"

"The Supreme One commanded me to seek you out," Chuang confirmed gravely. "'Go to Han. He is in great distress of soul, and consequently in everything he undertakes. He imagines he has found Me, yet he always seeks Me only when he despairs of himself. Actually he seeks himself!'"

"Did the Supreme One say that?" asked Han sadly. "Then help me, Brother, so that this may change. You shall be my chief adviser, as Lao-Tse was once my father's."

Chuang-Tse began by visiting the priests in the Temples of God, in order

265

to unite them all under his supreme authority. He found much that was wrong everywhere, but since he undertook nothing without receiving direction from the Supreme One, he arranged all things with wisdom and justice, and the people acquiesced.

After journeying through the Realm for about a year, he spoke to the Emperor about his sons.

"The Princes are frittering away their best years in idleness, O Emperor. Let them take part in the government. Install Chong as your representative in Chang-Chou, and give Chou a district in the north-west of the Realm; then the country will always be in readiness for any enemies. With regard to your sons, under your guidance they will learn what is to be expected by the people from their Ruler."

Han could not close his mind to the wisdom of the advice. He sent for his sons to announce that he had work for them. The joy of the Princes showed him how much he had wronged them by accusing them of hoping for his death. A strong bond was formed between father and sons, a bond that proved also to be of infinite benefit to the Realm. In the course of several years it began to flourish: out of work performed listlessly arose once more joyful activity; handicraft developed into art.

Once again men emerged who were skilled with the paint-brush. But they no longer restricted themselves to objects of kaolin or silk; they painted on parchment and on a similar material made from reeds, and called paper.

This paper was nearly as tough as parchment, but cheaper and therefore within the reach of ordinary folk as well. And another art arose among the people: poetry. Here and there appeared persons who expressed what they wished to say in verse, probably even singing it to the accompaniment of small instruments. This ability spread rapidly. It was not confined to any one class.

But Chuang-Tse took care that the knowledge of God, the worship of the Supreme One, was restored to first place. Although he did not have the vast knowledge of Lao-Tse, who could give advice and help everywhere, although he also lacked also the heart-winning kindness of his predecessor, he had never lost the connection with the Light, and that helped him to fulfil his difficult task.

But in addition he strove to record all the words of Lao-Tse that he still remembered. From time to time he read his notes to the Emperor, and Han recalled things that his teacher had said, which supplemented the Lama's records. At the same time, however, Han realised how rich his youth had been.

He had had the best of all teachers, who not only instructed him in the sciences, but filled his young spirit with the knowledge of God. His father had willingly encouraged everything that could help him to grow in fortitude and wisdom.

Nevertheless, all that once filled his soul with such brilliant radiance had descended to the commonplace over the years! And what had befallen him had likewise affected the whole country. The blazing flames kindled by Lao-Tse, which were to soar upwards in purity, continued to burn as a useful hearth-fire, sometimes smouldering, often already near to extinction. Suddenly the Emperor covered his face with his hands, and burst into a flood of tears.

"What could I have made out of my life, what could God have expected of me, and what have I allowed it to become!" he exclaimed in despair. "Everything has become shallow and meaningless! How could it have happened!"

Chuang-Tse stepped to his side, and placed his hand on his shoulder.

"You ask, my Emperor, how it could have happened? The answer is so simple. You never thanked God for what was given to you. Only when in need of help have you prayed to God, have you remembered Him. If each day anew you had felt inwardly in awe of God's Infinite Goodness, this feeling would have grown with you, and would have strengthened your volition and the flames within you. That which becomes habitual we no longer cherish. And your people did as you did."

"I see that you are right, my brother," said Han after a long silence. "But it is too late now. The damage can no longer be repaired."

At this Chuang flared up; he had not his teacher's calmness.

"How can you say that it is too late, Emperor!" he cried indignantly. "Only the Supreme One can say 'too late' when He pronounces His judgment. But man may, should, and must go on striving so long as there is still one breath in him. Believe me," he continued more gently, "you can still improve many things, if that is your earnest desire.

"Break with your old habits. Reflect on what you learned in your youth; seek God in His Works and in His Acts of Grace, of which you have truly been permitted to experience many. Seek God with a struggling soul, thank Him for all that you are, for what you have and what arises in you from out of the ruins of everyday life. But above all, my Emperor, in such hours forget that you are Emperor!"

Slowly the Lama walked from the room, leaving the Ruler to himself; but he prayed for him; and his entreaty drew down help for the deeply-humbled human being.

FOR THREE DAYS the Emperor remained in his apartment, and would see no one. For three days he contemplated his life up to then. Thereafter he felt a strength such as he had never known before, not even in moments when he knew that help from the Supreme One was close at hand.

"Supreme One," he implored, "add yet a span to the length of my life, so that I can begin anew and do better."

It could not remain a secret that the Emperor had withdrawn completely, and various conjectures were noised abroad. Some feared that he was angry about something, while others assumed that he was ill, and would probably die soon.

Those who thought so quickly learned better. Erect as in the days of his youth, the Ruler entered the assembly of his counsellors. His voice was clear and resonant, and reminded them of his father's.

He gave his orders briskly and firmly, asking his counsellors very little about their views. An inner voice seemed to tell him all he needed to know. That gave his spirit wings, which bore it joyously far beyond everyday occurrences.

Amazed, the mandarins stared at the changed Emperor. In many his words, and the tone in which they were spoken, touched kindred chords. The vigour of the Ruler seized them too, so that they had better thoughts than before. All kinds of ideas occurred to them which could benefit the country.

Later Han discussed with Chuang-Tse how best to fan into flame the smouldering little sparks of belief among the people.

"Let us send for as many Brothers as possible from Tibet, who shall tell of the Supreme One in the various Temples of God, perhaps even at the same time throughout the country. That will arouse the people, and encourage the good ones to reflect."

"But it will be a long time before the Brothers can arrive," the Emperor sighed.

"It is short in comparison with the years you have lost," answered Chuang implacably.

Meanwhile Han had sent messengers to his sons, summoning them to his presence. Chou came first; his was a shorter journey. When his father told of his newly-gained recognition, Chou became impatient.

"Believe me, Father, these are signs of old age, this brooding over lost time and a misused life!" he said in a loving, soothing way. "You were always the best of fathers to us, a great and just Ruler to your people."

Han tried afresh to convince his son. He held up to him the blossoming of the country under Hou-Chou.

"Grandfather had with him Lao-Tse, whom you had not. Chong and I are convinced that the Lama of all Lamas was no human being, but some being from the Luminous Heights. That is why God's Blessing rested upon everything he did and said. We human beings must be content with less. Do not brood, Father."

It was left at that. The son refused to enter into the thoughts of the father. Shortly after Chou had departed, Chong arrived.

The son's face was furrowed with serious thought; his eyes shone with unusual radiance. As soon as he entered, his father knew that he would find understanding here. Both had experienced and struggled through exactly the same; both were imbued with the same volition to improve first themselves and then the country.

This was a great joy to the father, for he saw his successor in this elder son. Chong would continue on the course he now followed, and carry the people upwards with him. All was not yet lost!

Overjoyed, Chong welcomed the thought of the preaching Brothers from Tibet.

"Believe me, Father, the people need such help for their very life. I can tell by the crowds that throng to hear anyone who has something new to say. With us in the south there seems to be a fertile ground for false teachings of all kinds. They spring up like weeds. Hardly is one uprooted than another rears its head somewhere else. They shout one another down, and that is even the good thing about it," he concluded, smiling. "In that way one silences the other, and there is no need to intervene every time."

"I had no idea that things were in such a bad state with you," said Han in surprise. But his son replied:

"I kept the news to myself until I could meet you, my father. It is so intangible that it cannot be put in writing. Rather it is in the air, it is palpable. And the fact that it is there, sinister, haunting, has made me finally reflect about myself.

"When you distribute the Tibetan Brothers, please think of our needs and send us as many as you can spare. I place great hopes on that."

The Emperor could not let his son leave without first speaking to him about his brother, whose way of thinking had so bitterly disappointed him.

"Chou has always regarded you as his example, my father," Chong explained. "Therefore it was bound to cut him to the quick when you tried to belittle yourself in his eyes. His love for you will not suffer that."

"Who is your example, Chong?" Han asked, although he was certain of the answer.

"Grandfather!" cried his son, looking radiantly at his father. "I know that you yourself would not have it otherwise."

A wave of joy surged through the Emperor. Here in this son nothing was yet spoilt! He would be a blessing to the country.

A FEW DAYS LATER Chuang-Tse entered the room unbidden, with every sign of the most joyful excitement.

"This is truly the Hand of the Almighty," he cried, without any preliminary. "News has just come that thirty Priests from Tibet are on their way to Kiang-ning under the leadership of a Lama. They may even arrive this very day!"

Deeply moved, the Emperor heard the news. Did the Supreme One want to show him that he was now on the right path?

The Priests came, venerable persons who, without exception, were bound to make a profound impression on anyone who came into contact with them. Their movements were peaceful, like their speech, their eyes radiant, they were sparing of words. Only now did Han grasp what Lao-Tse had told him about the monastery.

The Lama asked to speak with him alone, and told him that they had set forth at the command of Lao-Tse, in order to help the Emperor and the Middle Kingdom.

"We are to proclaim God anew, so that your people may find the way to Him again, O Emperor," said the old sage with calm dignity.

"But I have a message for you as well."

The Lama closed his eyes and placed his palms together as though he wished to shut himself off completely and listen only within:

"Tell my son Han that it is never too late to change, but one must change with all his strength and all his faculties. If but a single thought remains behind on the way, he is still bound to the past."

To Han it seemed that he had just heard the voice of his teacher. It was the soft yet firm tone that had guided his youth. Gratefully he absorbed the words. Then he discussed the distribution of the Brothers with the Lama, and the very next day the unwearied men set out on the journey to their new destinations.

The Lama, Hi-Wen-Yang, remained in the capital, and conducted the Hour of Worship in the Temple of God every day. Although up to now this had indeed taken place, only a few had attended. Now the multitudes began to flock, so that there was hardly room for them in the great hall.

What the Lama had to say was no different from what they all actually knew. But the way in which he said it held their attention. To most the thought of God had become a formality. They worshipped Him as their forefathers had worshipped the gods.

So deeply rooted in them was the concept of "sacrifice" that they had created divine sacrifices for themselves in the form of flowers, stones and fruits, which they brought to the altar. But they did this for their own gratification, it gave them pleasure.

From that point, however, Hi-Wen-Yang found the right words to breathe life into those dead forms. All at once some began to perceive intuitively that God is not merely a concept, but Power. Immediately they even sensed this very Power. That aroused their enthusiasm! It swept them along in the best and noblest way!

High-born and humble alike were affected. And when the right moment arrived, the Lama took more incisive action. He showed the people how they had blasphemed against God, how they had abused His Holy Name, by lowering themselves as they had done.

"Even the sacrifices you devised were not offered to God but to yourselves."

One day when he called that out to the crowd, his hearers were paralysed with fear. They had meant so well! He took up this thought, and showed them that what mattered was not the good intention but the actual deed.

"Each one of you must establish for himself a connection with the Supreme One, a connection which will give you strength, nourish and invigorate your soul, inspire and purify you."

From the spirit that now prevailed in the assemblies, Han observed that even the majority of his counsellors had made a fresh start. The petitions for favours ceased. Each strove only to do his duty for the sake of the Realm.

God's Blessing was also upon the sermons of the Brothers, although in some places it was much harder for them to penetrate to the souls of the listeners. There were towns where they met with such apathetic indifference that on some days not one came to the Hours of Worship.

So they visited the workshops, and began to speak to the men. It often took a long time to win their trust, but none lost heart. They all knew that it lay solely with themselves if their work was without apparent success. So they strove untiringly in ever new ways.

But matters were at their worst in the south, in the torrid region. The spiritually strongest Brothers, who were also masters in the use of words, had been sent there by Hi-Wen-Yang. It was as though a luminous cloud descended upon the land.

Chong perceived it intuitively in that way; but his eyes, accustomed to keen observation, saw even more. He saw how a dark mass opposed this luminous current. From every hiding-place all that he had long since been aware of, but unable to see or grasp, seemed to come creeping and crawling. Whatever shunned the Light was massing to offer resistance.

Chong was filled with loathing. But at the same time he began to doubt himself: how could it be that he saw things that were apparently hidden from others? When he looked straight at these things they assumed other forms, changed into ordinary human beings; and yet he knew that the way he had first seen them was the right one!

He had long since accustomed himself to taking all such thoughts upwards in prayer. He knew that if he was meant to have enlightenment, he would receive it. This time also he was helped:

"By the Grace of the Supreme One, Chong, you have been given second-sight," was the reply. "You are to see even what is so fine that it is usually hidden from human eyes. You are to read in the souls of men, in order to help them. Your people are in need of a helper."

Now Chong rejoiced over the gift, and vowed to use it with all his might as intended by the Giver. He looked about him more carefully, and saw again the mass of Darkness which could not help rebelling against the Light.

Those instruments of evil in human form had kept themselves well-hidden all these years. Now their master was summoning them to the battlefield, lest the province which he had conquered for himself be wrested from him. Chong now recognised this clearly.

They were to be found at all levels of society. Those who otherwise lived strictly apart came together here with the same aim: resistance to the end against the influx of the Light. And how they fought, what terrible spiritual weapons they had: mockery, temptation, slander, heresy, and the most flagrant lies!

And all this could develop in a country where a Lao-Tse had so recently lived and borne witness! It could develop before Chong's very eyes, in his immediate proximity!

"Where did all the dark beings come from?"

Shuddering with disgust, Chong asked the question again and again, until even to this he received the answer within him:

"By withdrawing themselves from the Supreme One, your people have offered the Lord of the Darkness the opportunity for his creatures, his servants, to incarnate here. Now these men of the Darkness will slowly poison their surroundings, unless this is checked. You, Chong, are allowed to see them so that you may realise what is at stake. Exercise your full authority in helping the Light to prevail in your Realm!"

The Lord of the Darkness! In what connection had Chong heard of him? Now he remembered: Lao-Tse, and with him all who had attended the address of the "Mysterious One", had seen him. His grandfather Hou-Chou had told him about it, and added:

"You too will one day have to deal with him, this most sinister of all beings. Once having set a goal, the Lord of the Darkness will never relinquish it. Then pray and watch, grandson, that the country may be safeguarded from him."

Yes, he would pray, watch, but also fight, even if he had to risk his life! Chong was furious.

He sent for the highest of the Tibetans, and asked him:

"What do you see in our province?"

For a moment the Priest looked at him penetratingly, then he said:

"The same as you, my Prince."

But Chong was not to be diverted by the ambiguous answer. He trusted the Tibetans implicitly, and therefore he now also described what he beheld daily and hourly, always in a different way.

The Priest nodded thoughtfully, then he replied:

"Blessed are you, Chong, that the Supreme One has opened the eyes of your spirit. You will know for what purpose this was done."

Chong assented, but then he implored:

"Wise one, let me be of assistance to you! Show me what I can do to overcome this horde of devils! I see them gloating and baring their teeth, because they hope to prevent the advance of the Light, and thus be able to seal the fate of the torrid region."

"If we need your help we will ask for it. But your way is not our way. You can oppose this danger, independently of us. Pray, and seek in the Light the wisdom you still lack."

The Prince, who would so gladly have been allied with them, was once more left entirely to his own resources. Alone? No, he could find help. Unceasingly he laid his petitions before the Supreme One. And the first answer came:

"Wait, but do not relax your vigilance!"

At the same moment the thought arose in him: perhaps it would be a good thing for me to make a list of those whom I recognise among the men

274

of the Darkness. He did not question whether this idea was his own or one given to him, but acted upon it promptly.

The first on his list was his footman. Next came the head gardener and one of the door-keepers of the Palace. In the assembly of counsellors he found three junior mandarins and one of the native priests. Even the water-carrier who always stationed himself beside the Palace garden was completely dark.

Then it struck Chong that all these people were between the ages of twenty and thirty. So that was when the decline had set in! Now he began to turn his attention also to younger people and boys. Here things were in a frightful state. He was forced to proceed with his notes in reverse order, and to list the luminous human beings.

And as the list grew longer another point became apparent: the majority were intelligent, educated men, or at least such as were reputed to be eminently gifted in their profession. That set him thinking.

Meanwhile the Brothers preached, and slowly the Houses of God filled up, even though many visitors came out of curiosity. Chong missed none of the Hours of Worship held in the main Temple of Chang-Chou.

Usually he arrived and left on foot, so that he could mingle with the crowd and listen to their talk. In doing so he noticed that some people were always stationed outside the Temple to receive the worshippers, and to pour out their nauseous blasphemy over all that the souls had just absorbed. That must not be.

Chong was about to carry into immediate effect his plan to prohibit by law any loitering around the Temples, when an inner voice cautioned him:

"Do nothing rash. First seek advice from above."

He did so, and received the answer:

"Let the Hour of Worship be held in the open air tomorrow."

Chong spoke to the Priest, who immediately consented. The square before the Temple was spacious enough to accommodate more than the usual number of worshippers.

"We must tell no one about this plan, my Prince," warned the Priest, "and we must absorb ourselves in prayer all through the night. We must pray as we have never prayed before; for it is a matter of battle with the Lord of the Darkness!"

Chong was happy. Not for a moment did he doubt the victory of the Light. He was not cautious by nature. He would much rather take action.

The worshippers were surprised to find the gates of the Temple locked, and the square adorned for the solemn Hour instead. A cloudless sky arched over those who wished to seek the Supreme One beneath it today. Word of this novelty had spread quickly, and countless people gathered round, driven by curiosity.

The Hour of Worship was about halfway through when a deafening noise – screaming, whistling, drumming, animal calls and insane laughter – interrupted the speaker. From one of the side streets a huge crowd approached, garishly attired, skipping and leaping in dance-movements to the sound of noise produced by every conceivable means.

The people had donned demon-masks like those formerly worn at temple-dances in the pagodas of the gods. They had blackened their hands and their bare legs to appear more sinister. Closer and closer they came, forming a circle around the devout, who thought their ears must split from the deafening uproar directly behind them. The disturbing element closed ranks, crowding the faithful further and further towards the centre of the square. Soon there would be no room for them to stand.

At that stage Chong, lithe as a panther, vaulted on to one of the low, crude wooden pillars that stood before the Temple, and were designed to carry bowls of incense. Now he stood, slender and upright, before the gaze of all. The noise ceased abruptly, and gave way to a shout:

"The Prince! The Emperor's Representative!"

Everyone shouted the words, some in joy, others in terror. They had not reckoned with his presence. But he was filled with great, holy Power. The voice within him had commanded what he had to do at the Behest of the Supreme One. His face shone with joy and confidence. He raised both arms and prayed, prayed in a loud, clear voice in the face of all Darkness:

"O Supreme One, Thou seest what sacrilege is taking place here. We have deserved no better, for we have forgotten Thee for a long, long time. But that the Lord of the Darkness may know that Thou art our protection, I beseech Thee to destroy this blasphemous circle which is about to close in on us."

He had hardly finished when a violent storm sprang up, heavy clouds raced across the sky that only seconds before had been deep blue; lightning flashed, and a cloudburst poured down upon the crowd, which scattered in all directions, screaming and terror-stricken. Within a few moments the square was cleared of the agitators, while the believers walked quietly through the opened Temple-gates. –

Among them were also many who had been lukewarm. But all were deeply shaken by the intervention of the Supreme One. This assault by the Darkness, therefore, had achieved the very opposite of its objective.

Nevertheless the Darkness made itself felt ever anew. Chong did not cease to implore for help, until a new Command of the Supreme One reached him.

Out to sea there was an island, difficult to reach; but fishermen who were driven on to it by storms reported that it was completely uninhabited and apparently fertile.

At a meeting Chong informed the mandarins and counsellors that he did not intend to leave this large island, Tai-Wan, unused in the sea.

He described its wealth of mineral resources, arable land and fruit-bearing trees; moreover he promised the necessary assistance to all those who would like to settle there. But everyone willing to live henceforth on this island should report within a certain time-limit.

The province was overpopulated; the suggestion of the Imperial Representative seemed worthwhile to all. Many more than were expected came forward. Chong asked for all the lists to be submitted to him, and compared them with his notes. And as he had been promised, he found most of the dark ones among those eager to emigrate. Whoever was not dark was held back; a reason could always be found for it.

But there were still a great many about whom Chong could make no decision from their names alone. These were all summoned on a certain day to the Palace, where they had to walk past the Prince. His spiritual eye was opened wide. He saw who was dark, and a few weeks later when the people had embarked, three large vessels were filled with servants of the Darkness.

Four additional vessels carried their utensils and personal effects. The priest went with the men; the mandarins were instructed to divide the island into districts and then to administer them. The vessels, however, had orders to return immediately after the disembarkation.

Only when the ships were back in harbour did Chong rejoice over the successful undertaking.

"Now we can breathe again without being choked by the Darkness," he said, delighted, and the Tibetans too rejoiced.

But no one knew the actual reason why this emigration had had to take place; only the highest of the Priests suspected it. But even to him Chong did not speak about it.

Quieter times now followed for the torrid region. The Priests declared that the time had come for them to return to Tibet; the Tibetans from all the other regions had already gone back. But Chong explained so urgently why they could not possibly leave him and the endangered country just now, that they decided to stay longer.

Then Chong set out for Kiang-ning, to give a report to his father, whom he found very aged, but more cheerful than he had ever seen him. Good news had come from all the provinces. Before returning home all the Priests had given the Emperor an account of the condition in which they had left the country.

Nowhere had things been as bad as in the torrid region. The idea of ridding oneself of the Darkness by means of three ships and an island pleased the Emperor immensely, and even Chuang-Tse was delighted with . it.

"But what will you do if they come back?" Han asked.

"There is little likelihood of that, Father," said Chong good-humouredly. "The vessels have returned. They have no boats, nor any tools with which to build sailing vessels. There is not a single boat-builder among the emigrants – I made sure of that. The Lord of the Darkness would indeed have to send them ships; in no other way could they gain possession of them."

CHONG DID NOT stay long in the capital. All his thoughts were with his province. He still saw Darkness gathering here and there, but usually he was able to subdue it promptly. He intervened relentlessly at the least provocation.

Despite his oft-manifested severity, he was loved by the people. They

278

urged him to marry, so that there would be an heir after his death one day. He could not come to a decision. His brother Chou had married long ago, and rejoiced in his numerous offspring. Let one of the young Princes be Emperor one day! But the counsellors continued to urge and exhort him.

One evening he was strolling in the garden, thinking about all the exhortations just made to him. It was strange, he had neither wife nor child, nor a single human being whom he could call his friend. Was that his fault? Or was it so willed to enable him to serve his people with undivided attention when he became Emperor?

"When I am Emperor," he whispered to himself, deeply wrapped in thought.

And within him sounded a response:

"You will never be Emperor, Chong. The Supreme One has decreed otherwise."

The Prince was overcome with amazement. Why should he not be allowed to look after the whole Realm? And who would do so in his stead? His brother Chou?

"Idle questions," he reproved himself. "If the Supreme One has so ordained it, it will be good for the country and for me."

"Chong, the country is heading for decline which you cannot arrest. You would sacrifice yourself in vain. The Supreme One has other tasks for you."

"Grant me then, O Supreme One, that I may recognise these tasks clearly and serve Thee joyfully, wherever it may be!" cried Chong. A harsh, raucous voice answered:

"You will serve no one any more, either for better or worse, for your last hour has come!"

Chong did not grasp the final words; a sword had plunged through him from behind. Covered with blood, he collapsed. Only after some hours was he found by the servants who had come to the garden to call their master to his meal.

He was no longer alive. His mortal remains were taken to Kiang-ning and buried under the Temple. But Emperor Han could not understand why his best son had been taken from him. No trace of the murderer was ever found.

Han reigned in outward peace for a few more years; then the Emperor, who had grown very old, was allowed to pass on, and Chou became Emperor in his place.

He assumed office with the best of intentions, but soon found that it was easier to govern a single province than such a vast, complex realm.

On the advice of Chuang-Tse he had sent a trustworthy senior mandarin to the torrid region as his representative. in doing so, he believed that he had done enough for this province. He held a grudge against the province, because it was there that his brother had been murdered. This was also the objection he raised whenever Chuang-Tse tried to persuade him to see for himself that everything was in order there.

In the second year of Chou's reign, however, news came from the south that the great sage Con-Fu-Tse was teaching there, and had formed a large circle of students around him.

"Master Kung is dead," said Chuang-Tse firmly, "Emperor, you must find out who is using his name."

"How do you know that Kung is dead?" asked Chou indifferently.

"Lao-Tse said so. A sage who called himself the "Mysterious One" appeared here. Lao-Tse unmasked him as an impostor, and the Supreme One Himself judged him."

"But need this mysterious one have been Kung?" Chou asked once more.

Chuang-Tse was silent, but resolved to make the necessary enquiries himself. To this end he set out on a journey to the south, and soon found the one he sought.

He joined the circle of listeners for a few days, then he knew enough. He thrust his way close to the speaker, and asked how it was that he claimed the title of Lama. Con-Fu-Tse, as the man called himself, regarded him scornfully.

"This question was put to me once before, in fact by no less a person than Lao-Tse himself," said he casually.

"That is no answer to my question. But I am entitled to demand one from you, since I am a Yellow Lama."

"So am I," was the man's answer. "Then we are on equal ground; you merely have the advantage of age. But let me ask you: in which monastery did you acquire your rank?"

Chuang-Tse was not equal to this effrontery. Without a word, he turned away.

He went to the mandarin who was Chou's representative, and explained to him that Master Kung had died long ago. This man must be an impostor. Even if the "Mysterious One" at that time was not Kung, this man could not possibly be Kung, for he was too young.

The mandarin, who until then had not concerned himself about the teaching sage, promised to investigate the matter. At first he forgot about it, but Chuang-Tse kept on questioning, until the mandarin decided to send for the sage. But he insisted that Chuang-Tse should confront him.

This proved that he himself was not at all interested in the outcome of the investigation. It grieved Chuang-Tse, who foresaw that the Darkness would triumph.

The mandarin began his examination very cleverly. After eliciting from both Lamas that they were true Lamas, he asked the one who called himself Con-Fu-Tse how old he was.

The man stated an age which could well correspond to that of the real Kung if he were still alive, but which was in no way consistent with the appearance of the speaker. When the mandarin pointed this out to him, the man laughed and said:

"I see that you have not yet seen many sages, Illustrious One. Know then: the pursuit of learning keeps the body young, especially if one lives as a servant of the Supreme One."

"Nothing can be said against that," said the mandarin admiringly. "But tell us about your teaching. What do you preach?"

"I preach that all the torments taught by the Priests are not essential to a happy life. We need not abstain from either prosperity or earthly pleasures. Of what use would that be to God? Does it serve Him if we torment ourselves and sigh over our sinfulness?"

"And do you really believe that God will be satisfied with such a life as you preach?" the mandarin wanted to know.

Chuang-Tse perceived that the mandarin was moved to enthusiasm, and he was horrified.

"Just try to live according to my teachings, Illustrious One, and you will experience how happy and contented you can be. The people will love you, and honours will be heaped upon you. I will admit you to the circle of my pupils, and you will partake of all the blessings which I am able to bestow."

"Enough of this blasphemy!" shouted Chuang-Tse at the top of his voice.

But Con-Fu-Tse laughed scornfully:

"You of course are too old and too encrusted to grasp new ideas. The best thing for you would be to return to your monastery. There is no more room here for such as you."

Chuang-Tse left the room without a word. He prayed to God for help to confront the fiend. Instead of the help for which he prayed, there came the Command to return to Tibet.

WITH HIM was gone the last person who could restrain the Emperor from likewise occupying himself with the teachings that were preached. It was as though the Supreme One had left the Realm on which He had once bestowed the Light entirely to itself.

The false Con-Fu-Tse however was free to teach, and gained an ever greater following. He knew how to interweave the knowledge of the Supreme One in subtle ways with his false teaching.

If anyone had really examined his words, they would soon have discovered the discrepancy. But no one took the trouble to do so. They were all as though in a frenzy. For indeed it was made so easy to attain to happiness here on earth, and later to enter the Eternal Gardens, so generously promised by Con-Fu-Tse to all his adherents.

But whenever a thoughtful person asked why there was more suffering, why more epidemics and famine, more misery and poverty now than there had been in Hou-Chou's times, he received the answer:

"Because the wrong teaching arose under Hou-Chou, and the people have been living according to it ever since. Just wait, everything will soon become better."

When Con-Fu-Tse had been travelling through the provinces for several years, he came also to Kiang-ning, where he intended to settle. There was probably no longer anyone alive who had known the real Master Kung. He could no doubt risk it.

Chou received him with great joy. Con-Fu-Tse was a past master of flattery. To honour the sage, the Emperor invited him to conduct the Hour of Worship in the woodland Temple of God on one of the following days. Con-Fu-Tse gladly accepted. He could ask for nothing better.

But that was not to be. The night before, a violent earthquake shook the capital, laying many buildings in ruins. Worst affected was the Temple of God, which was razed to the ground. It was as though the animistic beings, who had once helped to build it, had torn their work asunder with avenging fists. Several other temples had also collapsed. They were not rebuilt.

Con-Fu-Tse dropped his mask ever more openly. When Chou died after a brief reign, and his son Han became Emperor, Con-Fu-Tse re-introduced idolatry everywhere. Slowly China sank into Darkness and horror.

The vast Realm, which expanded still further in the course of centuries, never again acknowledged the Supreme One as its God.

Abd-ru-shin

In The Light Of Truth: The Grail Message

The Author was born in 1875 in Bischofswerda, Germany. His given name was Oskar Ernst Bernhardt. After being educated and trained in business, he established himself in Dresden and became financially successful. In the years that followed, he made many journeys abroad, and wrote successful travel books, stories, and plays.

After residing for some time in New York, Mr. Bernhardt journeyed to London, England. There, the outbreak of World War I took him unawares, and in 1914 he was interned on the Isle of Man.

The seclusion of internment brought with it an inner deepening. He reflected continuously over questions connected with the meaning of life, birth and death, responsibility and free will, God and Creation. More and more the desire awakened within him to help humanity. He was released in the Spring of 1919 and returned to Germany.

He began to write the first lectures for *In the Light of Truth: The Grail Message* in 1923. His explanation of the Knowledge of Creation resounded among his hearers.

In 1928, Abd-ru-shin settled in Austria, Tyrol on a mountain plateau called Vomperberg, where he continued writing *The Grail Message*. The seizure of power in Austria by the Nazis in 1938 ended his work there. He was arrested, and his land and property were appropriated without compensation. Abd-ru-shin was exiled to Kipsdorf in the Erzgebirge, where he was under surveillance by the Gestapo. He was forbidden any further work for making *The Grail Message* known publicly.

On December 6, 1941, Abd-ru-shin died from the effects of these measures. After the war his family returned to Vomperberg, and carried on his work.

If you have questions about the content of this Work,
please contact Reader Services at:

Grail Foundation Press
P.O. Box 45
Gambier, Ohio 43022
Telephone: 614.427-9410
Fax: 614.427-4954

IN THE LIGHT OF TRUTH: THE GRAIL MESSAGE
by Abd-ru-shin

Linen edition, three volumes combined
ISBN 1-57461-006-6
5.5" x 8.5"
1,062 pages
Paper edition, three-volume box set
ISBN 1-57461-003-1
6" x 9"
1,096 pages

Original edition: German
Translations available in:
Czech, Dutch, English, Estonian, French, Hungarian,
Italian, Portuguese, Rumanian, Russian,
Slovak, Spanish

Available at your local bookstore
or directly through the publisher.

Grail Foundation Press
P.O. Box 45
Gambier, Ohio 43022
1-800-427-9217

Publisher's catalog available on request

Further Writings by Abd-ru-shin:

THE TEN COMMANDMENTS OF GOD
THE LORD'S PRAYER
72 pages
Linen clothbound
ISBN 1-57461-007-4
Paperback
ISBN 1-57461-004-X

QUESTIONS AND ANSWERS
232 pages
Clothbound
ISBN 3-87860-145-X

PRAYERS
16 pages
Paperback
ISBN 3-87860-138-7

Available at your local bookstore
or directly through the publisher.

Grail Foundation Press
P.O. Box 45
Gambier, Ohio 43022
1-800-427-9217

Publisher's catalog available on request